ARTHUR
LEGEND, LOGIC & EVIDENCE

ARTHUR
LEGEND, LOGIC & EVIDENCE

ADRIAN C GRANT

Arthur: Legend, Logic & Evidence

By the same author: *Scottish Clans: Legend, Logic & Evidence*
Forthcoming by the same author: *St Patrick: Legend, Logic & Evidence*

First Published in 2017 by FastPrint Publishing, Peterborough, England.

Copyright © Adrian C Grant, 2017

The moral right of Adrian C Grant to be identified as the author of this work has been asserted by him in accordance with the Copyright, Designs and Patents Act 1988 and any subsequent amendments thereto.

All rights reserved. No part of this book may be reproduced in any form by photocopying or any electronic or mechanical means, including information storage or retrieval systems, without permission in writing from both the copyright owner and the publisher of the book.

A CIP catalogue record for this book is available from the British Library

Paperback ISBN 978-178456-501-5

Printed and bound in England by www.printondemand-worldwide.com

www.fast-print.net/bookshop

CONTENTS

Introduction.	1
Part I: Exploring the Sources	7
Part 2: Background – Scotland before Arthur	23
Part 3: Identifying the Battle Sites	63
A. Battles 2, 3, 4 and 5 – Glen Douglas.	66
B. Battle 7 – Cat Coit Celidon	75
C. Battle 1 – The Mouth of the River Glen	78
D. Battle 6 – The River Bassas	83
E. Battle No. 8: Guinnon Fort	86
F. Battle No. 9: The City of the Legion	88
G. Battle No 10: On the bank of the River called Tribuit	90
H. Battle No 11: On a hill called Agned	92
I. Battle No 12: Badon Hill	95
Part 4: Who was Arthur and What he did next	99
0. Who Arthur was not	100
1. Identifying Arthur	102
2. Camelot and Guinevere	108
3. "Kardoel"/"Carduel"	112
4. "Norway"	114
5. What Arthur did next	116
Appendices	
1: An Arthurian Who's Who	121
2: The Earldom of Lennox	139
3: St Serf and others	181
4: The Faroes: The Island of Thule Identified	199
5: Notes on the cover Illustration	203
Conclusion	205
Postscript: What if…?	207
Acknowledgements	211
Bibliography	212

LIST OF ILLUSTRATIONS

1. 85AD: The Roman Front Line — 25
2. Ptolemy's Scotland (from Macbain) — 28
3. Correcting the location of the Caledonii — 35
4. Redrawing Ptolemy's Scotland — 36
5. Proposed distribution of Tribes mentioned by Ptolemy — 37
6. Proposed Southern Scotland c45AD — 44
7. Proposed map of kingdoms just before Arthur — 47
8. Dalriada just before Arthur — 58
9. The Battle Sites - summary map — 64
10. Glen Douglas and Loch Lomond — 66
11. Cat Coit Celidon — 75
12. Mouth of the River Glen — 78
13. River Bassas — 83
14. Guinnon Fort — 86
15. City of the Legion — 88
16. River Tribuit — 90
17. Agned Hill — 92
18. Badon Hill — 95
19. Arthur's Pedigree — 104
20. Owain's Pedigree — 129
21. Colour Plates of Coats of Arms — 140/1
22. Galbraith Arms — 142
23. Dunbar and Lennox Arms — 150 & 151
24. MacAulay Arms — 159
25. Colquhoun Arms — 162
26. Haldane Arms — 163
27. Buchanan Arms — 165
28. MacAuslan etc. Arms — 171
29. Forbes Arms — 175
30. Forbes home area — 176
31. Firth of Forth — 187
31. Ptolemy's Scotland including Thule — 201

INTRODUCTION.

A. Arthur: the story so far

"History is Bunk," Henry Ford

"History is the distillation of rumour" Thomas Carlyle

"History is written by the victors," Winston Churchill

"History is a set of lies agreed upon," Napoleon Bonaparte

To these we may add that much so-called history is no more than an expression of the author's desire for some sort of reflected glory whether through inheritance or by more general association with the person/people being written about.

For more than a thousand years legend has built up about "King Arthur" and his "knights of the round table". Much of it is indeed bunk – which can so easily become rumour, ie based on hearsay rather than any rigorous knowledge or understanding. As we shall see, I suggest that much has been made up and was never intended as historically accurate – and I adduce specific evidence for this. Many elements of the legend have indeed become a corpus of agreed lies and they have indeed been promulgated by those in power.

However I intend to show that much of the truth does lie out there, waiting to be brought to light.

B Why I started this

The initial purpose behind my previous book, "Scottish Clans: Legend Logic & Evidence", had been simply to examine and, hopefully, to establish the true origins of the Clan Grant. As the research progressed it became necessary also to examine much else besides, including exposing the supposed history of the origins of many clans as commonly promulgated and (mis-)understood for what they were, identifying the lies and the reasons for the lies, thereby creating space for the truth to emerge.

In "Scottish Clans..." passing reference was made to "king Arthur" for two separate reasons: I needed (i) to correct a(n albeit posthumous) misattribution of a particular coat of arms to him and (ii) to discount the proposition being advanced by far too many MacArthurs (and their fellow travellers) – that prince Arthur mac Aedan (from whom they claim a direct male line descent) was "the" true Arthur of legend (as we will see, this is not at all possible). I gave no serious further thought to Arthurian legend, although, simultaneously with the researches for my book, I had read and been somewhat intrigued by Alastair Moffat's "Arthur and the Lost Kingdoms". [As it turns out Moffat is far too far off the mark in too many respects.]

When "Scottish Clans..." was published I sent a copy to one of my old schools, first for its library and second in the hope that a review might boost sales. In the event the reviewer was supercilious and Onanistic – so I will not dignify him by naming him! He took the opportunity of the magazine space made available to him not to consider what was actually in my book, but rather to parade his Anglo-centric smugness by rehearsing the rubbishing of many "well known facts" about Scotland, most of which I had not even mentioned and which were in any case completely irrelevant to the various original propositions advanced in the work. While what he said was technically true, the tone was inappropriate; in essence it was not a "review". In one specific instance he went out of his way to highlight what had been my tangential references to the Arthur of legend, quoting an academic friend as saying that "not much" could be said about Arthur at all.

This double dose of disdain stirred my blood; so far as I was concerned a gauntlet might as well have been thrown down and so I decided to examine the matter further.

C My Approach

Exploring the commentaries on the very few historical references I was amazed by the way in which the commentators had been in thrall to preconceptions which they had failed to observe in themselves; they all seemed to want their particular answer to be true. They could not see, far less acknowledge, this weakness of intention in themselves – so naturally it was not possible for them to free themselves of these self-imposed distorting lenses.

I hope that I am free from such constraints. In 2005, well before "Scottish Clans...." was in any real shape, I had my DNA tested – and this confirmed our family lore: I am born of mongrel peasant stock (with all the genetic resilience implied!) – not in any way connected to any chiefly line. Thus I was not invested with any interest in any particular outcome of my researches into any clan's origins. And so it is with this examination of "king" Arthur. I am connected neither by family nor by geography to anything directly to do with my subject. Nor do I "care" in any way what the outcome might be. Thus I believe that I bring to this study an independence which should be a firm support for objectivity – but you, the reader, will decide.

Thus freed from what would otherwise be severely constrained perspective I have been surprised by just how much can be gleaned very quickly: how many threads of the hitherto seemingly Gordian knot can be untangled. But perhaps you, the reader would be inclined to think that I would say that – so it will be for you to judge also just how far I have managed to stick to this, how many problems I have resolved and how dubious any residual issues may be.

Convinced of the power of rigorous logic – which I have found of enormous use in resolving problems in many areas of life, I am a devotee both of William of Occam and of Star Trek's Spock. Thus I was much taken by this exchange in the film version of Harry Potter and the Deathly Hallows (Part I):

> Harry: "You are brilliant, Hermione…. truly".
>
> Hermione: "Actually, I'm highly logical, which allows me to look past extraneous detail…and perceive clearly that which others overlook."

[see http://www.springfieldspringfield.co.uk/movie_script.php?movie=harry-potter-and-deathly-hallows-part-1]

I have sought to apply this throughout my research.

What has transpired is remarkably parallel to how "Scottish Clans…." worked out. The legends as told are so far off the mark that the "obvious" thing to do is to dismiss them altogether and historians seem divided between those who would throw up their hands, claiming that there is nothing which can be said about any Arthurian character and those who discount the legend altogether. This has left the territory free for a host of romanticists to invent and promulgate ever more elaborate stories to suit their own fantasies and/or prejudices.

Yet just as in "Scottish Clans…." it was possible to tease out the many strands of truth lying within the legend and recombine them into a coherent narrative which makes sense and conforms to a feasible time line, so it is with Arthur. And if my analysis does find favour, then this may allow others with specific interests beyond the immediate scope of this work to address them in a more focused way.

I started this work objectively, but now that I have undertaken the research I am ready to defend vigorously such definite conclusions as I have been able to reach!

[NB References to "Scotland" and to "England" will be as understood today even though neither such country existed at the time. I hope that this will be an aid to the reader. Thus for "England" the reader should understand "that part of Britain which is now England" and so forth.]

D. Structure of the book

I wanted to write this book in the way many others in this genre have done – taking the reader along with me on my voyage of discovery. But my journey was not linear. My track was back and forth and round and round in circles! Not only that, but the material is not suited to "chapters" in the conventional sense. My self-imposed task in researching this book was to identify the sites of Arthur's famous twelve battles, the broad time-scale within which this military campaign took place and hopefully go on to get a handle on who Arthur may have been. In the event I hope that the reader will agree that I have achieved rather more than I set out to do. But there is more..... colour and depth which can be added to this bare story – and superficially extraneous detail which will act as powerful circumstantial evidence and thus help to make the proposition even more certain – and these are set out in the Appendices.

So this is the structure I have settled on for this work:

Part 1. An examination of the sources. I hope the reader will agree that this demonstrates that the famous 12 battles identified by Nennius (see below) were in what is now Scotland and that the relevant time window for them is 495x520.

Part 2. A review of the historical, political and geographical context – what had been going on, where and who was involved – which led to the necessity for the 12-battle campaign.

Part 3. Consideration of each battle – identifying the site and why it occurred. In the course of these considerations a few characters in Arthurian Legend will be identified.

Part 4. The identification of Arthur and many of those not already identified with whom he came into contact followed by other people who feature in Arthurian legend.

Part 5: Appendices

1: Arthurian Who's Who This appendix has a look at a selection of the characters appearing in Arthurian romance.

2: The Lennox This appendix considers the principal families of the Lennox and the way in which their pedigrees – real and/or fabricated – reflect the power struggle of the Arthurian period. I go on to show how this power continued to shift over several centuries. In their heraldry and, particularly, in the way these families sought to fabricate their true origins, we find powerful support for the main thesis set out in this book.

3: St Serf This appendix considers the life and times of St Serf. This is technically completely irrelevant to Arthur himself, but serves, hopefully once and for all, to debunk the claimed link between St Serf and St Kentigern – leaving the way open for a more rational consideration of Theneu and her son Kentigern who were, respectively, Arthur's niece and grand nephew.

4: Identifying the Island of Thule This appendix arises purely from my examination of Ptolemy's geography of Scotland. I hope that this supports – and so will infuse the reader with enthusiasm for – the other, far more directly pertinent, conclusions I have drawn regarding Ptolemy's work.

PART I:
EXPLORING THE SOURCES

EXPLORING THE SOURCES

Let us begin our investigation into "king" Arthur by considering the early sources we have available to us which are relevant (remembering that much has been lost – some deliberately destroyed). I have found it quite difficult to decide how best to present this survey because the argument tacks back and forth between the disparate elements, In the end I have chosen to introduce and discuss each one in turn even though the overall pattern will only emerge towards the end.

The examination will be of extracts from these sources:

St Gildas   "The Ruin of Britain" ("*De Excidio et Conquestu Britanniae*")
   http://www.vortigernstudies.org.uk/arthist/vortigernquotesgil.htm#_ednref42

Aneurin   "Y Gododdin"
   http://www.maryjones.us/ctexts/a01b.html

The Venerable Bede   "Ecclesiastical History of England"
   http://www.gutenberg.org/files/38326/38326-h/38326-h.html#toc39

Nennius   "History of the Britons" ("Historia Britannorum")
   http://sourcebooks.fordham.edu/halsall/basis/nennius-full.asp

Anonymous   "Welsh Annals" ("Annales Cambriae")
   http://sourcebooks.fordham.edu/source/annalescambriae.asp

M. Swanson (tr & ed)   The Anglo-Saxon Chronicle (Dent 1996)

Marie de France   "Lanval"
   http://www.arthuriana.org/teaching/Marie_Lanval_Shoaf.html
   http://users.clas.ufl.edu/jshoaf/Marie/lanval.pdf

Chrétien de Troyes   "Four Arthurian Romances"
   http://www.gutenberg.org/files/831/831-h/831-h.htm

Geoffrey of Monmouth   "History of the Kings of Britain" (books 7-11)
   http://www.indiana.edu/~dmdhist/arthur_gm.htm#7.1

Thomas Malory   "Le Morte d'Arthur"
   http://www.sacred-texts.com/neu/mart/index.htm

Anonymous   "Sir Gawain and the Green Knight"
   http://quod.lib.umich.edu/c/cme/Gawain/1:1?rgn=div1;view=fulltext
   http://d.lib.rochester.edu/camelot/text/weston-sir-gawain-and-the-green-knight

Amplification of some points comes from:

Ruys: "Life of Gildas"
   http://www.maryjones.us/ctexts/gildas07.html

Caradoc of Llanfarcan   "Life of Gildas"
   http://www.maryjones.us/ctexts/gildas06.html

Source 1: Gildas

Although Arthur is not mentioned by name, the earliest reference we have now to an event in which he is supposed to have taken part is in a diatribe "The Ruin of Britain" ("*De Excidio et Conquestu Britanniae*") written by a monk called St Gildas. One good place to see his work, because the English is set next to the 'original' Latin is http://www.vortigernstudies.org.uk/arthist/vortigernquotesgil.htm#_ednref42

It should be noted that Gildas' "chapter" numbers and the subheadings are later additions by editors – hence not relevant to the original.

In Chapter 24 Gildas explains how the Britons were attacked by the Saxons who were supposedly here to protect them from the Picts and Scots. In Chapter 25 he goes on to explain how the Britons were between a rock and a hard place until the extremity of their plight united them under Ambrosius Aurelianus and they took on and beat the enemy. The problem we have in gaining a proper understanding of this is that all the subsequent commentators have supposed that by now the Anglo-Saxons were "the enemy". But this is unfounded assumption on their part. An unbiased reading of the text shows that despite the bad treatment by (in particular) the Saxons there is no alteration of who "the enemy" was. So we should follow the flow of the text and understand that in fact "the enemy" continued to be the Picts and Scots.

The first paragraph of Chapter 26 says:

> 26. ex eo tempore nunc ciues, nunc hostes, uincebant, ut in ista gente experietur dominus solito more praesentem israelem, utrum diligat eum an non: usque ad annum obsessionis badonici montis, nouissimaeque ferme de furciferis non minimae stragis, quique quadragesimus quartus (ut noui) orditur annus mense iam uno emenso, qui et meae natiuitatis est.

which has been translated as:

> 26. From that time, the citizens were sometimes victorious, sometimes the enemy, in order that the Lord, according to His wont, might try in this nation the Israel of to-day, whether it loves Him or

not. This continued up to the year of the siege of Badon Hill, and of almost the last great slaughter inflicted upon the rascally crew. And this commences, a fact I know, as the forty-fourth year, with one month now elapsed; it is also the year of my birth.

So, contrary to the interpretations of others from the Venerable Bede onwards (see below), my conclusion is that in the first instance the 44 years are those following the victory of the Britons under their leader Ambrosius Aurelianus. Not only that but this is supported in general terms by his commentary on Ambrosius:

> "uiro modesto, qui solus forte romanae gentis tantae tempestatis collisione occisis in eadem parentibus purpura nimirum indutis superfuerat, cuius nunc temporibus nostris suboles magnopere auita bonitate degenerauit, uires capessunt, uictores prouocantes ad proelium:"

Translated as:

> He was a man of unassuming character, who, alone of the Roman race chanced to survive in the shock of such a storm (as his parents, people undoubtedly clad in the purple, had been killed in it), whose offspring in our days have greatly degenerated from their ancestral nobleness.

In other words Ambrosius belongs to a time roughly two generations prior to the Battle of Badon Hill – and at least another one before the time of writing. But as to whom the victory was over is far less clear.

Dating Gildas' work

We can date Gildas' writing to some time before 540, for one of the kings he excoriates (in Chapter 31) and addresses in the present tense, Vortipor (Prince of the Demetae in Dyfed), died that year (see http://www.britannia.com/bios/ebk/gwrthdf.html)

There has been argument about the date of this work for two main reasons: (i) because this "obvious" date does not accord with many authors' preconceptions and prejudices and (ii) because Bede lifted the "44 year" idea from Gildas, but misunderstood it – probably because of his understandable prejudice against pagan Anglo-Saxons. However my impression is that the tide of current thinking is to revert to the 'obvious' date and I am very much sticking with it.

Gildas: Why no mention of Arthur?

It would be legitimate to ask that if Gildas was so knowledgeable about these battles – and both the Annales Cambriae and Nennius (See below) ascribe the leadership of the victorious forces at Badon Hill to Arthur – why then did Gildas not mention Arthur by name?

An answer may be gleaned from his biographers. There are two lives of Gildas which may be read here:

1. http://www.maryjones.us/ctexts/gildas07.html by a monk of Ruys
and
2. http://www.maryjones.us/ctexts/gildas06.html by Caradoc of Llanfarcan

In Section 5 of his work, Caradoc claims that Arthur had killed Hueil, Gildas' elder brother, while Hueil was on a plundering expedition. The story as related by Caradoc (writing in the middle 1100s when the legend was already gathering pace – he was, after all, a contemporary of Geoffrey of Monmouth) cannot be wholly true, as Caradoc styles Arthur as the "king of the whole of Britain", but it seems likely that there is more than a germ of truth lying within. Bad blood between Arthur and Gildas, coupled with Gildas' knowledge that his brother was in the wrong, is just the scenario likely to lead to a deliberate decision to exclude Arthur from his comments altogether, while not actually attempting to blacken Arthur's name.

Gildas' Life

I have no *a priori* reason to challenge the date of Gildas' death offered by the Annales Cambriae: 570. Most Commentators seem to offer a date around 500 for his birth, and it would be fit and proper for a 35-40 year old to be railing against the iniquity of the country's rulers. However the earlier "life", generally regarded as more reliable, claims that St Bridget invited him to Ireland having heard of his renown. She was certainly dead by 525 and I think that it would be pushing it for Gildas to be of "renown" much under the age of 30. So let us suppose that the visit took place as late as 520: an extra ten years would also add considerable gravitas to his criticisms of the British aristocracy. So I would prefer a date of c490 for Gildas' birth, making him nearer 80 at death, by no means especially remarkable (compare also Kentigern below). However we have also to deal with the genealogical tables – which make Gildas a 4xgreat grandson of Old King Cole. This makes a date as early as 490 difficult – 495 rather more feasible. Adding 44 years to this date we find ourselves at 539 – which being just before the 540 date noted above as too late is also feasible.

Thus my interpretation is that the siege of Badon Hill was relieved 44 years after Ambrosius Aurelianus relieved Dumbarton Rock – and Gildas is saying "Oh... what a coincidence, because that is how old I am now!" This makes the time window for Gildas' birth quite small – 495 +/- 2 at most, +/-1 more likely. As we shall see, this means that Gildas was born just when Arthur's campaign was starting.

Source 2: Aneurin

The earliest reference to Arthur by name is contained in a poem called "The Gododdin" composed by a bard called Aneurin about the battle of Catterick which took place around the year 600AD. In this poem, which must have been written in the immediate aftermath of this battle, Arthur is already a legendary figure.

This reference will not help us a great deal, but the single verse (§102) actually about Gwawrddur, is reproduced here for the sake of completeness. The entire poem can be found online at: http://www.maryjones.us/ctexts/a01b.html

> *CII*
> He thrust beyond three hundred, most bold,
> He cut down the centre and far wing.
> He proved worthy, leading noble men;
> He gave from his herd steeds for winter.
> He brought black crows to a fort's
> Wall, though he was not Arthur.
> He made his strength a refuge,
> The front line's bulwark, Gwawrddur.

Source 3: Bede

The venerable Bede, wrote his "Ecclesiastical History of England" principally in the late 720s. As we shall see, he clearly had access to, but misunderstood, the work of Gildas. It is this misunderstanding which opened up the scope for the misunderstanding of the life of Arthur. Here is the relevant extract from Bede's work (the italics are mine).

> **Chap. XVI. How the Britons obtained their first victory over the Angles, under the command of Ambrosius, a Roman.**
> When the army of the enemy, having destroyed and dispersed the natives, had returned home to their own settlements, the Britons began by degrees to take heart, and gather strength, sallying out of the lurking places where they had concealed themselves, and with

one accord imploring the Divine help, that they might not utterly be destroyed. They had at that time for their leader, Ambrosius Aurelianus, a man of worth, who alone, by chance, of the Roman nation had survived the storm, in which his parents, who were of the royal race, had perished. Under him the Britons revived, and offering battle to the victors, by the help of God, gained the victory. *From that day, sometimes the natives, and sometimes their enemies, prevailed, till the year of the siege of Badon-hill, when they made no small slaughter of those enemies, about forty-four years after their arrival in England.* But of this hereafter.

[For the whole work see: http://www.gutenberg.org/files/38326/38326-h/38326-h.html#toc39]

As we can see, Bede supposes that the battle of Badon Hill took place 44 years after the arrival of Hengist and Horsa – no later than 450AD. As we have seen, this is a mistake.

Source 4 Nennius

The earliest list of Arthur's principal achievements, including detail of the 12 battles, are in the "History of the Britons" ("Historia Brittonum") attributed to another monk – this one based in Wales and usually called Nennius. It seems generally agreed that this work was composed around 830AD.

There are several editions of Nennius' History of Britain – and they do vary one from another. In one edition (Giles' translation) Arthur's battles are listed in chapter 50, while in another they are in chapter 56.

The relevant part of Nennius' work (in Latin) can be found online at: http://www.kmatthews.org.uk/history/hb/historia_brittonum15.html

The whole of Nennius' work can be found here:
http://www.yorku.ca/inpar/nennius_giles.pdf
http://sourcebooks.fordham.edu/halsall/basis/nennius-full.asp

Nennius is careful to put Arthur in his right social place:

> "....though there were many more noble than himself, yet he was twelve times chosen their commander, and was as often conqueror."

Nennius goes on to identify for us the locations of the 12 battles

- The first battle was at the mouth of the river called Glein
- The second, third, the fourth and the fifth were on another river, called the Dubglas, which is in the region of Linnuis

- The sixth battle was on the river called Bassas
- The seventh battle was in the Caledonian Forest, that is, the Battle of Cat Coit Celidon
- The eighth battle was in Guinnon fort, and in it Arthur carried the image of the holy Mary, the everlasting virgin, on his shoulders, and the pagans were put to flight on that day, and through the power of Jesus Christ and the power of the virgin Mary there was great slaughter
- The ninth battle was in the City of the Legion
- The tenth battle was on the bank of the river called Tribruit
- The eleventh battle was on the hill called Agned
- The twelfth battle was on Badon Hill and on which fell 960 men from one charge by Arthur; and no-one struck them down save Arthur himself

Source 5: The Annales Cambriae

The earliest assertion of particular dates associated with Arthur are in the anonymous "Annales Cambriae", probably completed around 954AD (the date of the last entry). These Annals can be found online at: http://sourcebooks.fordham.edu/source/annalescambriae.asp

Here is a relevant extract (I have also cut out some events which cannot be verified at all). Many people have sought to challenge the dates given in these annals so to illustrate just how much accuracy we should attribute to them I give not only the date offered by the Annals but also the best estimate agreed by modern scholars.

As we can see (my bold type!) the Annals are unequivocal in dating the battle of Badon Hill to the year 516. Moreover they go on to say that Arthur died at the battle of Camlann in 537.

What we can see from this table is that the great majority of historians are not inclined to do any more than quibble with the dates given. I make two reservations: in the case of the Synod of Victory, the Anglo-Saxon Chronicle does recognise a rout of the Anglo-Saxons the year before – so the date in brackets is implied. The other problem is the first entry listed. We have to remember that the Annales were put together well after the Catholic Church had promulgated its "story" about St Patrick. In the case of this entry in the Annales it is difficult to be sure what they are actually referring to. I am inclined to the idea that the modern date is correct, the date in the Annals being made up to suit the Bowdlerisation of the life of St Patrick. St David may well have been born 30 years following some significant event – whether or not actually involving St Patrick. But this need not detain us.

Date given	Event	Modern assumed date
458	St. David is born in the thirtieth year after Patrick left Menevia.	c500
468	Death of Bishop Benignus	467
516	**The Battle of Badon, in which Arthur carried the Cross of our Lord Jesus Christ for three days and three nights on his shoulders and the Britons were the victors.**	
521	St. Columba is born.	521
521	The death of St Brigid	c524
537	**The battle of Camlann, in which Arthur and Medraut fell:**	
544	The sleep [death] of Ciaran.	544
558	The death of Gabrán, son of Dungart.	
562	Columba went to Britain.	563
565	The voyage of Gildas to Ireland.	
569	The 'Synod of Victory' was held between the Britons.	(568)
570	Gildas wisest of Britons died.	
573	The battle of Arfderydd between the sons of Eliffer and Gwenddolau son of Ceidio; in which battle Gwenddolau fell; Merlin went mad.	
574	The sleep [death] of Brendan of Birr.	c572/3
589	The conversion of Constantine [king of Britain] to the Lord.	
594	Aethelbert reigned in England.	589-616
595	The death of Columba.	597
	The death of king Dunod son of Pabo.	
	Augustine and Mellitus converted the English to Christ.	595
601	The synod of Urbs Legionis [Chester].	
	Gregory died in Christ and also bishop David of Moni Iudeorum.	604
606	The burial of bishop Cynog.	
607	The death of Aidan son of Gabrán	c609
612	The death of Kentigern and bishop Dyfrig.	614
613	The battle of Caer Legion [Chester]. And there died Selyf son of Cynan. And Iago son of Beli slept [died].	
616	Ceredig died.	c617
617	Edwin begins his reign.	616

From this table we can see that the Annales are broadly correct, sometimes to the precise year, at other times to within two or three years.

Source 6: The Anglo-Saxon Chronicle

We also need to bear in mind, however, just how accurate the Anglo-Saxon Chronicle may be. Here we may call modern science to our assistance, for the Chronicle records a solar eclipse in June 540. Today we can extrapolate backwards and so http://eclipse.gsfc.nasa.gov/SEcirc/SEcircEU/LondonGBR2.html is able to tell us that there was indeed an annular eclipse, but it was in 536, giving us a useful guide as to the accuracy of the Chronicle – on the one hand far from made up, on the other hand in essence no more accurate than the Annales.

Broadly the Anglo-Saxons record their own success and the fact that they made so little progress in the course of over 70 years indicates how tough the going was for them. Had there been anything different at least one might have expected the Peterborough MS to note it – but no, except for another eclipse in 538 as well as 540. [NASA recognises 527, 536 and 550.]

473 is one date noted. According to the Chronicle:

> Hengest and Aesc fought against the Welsh and seized countless war-loot. And the Welsh fled from the English like fire.

Here it is generally agreed that the term "Welsh" is used in its correct form to mean "native Briton" of whatever variety.

In the Anglo-Saxon Chronicle, the whole period 473 to 514 is delineated in just 25 lines, with 519 to 540 (the eclipse noted above) dismissed in 13 lines. The next entry is for 544 (a natural death). All the events noted are south of the River Thames – Kent, Sussex, Hampshire and the Isle of Wight. Especially in the light of what was to follow – the way the Anglo-Saxons took over England – to suggest that anything like a "final victory" over them could have taken place in 516 is at best risible.

According to the Anglo-Saxon Chronicle, Hengist and Horsa arrived in 449 – add 44 years and we reach 493, which is definitely not the date for the battle of Badon Hill; however 516 is 44 years after 472 – for which, I suggest, read 473. If Hengest and Aesc took advantage of absence of Ambrosius Aurelianus and the cream of the British Army being away relieving the siege of Dumbarton Rock not only can we understand the victory, but everything else also begins to fit.

As logicians and lawyers know only too well, absence of evidence is not evidence of absence. So given that Arthur was not otherwise excessively busy in the period 520-535 and given, as we shall see, that there is good reason to suppose that he was "away from home" for at least some of this period, the way is left open for him to have delivered otherwise unrecorded defeats whether of the Anglo-Saxons or of others during this period – but this is not something to which I will be giving any serious attention, leaving it to those enthusiasts of the traditional Arthur and Arthuriana to recast their theories within the constraints I am providing in this work.

Source 7: Marie de France

I am grateful to Jacqueline Eccles for bringing the work of Marie de France to my attention. Marie wrote a series of "lai"s in Norman French in the later 1100s. These were designed as entertainment, but had a moral tone to them. Clearly they were not intended as history. Nevertheless there is something to be gleaned from one of these lais, called Lanval, after the hero, which has an Arthurian setting. Judith Shoaf has translated it using the text edited by Alfred Ewert and published as "Marie de France: *Lais*" by Basil Blackwell, Oxford in 1944. There are two items which we may draw from this work.

1. Marie on Arthur (Ewert lines 4-10)

> A Kardoel surjurnot li reis,
> Artur, le pruz et li curteis,
> Pur les Escoz e pur les Pis,
> Que destruieient le païs;
> En la tere de Loengre entroënt
> E mut suvent la damagoënt.

Which Judith Shoaf translates as:

> King Arthur was staying at Carduel -
> That King of valiant and courtly estate -
> His borders there he guarded well
> Against the Pict, against the Scot,
> Who'd cross into Logres to devastate
> The countryside often, and a lot.

What Marie tells us is that Arthur's job was on the border defending against attack of Pict and Scot.

"Logres" (variously Loengre and elsewhere Loegres) is clearly a variant of 'Lloegr' the Welsh word for England – a distinction which did not exist in Arthurian times (a useful discussion of this is to be found at: http://www.omniglot.com/blog/?p=532) – so the very name itself is anachronistic. The feel I get from these words is that Marie was NOT of the view that Arthur had been the king of 'Logres'. We should note also that Scottish and/or Pictish attacks on Wales were far fewer and less devastating than raids into what is now England. [The converse held, of course, for Irish pirates.]

Wikipedia cites many sources in suggesting that "Carduel" is the form used for "Camelot" on the continent. This variation deserves some exploration. On the one hand we could suppose that this stems from a resiting of the action to suit later story tellers, but this does not sit well with Marie's locating Arthur on the border with the Picts and Scots. Moreover whoever wrote the Wikipedia page seems to have overlooked the fact that Chrétien de Troyes refers separately to Camelot (in his "Lancelot") and to Carduel (in "Erec and Enide" and in "Yvain").

Parsing the word we can see that "Car-" is in all likelihood "Caer-" ie castle/fort. For "-duel" we should look to Welsh, where the best I can come up with is "dubwll" meaning "grave". One might reasonably expect a good deal of fighting, death and consequent burial in the environs of more or less any fort from those times, so even if this is the correct understanding, by itself it does not help us to locate Carduel. As an alternative, we should also consider parsing "-duel" – especially because it is elsewhere spelled "-dowal". The first part "Du-" is likely from Dubh – ie "black" – (and in several parts of Scotland "dubh" is still rendered as "dow") while "-el" could easily be a variant of "-ail" – "rock"; so all in all "Blackcastle" or more completely "Blackrock castle". [While the Gaels tended to place the adjective after the noun, it appears that the Picts were not so particular.] So I say that Camelot and Carduel were indeed separate places; their locations are discussed in Part 4.

2. Marie on Guinevere Ywain and Gawain (Ewert lines 223-6 & seq.)

Much of the story of Lanval hinges on Marie's suggestion that it was Arthur's (unnamed) wife who was the initiator of sexual encounters with other men. Spurned by Lanval she covers her embarrassment by claiming that he must be gay. For the purposes of my work, the specific story, which I assume to be wholly fictitious, is irrelevant. But for it to be of interest to contemporary listeners it needed to ring true – and so I take it that Marie's audience would have found this characterisation of Guinevere unremarkable. This in turn should inform us regarding her apparent liaison with Lancelot – ie it is of no consequence whether such a liaison was intended to be supposed to be true, but it was understood that Guinevere was the sort of woman who might well try this on.

Marie specifies that Owen (Ywain) and Gavin (Gawain) were cousins. This fits with the idea that their mothers were (Arthur's) sisters. However this could have been drawn from her prior knowledge of Geoffrey of Monmouth's work.

Source 8: Crétien de Troyes

The work of Crétien de Troyes, writing in the later 1100s is the most removed from an attempt to place Arthur and his entourage in historical situations. He need not concern us here, but later we will have cause to consider two of his characters: "King Lac" and his son "Erec". We have noted already his separate references to Camelot and to Carduel.

A good summary of his work, together with further references may be found at http://www.gutenberg.org/files/831/831-h/831-h.htm

Sources 9 & 10: Monmouth and Mallory

We can discount as a reliable source the fantasy about Arthur in "The History of the Kings of Britain" by Geoffrey of Monmouth, writing in the middle 1100s. However for any fantasy to work it must contain sufficient elements regarded by the intended audience as true, so the text is worthy of careful, albeit sceptical exploration.

We may discount also "Le Morte d' Arthur" (dating to the later 1400s) by Thomas Malory; but it is well, nevertheless, to pay attention to much of the text – not for the main thrust of the story which we know to be untrue, but rather for items which it is easy to dismiss as embellishments to make a good story, but which nevertheless represent in some way elements of the lore upon which he drew.

In Book XI Chapter IX, Geoffrey of Monmouth refers to Lot(h), king and eponymous of Lothian.

[See http://www.indiana.edu/~dmdhist/arthur_gm.htm]

Mallory refers to Loth also (Book II chapter 10), albeit making him king of Orkney.

[See http://www.sacred-texts.com/neu/mart/mart036.htm.]

Both are agreed that he was married to Arthur's sister. This is relevant and important because it was Lot's daughter (St Theneu) who was the mother of St Kentigern. For a more full discussion of St Kentigern see the Appendix.

The Catholic Encyclopaedia (http://www.newadvent.org/cathen/08620a.htm) gives St Kentigern's dates as c518-603. Meanwhile as we can see above the Welsh Annals prefer 612 for his death and the modern view is c614. If the encyclopaedia has his life span correct then the alternative birth epoch would be c528.

For a more full discussion of St Kentigern see Appendix 1 Section 3

Source 11: Anonymous/"The Pearl Author"

The reader may be just a little surprised by this entry amongst the "sources", but, spurred on by the nuggets to be found in the Lais of Marie de France and really only as an afterthought I took a look at the story of Sir Gawain and the Green Knight. It is not my intention to question the general conclusion as to the date and location of the writing of this story (the general consensus would appear to the later 1300s and the Cheshire area). The way the story is set out reflects the times in which it was written. It is "obvious" that the writer draws on earlier sources if only because he refers to Arthur, Guinevere and Gawain – but I suggest that the basis of the story is a much older tradition. There are three items I will draw from it.

1. Here is an extract from the Tolkien and Gordon edition:

Bot Arthure wolde not ete til al were serued,
He watz so joly of his joyfnes, and sumquat childgered:
His lif liked hym lyȝt, he louied þe lasse
Auþer to longe lye or to longe sitte,
So bisied him his ȝonge blod and his brayn wylde.
And also an oþer maner meued him eke
Þat he þurȝ nobelay had nomen, he wolde neuer ete
Vpon such a dere day er hym deuised were
Of sum auenturus þyng an vncouþe tale,
Of sum mayn meruayle, þat he myȝt trawe,
Of alderes, of armes, of oþer auenturus,

which Jessie Weston translates in this fashion:

"But Arthur would not eat till all were served, so full of joy and gladness was he, even as a child; he liked not either to lie long, or to sit long at meat, so worked upon him his young blood and his wild brain. And another custom he had also, that came of his nobility, that he would never eat upon an high day till he had been advised of some knightly deed, or some strange and marvellous tale, of his ancestors, or of arms, or of other ventures."

So this fantastical tale claims, self-referentially, that tales such as itself were a commonplace at Arthur's 'court' as an integral part of any celebration/feast. I was delighted by this as I had long since come to the conclusion that the vast majority of surviving "tales" told about Arthur and his contemporaries were just that – intended not as truth, but as entertainment.

2. But the story features, among others, Sir Gawain – a real person whom we know from elsewhere as Arthur's nephew. This gives us an extra layer of understanding: that the fictional tales nevertheless featured real people, often people in the room at the time. Thus a good laugh could be had at their expense by the exposure though caricature of some weakness, or some strength or genuine good deed of derring-do could be extolled in a fantastical way. When we are confronted by characters in Arthuriana, therefore, we need to consider whether they are real, or purely fictitious, or real but fictionalised eg in a satirical way which everyone present would have understood.

3. An excellent example of this (2 above) is the Green Knight himself, ultimately revealed as "Bertilak de Hautdesert". I propose that the writer has misunderstood a different name (presumably from an oral source). Bertilak should be parsed as Ber-ti-lak where "-ti-lak" is a corruption of "du lac". Thus Bertilak is actually another real person, a member of the extended "du lac" family, for which see the "Who's Who" appendix. We may note in passing that in Welsh "Byr" and "Ber" mean "short" – thus the name Bertilak itself could be satirical ("the dwarf of the du Lac family" or whatever – perhaps intended ironically to indicate large size). However "Bêr" means "spear" or "lance", so this could be a byname for Lancelot (du Lac – see in the first section of part 3 of this work) or a member of his immediate family. Not only that, but the story is intended to caricature/illustrate some real underlying truth about the real relationship between Gawain (and his family?) on the one hand and the du Lac family (in general or this particular member) on the other.

Conclusions:

The general conclusion we should draw is that if we should seek to depart by more than five years from the dates offered by the Annales then, given its general reliability, it would be necessary to construct a really strong case. All the evidence we have is consistent with

1. the date offered for Annales Cambriae date given of 516 (+/-3) for the battle of Badon Hill, described by Gildas as the final victory over "the enemy".

2. "the enemy" in question being the Picts and Scots.

PART 2:
BACKGROUND – SCOTLAND BEFORE ARTHUR

The situation confronting the tribes of Southern Scotland, Ambrosius Aurelianus and Arthur in the last quarter of the 400s is best understood if we can get a sense of the ebb and flow of tribal power in Scotland over a considerable period of time preceding their own. In particular we need to understand the distribution of the various tribes in Scotland – and this is by no means easy, as is demonstrated by the way in which so many writers have got so much wrong.

In this part I will take you, the reader, through the proposition systematically and then provide a "narrative summary" at the end.

SCOTLAND BEFORE ARTHUR
1: SCOTLAND 80 – 140AD

We may usefully begin this survey with the Roman invasion of Scotland. For a general reference here I would recommend

http://roman-britain.co.uk/ and
http://www.antoninewall.org/

1.1 Timeline: The Roman Invasion of Scotland

43AD: Our starting point is the peace treaty between the (unnamed) king of Orkney and the Roman Empire on the occasion of the invasion of the British Isles. There is the suggestion that diplomatic relations may have been established earlier still – we may wonder why such an effort to be included in such a treaty may have been made.

85AD Having already done two tours of duty here, Agricola was governor of Britain in the period 77-85AD and during this time he invaded Scotland – an invasion which included his famous victory at Mons Graupius in 83AD (there are now some who doubt this event). He built a series of forts extending through the whole of the central belt and even across Buchan to Elgin and, in effect, Inverness if not beyond. It is also argued that from the north coast he penetrated deep into Strathspey. Much of this was recorded (some now claiming that this was 'over-glowingly' ie exaggerated) by his son-in-law Tacitus.

120AD The Romans were overstretched – or stretched beyond the energy and resources they were willing to apply to the problem. Inchtuthil fort near Dunkeld was never completed; it was abandoned after a very few years. From the vast horde of nails discovered there recently it has been inferred that they had plans for a much more muscular presence in Scotland which they then decided against. So this intrusion was not maintained and as we know the Romans retreated to build what is now Hadrian's wall in the 120s.

To round off the matter of the time window we should note that:

140AD The Roman retreat was not to last long as a new invasion under Lollius Urbicus at the behest of the emperor Antoninus Pius led to the establishment of the Antonine Wall shortly after 140AD.

160AD However this was abandoned shortly after 160AD

208AD only to be reoccupied by Severus around the year 208 AD following aggression principally from the Maeatae especially after 197 (see James E Fraser "From Caledonia to Pictland" pp26 et seq.). [He took the opportunity of this punitive expedition to burn many of the Picts' forts which thereby became vitrified.]

213AD and then abandoned again c 213.

1.2 85AD: the Roman/Pictish Front Line

The result of Agricola's campaign was a line of Roman Forts which are now usually referred to as the "Glen blockers". From the map below, however, we can see that the function of the forts was not some merely theoretical glen blocking, but was an active front line where the Romans opposed established Pictish strongpoints.

85AD: The Roman Front Line

Pictish Forts ●   ● Roman Forts

Key	Pictish Fort	Roman Fort	Separation
1		Raedykes	
2	?Drumsleed	Kair	4 km
3	Catheruns	Stracathro	6.5 km
4	Castlehill	Inverquharity	1.3 km
5	Barry Hill	Cardean	1.2 km
6	Rohallion	Inchtuthill	3 km
6		Bertha	
7	Dun Mor	Fendoch	700m
8	Dundearn	Dalginross	2 km
9	Dunmore	Bochastle	500m
10	Doune Hill	Malling	2 km
11	?Catter Law	Drumquhassie	800m

We should consider why the Pictish forts were there in the first place. I surmise that all was not peace and harmony between the Pictish tribes before the advent of the Romans. This in turn informs us of the Romans' strategy – which was to try to encourage the lowland tribes to accept union with Rome by providing the protection which they clearly needed. The coastal Lowlanders were then on the horns of a dilemma. If they exchanged one set of masters for another the Highlanders would surely interpret this as treachery. How reliable and sustained would the Roman support prove to be? Where would their advantage lie?

The Romans had no real expectation that the tribes in the Central Lowlands would be won over – and so these tribes (sadly left unnamed to history) were bisected by a second chain of forts running from Stirling up the route of the current A9 to Perth, including the huge fort at Ardoch. [We should note also that at that time the bulk of the Forth/Teith valley was marsh incapable of sustaining a substantial population.]

We will consider this twin line of forts in order – north to south, but please note that although I have taken Raedykes, north east of Stonehaven as the starting point for the purpose both of the illustration and for the bulk of the discussion, Agricola did not stop there. From there he struck inland to Kintore whence via Huntly to Elgin and Cawdor – with a view to following the line of the A9 North of Inverness. As will be seen from the maps later on we may take it both that the tribe called the Taexali were broadly friendly and that I can concur with the bulk of modern opinion which is that there was a battle of Mons Graupius and that it took place near to Bennachie.

Most commentators seem to think that Raedykes was but a day's march from Stracathro – but at well over 30 km I am sure that at the very least there would be a good deal of grumbling and fractiousness amongst the troops. Fortunately this is not an issue as there was a Roman Camp at Kair – almost exactly half way between. There is no evidence of a Pictish fort to oppose here, but there is a quarry at Drumsleed which is the sort of headland ideal for that sort of defence. So it would not surprise me if there had been something there. But this is pure speculation – whence the question mark.

Stracathro is rather further from the Catheruns than would have been ideal, but the siting options were constrained by the lie of the land; we may infer further that the risks here were relatively small. Indeed the rather larger distances in Angus and the Mearns, with the rather more relaxed atmosphere implied, follow directly from the fact that this was not the primary route for any substantial aggressive raid – ie beyond local plundering.

And so it is that we come to Strath Tay. The "Rath" that was called Rohallion ("The Rath of the Caledonians") is in Birnam Wood and is now called Duncan's Seat. From here there is line of sight all the way to Dunsinane Hill in the Sidlaws, made famous by Shakespeare. Inchtuthil is on the other side of the river from this fort, but it is close enough for the Romans to be sure of what was going on. If the Picts launched their sortie on the west side of the Tay it would have still been easy for the Romans to meet them from their base at Bertha – which was just north of present day Perth on the North bank of the River Almond, relatively easily reinforced from Carpow (near Abernethy, just nine miles to the South).

The reader will have noted already the question mark also regarding Catter Law. This is generally described as a "motte" and assumed to be of mediaeval construction – but the mediaeval mottes usually had baileys (larger areas of defensible space, usually higher than the surrounding environment) surrounding them. This one lacks a bailey. There are other mottes like this (at Kennoway in Fife, for example) so this interpretation of it is far from impossible, but it would make a great deal of sense for it to have been much older – a rath rather than a motte – so I have included it, as a possibility, for the sake of completeness.

Not included on this map is Dumbarton Rock – which will be considered later. There is no reason to suppose a direct Roman connection.

1.3. c120AD: Ptolemy's map of Scotland
a: Capes and Bays

So now we can come to the work of Claudius Ptolomeus (otherwise Ptolemy), who lived in Alexandria and never visited Scotland.

Sources:

http://roman-britain.co.uk/ptolemys-geography.htm

http://penelope.uchicago.edu/Thayer/E/Gazetteer/Periods/Roman/_Texts/Ptolemy/2/2*.html

ALF Rivet & Colin Smith: "The Placenames of Roman Britain" (Batsford 1979)

Prof. Alexander McBain: "Outlines of Gaelic Etymology" (Mackay 1909)

Alastair Strang "Explaining Ptolemy's Roman Britain" Britannia Vol 28 pp1-30 (1997)

Christian Marx: "Rectification of position data of Scotland in Ptolemy's Geographike Hyphegesis"   Survey Review 46: 231–244, DOI (2014)

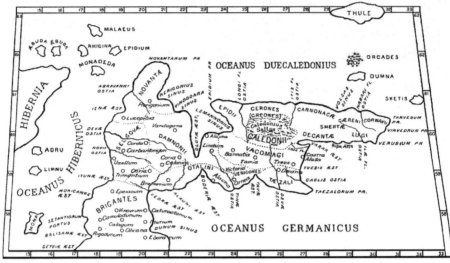

PTOLEMY'S MAP OF SCOTLAND.
(Founded on Muller's text of 1883 and Map of 1478 by the Editor).
(from Macbain, 1909)

b. Dating Ptolemy's work

We see that the Damnonii were on both sides of the line of the Antonine Wall so the data cannot be from after 140 or even some years before. The fact that Ptolemy does not even mention the River Tyne preferring the nearby Wear shows us that the line of Hadrian's Wall had not yet been confirmed. So the information could not be significantly into the 120s. Nevertheless it does seem that the Selgovae and the Goddodin were to the North and the Brigantes to the South of the broad line which would become Hadrian's wall.

Because of the building of the Antonine Wall substantially south of the line of the "Glenblocker" forts, we know that Scotland rebounded from the weight of the Roman yoke – and it is clear that Ptolemy's map represents a situation well before that process was complete. Thus we can go along with the generally accepted proposition that he did his work on Scotland in the early 120s AD (or, to be rather more precise, the early 120s represents the date of the most recent information available to him). In this context the reader is urged to be extremely cautious about maps eg on the internet purporting to show the distribution of tribes "c150".

Ptolemy relied on reports, often remarkably exact and contemporaneous, of Roman measurements and whatever was left of the work of Pytheas, a Greek adventurer based at Marseille (now France) who had circumnavigated the British Isles sometime in the decades immediately before 300 BC (ie nearly 450 years earlier).

We now need to consider the information that Ptolemy recorded and we should begin by understanding the problems we encounter in trying to understand it. The first thing to bear in mind that Ptolemy drew no map – indeed he discouraged it on the basis that there would be mistakes made and that these mistakes would be so great as to render the result seriously problematic in practice; however this has not prevented many people from trying to draw such a map. The second problem we have is that in the process of other people copying and recopying the information many mistakes – indeed many contradictions – have been introduced. So it is very difficult to make definitive assertions about much of the information, as will become clear below.

c. Ptolemy's "obvious" mistake

Anyone who has ever looked at maps based on Ptolemy's data will have seen that the first glaring mistake he made was to put Scotland on its side – so the western coast appears to be the north coast, while the east coast appears to be the south – as the outline sketch above shows. I say that this misrepresentation was deliberate.

Latitude

The problem arose from a fundamental inaccuracy in his tables of Latitude. This can be illustrated by his coordinates for Morecambe Bay – for which Ptolemy gives a latitude of 58° 20' N. In fact Morecambe Bay is just 54° 10'N – an error of over 4 degrees. In other words Ptolemy was working on the assumption that Morecambe Bay was some 280 miles North of its true position.

Constraining him at the other end was the "well known fact" – which he took as axiomatic – that Thule was at 63°N, which is highly ironic as it is as good as exactly true: the northern tip of the Faroe Islands (Thule) are in fact at 62° 23'N (the southern tip of Iceland (Ultima Thule?) is 63° 20'N. [For a discussion of Thule and my identification of it as the Faroe Islands, see the relevant appendix in this book.] Thule excepted, it would appear that the inaccuracies in the data with which Ptolemy had to work got worse the further North he was trying to map. His data for Morecambe Bay shows double the error which he has for the mouth of the River Tamar at Portsmouth – which he lists as 52° 10'N, whereas it is really only 50° 20'.]

Longitude

Solving the problem of Longitude resisted the lure of huge rewards offered by many monarchs into the 1700s, so how Ptolemy (or before him Pytheas) approached it is problematic – the wonder is how (after Marx's emendations) so much of the data offered was as accurate as it turned out to be. Ptolemy and Pytheas had a good understanding of the overall size of the globe of the Earth, so my conclusion is that the longitude was calculated partly using trigonometry and was based on measurements of length taken on the ground.

So Ptolemy had to recalculate his raw data to try to make Scotland squash into the limited space he understood to be available for it. Given the distances that he was aware of, the only solution lay in a complex set of rotations to fit with what he "knew" the underlying truth/constraints to be. My guess is that Ptolemy knew perfectly well that something was not right – but he did not have any opportunity to work out just where the error lay. What he offered was the best that he could do under the circumstances. Various attempts have been made to devise a mathematical system to rectify this problem – with several points identified as possible centres of rotation to account for what ends up as a nearly 90 degree shift. Two such efforts commend themselves to our attention: the work of Alastair Strang and of Christian Marx. It would appear that Marx has cracked the problem of recalculation – so this is a very helpful start – but it is only a start. Where Marx has scored over Strang is that he has been fiercely logical. Strang could see that, even after the transformations had been computed, there were "obvious" mistakes – and he sought to offer what he saw as logical explanations and alternatives. Marx just tells it how it is leaving others to deal with the errors in the original data.

Oceanus Duecaledonius

We shall discuss below the location of the tribe called "Caledonii". But there is a conceptual problem which needs to be highlighted here.

We should start by noting that according to the ancient Greeks the sea which completely surrounded the land on which people lived was simply known as "Oceanus". The name "Atlantic" Ocean (known in this way since the mid 500s BC and apparently named after Atlas) referred specifically to that part of "Oceanus" beyond the Pillars of Hercules, but also, at least since Plato (fl 420s-340s BC) evokes the place Atlantis which was overwhelmed in a flood (modern day opinion is split between those who would dismiss the story as pure fiction and those who think that this is a reference to the volcanic eruption on Santorini/Thera which largely destroyed the Minoan civilisation) – but it is not clear how far that name was intended to apply at that time. Another part of it, which we now call the North Sea, Ptolemy calls "Oceanus Germanicus".

In Greece there are the remnants of a place called Calydon (not far from modern day Messolonghi) – named after the mythological king of the same name. Calydon had a great-grandson, also king of Calydon, called Oeneus (compare this with Oengus/Angus common in Pictland). Calydon was a 3xgreat-grandson of Deucalion, who, with his father, survived a flood sent by Zeus by building a chest. Deucalion was the son of Prometheus. The name Deucalion includes the idea 'sailor' as well as 'sweetness/wine' and his wife Pyrrha's name contains the idea 'ginger haired' (a genetic quirk particularly (though not exclusively) characteristic of Cruithin people (see below)).

Thus my guess is that the (Scottish) Caledonians were known to Pytheas and that they were somehow conflated with Calydon in Greece (and there is the legend that the Picts came from Scythia). Thus Oceanus "Duecaledonius" is a misreading by someone along the way – Ptolemy himself at the latest – for "Deucalionid" or some such. This conflation and confusion led Ptolemy – or such of his copyists through whom we have access to his work – to associate the Caledonians and the Duecaledonian Ocean more closely than was in any way warranted.

This in turn led to later Romans (eg Ammianus Marcellinus in the later 300s AD) renaming the Caledonians as "Dicaledonians" (no-one has been able to identify any tribe of this name – leading to considerable speculation founded on nothing).

Ptolemy's Data

Ptolemy provides a list of "Capes and Bays" – ie a sequence of landmarks which someone sailing round the coast might expect to encounter – with their latitude and longitude as he understood it. He also provided a list of tribes with a general explanation of their position relative to each other – but with hardly any specific ties in to any of the capes and bays mentioned. He went on to list a number of settlements (with their coordinates) which he groups according to which tribe they "belong" to.

For a full list of these see, for example, Rivet & Smith – but they can also be found online at eg

http://penelope.uchicago.edu/Thayer/E/Gazetteer/Periods/Roman/_Texts/Ptolemy/2/2*.html or

http://roman-britain.co.uk/ptolemys-geography.htm

d. Places identified by Ptolemy that we may be sure of:

Ptolemy's name	Name Today
Rerigonius Bay	Loch Ryan
Vindogara Bay	Estuary of the Ayr
Clota Estuary	Clyde Estuary
Navarus River	River Naver
Deva River	River Dee (Galloway)
Novius River	River Nith
Itunae Estuary	River Eden (Carlisle)
Varar River	River Farrar
Loxa River	River Lossie
Tuesis River	River Spey
Deva River	River Dee (Aberdeen)
Boderia Estuary	Firth of Forth
Trimontium	Newstead (Eildon Hills)
Bremenium	High Rochester (Northumberland)

From what I can understand of Marx's work, river mouths map to river mouths and settlements map to settlements (often Roman Forts). The residual problem is that often the name of the river does not match the reality – so also with the settlements. Thus, even after recalculation, the coordinates Ptolemy offers for the river Tay actually take us to the Montrose Basin – which is some 20 miles to the North of the Tay. [In this case Ron Greer of the Antonine Guard advises me that the Montrose Basin was an important Pictish naval base – so it is easy to understand why it would have been a place whose location was noted by Roman cartographers – providing the opportunity for the later mix-up.] Similarly, Ptolemy identifies the Tweed but calls it the Aln – which is about 33 miles away to the South. In the case of the river "Itis", Macbain makes a strong case that etymologically this should be Loch Etive, yet Marx shows that its readjusted coordinates map to Loch Alsh – over 50 miles away. In the case of the river Caelis (variously Celnius) while all agree that the River Deveron is intended (and mapped to) nevertheless, as Macbain asserts, the name more suits Cullen, some ten miles farther west.

[In the Moray firth some editions of Ptolemy have eg the rivers Lossie and the Farrar in the wrong order.]

So my general conclusion is that it is a fruitless exercise to try to say "what" Ptolemy means as if there is a single answer. Instead we should accept the duality of (i) the place mapped to and (ii) separately the name of the place – albeit allowing that in some cases they will indeed coincide. This implies that the original data included at least all the places named AND all the places mapped to!

e. The Nature of Political Boundaries

Before we move to trying to understand the nature and distribution of the tribes named by Ptolemy, we need to consider the nature of boundaries.

Today with air photography and various satellite based Ground Positioning Systems (GPS) we can identify any location to within a very few metres; maps can be drawn with an accuracy far beyond anything anyone could even dream of before the advent of space and other modern digital technology. On this basis, in any country with an effective system of law and government, we can say exactly who owns and/or is responsible for what and where it is.

Before our current time, it was possible, of course, to use many items in the landscape and reasonably accurate measurement to identify boundaries and so settle who controls which parcel of land – written down in charters and title deeds. But for this to be effective, reasonably widespread literacy and the ability to enforce the rule of law were necessary.

If we step back one further pace – to a time of reasonably effective government but no written charters – then natural barriers are the best features to use. Especially in mountainous areas, watersheds between different valleys were highly convenient; as were those rivers which are not easily crossed. Where land could not be divided in this way, some minor water courses were used nevertheless – in Pictish times these were often given the name "Creichie" – meaning "the boundary burn" – and elsewhere it was often the case that official marker stones were set up to show where just where the boundaries were.

Where there is no effective government then a free-for-all can develop. We see this in places like Afghanistan today – where the mountains can serve as a hideout. In these circumstances the watersheds can sometimes still be of value, but more often the distinction is between (a) the wild mountains and (b) the more settled lowlands. Although the lowlands are more fertile and so can sustain a higher population, nevertheless it is difficult for the larger lowland population to dominate the smaller highland one. Once sufficiently aroused the lowlands can put together a force – an army – for a punitive expedition to inflict damage on the highlands, but maintaining a presence sufficient to exercise permanent control tends to prove excessively burdensome. Indeed the continuing existence of countries such as Switzerland, Liechtenstein and Andorra bear witness to the persistence into modern times of the same underlying principles on mainland Europe.

So it has been in what is now Scotland. Written charters came in with feudalisation, broadly post 1100. It was this which allowed the large Mormaerdoms to be broken up into smaller Earldoms and smaller still free baronies. For some hundreds of years before feudalisation, the Mormaerdoms, largely based on watersheds, were small enough for a strong man to exercise a good deal of control – but this was always quite fragile. Even well into historical times the Border rievers were beyond central control and serial attempts to control the Highlands were really only concluded with the military roads and the population clearances which followed the battle of Culloden in 1746.

In Ptolemy's time, as we shall see, the most important confrontations were between Highland and Lowland. Not only that but the situation was exceptionally fluid. Despite this, many writers have been extremely casual about the dates they throw about. I have already cautioned about the "about 150" phrase. Furthermore although scholars are making progress, note how in many cases the maps do not match the text. [It is easy to emend/update text, often a real trial to redraw the accompanying map.]

With these reservations in mind, we may now proceed to consider Ptolemy's tribes and settlements.

f. Ptolemy's Tribal areas

We must start by noting the way Ptolemy uses weasel words such as "above and below" when describing the relationships between tribes. What does this mean, especially in a Highland context? Does it mean "more to the north/south (whence, by rotation, east/west) or does it actually refer to the height of the land? Might it mean different things in different contexts?

The map used by Professor Macbain shows a "commonsense", albeit literalist, interpretation of the distribution of the tribes broadly as Ptolemy described them, but the Caledonians in particular pose a problem for it is only too easy to translate the words, apparently "literally" (as on the map above) to show the Caledonii occupying the area of Urquhart and Glenmoriston. Urquhart and Glenmoriston is poor land with a carrying capacity quite unable to sustain the sort of population necessary to provide leadership for all the Picts. But in his "Agricola", Tacitus, writing about the Battle of Mons Graupius, describes his enemy as "Caledones and other Picts" – in other words the Caledones were the principal grouping within the Pictish confederacy.

Fortunately the Picts did leave placenames. Thus we have the mountain Shiehallion – the Mountain of the Caledonians (I resist the often supposed "fairy" allusion) and Rohallion – the rath (fortified place – cognate with the English "-worth") of the Caledonians. Somewhat later we have Dunkeld – the fort of the Caledonians. These are in upper Perthshire (for a long time

"Atholl"), miles away from Urquhart and Glenmoriston. This is far more promising in every respect. Thus we can see that Ptolemy got his geological faults confused – and he placed the Caledonii on the Great Glen Fault when he should have placed them in the parallel position on the Highland Boundary Fault. Conversely when he said that the Caledonii were "above" the Vacomagi, he was right – provided that the dimension was height above sea level.

Professor Macbain (p44) wrote:

> "The Caledonians are definitely located; they stretch, says Ptolemy, from Lemman Bay to the Estuary of the Varar – from Loch Fyne to the Inverness Firth; above them, that is, west of them, is the Caledonios Drumos or Forest. The last, as Skene says is Drum Alban and the Western Grampians. A line from Loch Fyne to Inverness goes right along Drum Alban for half the way; in fact the district so defined is impossible for two reasons. The Caledonians were east of Drum Alban; secondly Dunkeld, which most writers allow as containing their name shews that Perthshire was occupied by them. In fact the Caledonians inhabited Perthshire and easter Inverness."

So this problem was recognised over 100 years ago, yet no-one seems to have attempted to redraw the map with this in mind. I propose that we do.

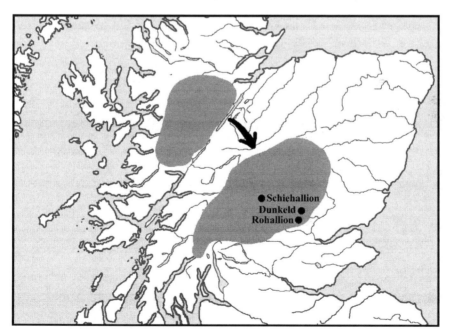

Correcting the location of the Caledonii from Ptolemy's data

Distribution of Tribes

Particularly with regard to settlements, Ptolemy not only identified them by latitude and longitude, he also specified the tribe within whose ambit they lay. This has generated more misunderstanding and consequent failures of cartography – for if the names are misallocated in space then any literalist will conclude that the tribe mentioned must have controlled that area. But, as we have seen, many of the names have indeed been misplaced (cf the River Tay noted above). Not only that, but there are tribes which we know of – sometimes quite substantial tribes – which find no mention (for example the Maeatae and the Verturones).

When I started on my study of Prolemy, my previous experience encouraged me to suppose that watersheds would be key to tribal boundaries, but from the location of Rohallion, occupied by the Caledonians and most of the way down the River Tay and from the location of Trimontium, just downstream from Melrose and thus midway along the river Tweed, I have had to reset my thinking completely. The dominant antithesis here and then was highland and lowland – reinforcing the need for caution in interpreting Ptolemy's "above" and "below".

The map used by Macbain is cluttered, so I redrew it leaving aside the tribes and using a similar graticule developed by Barri Jones and David Mattingly ("An Atlas of Roman Britain" 1990 p19) which was good enough for Alistair Strang to use in his own paper (Britannia Vol. 28 (1997) pp1-30).

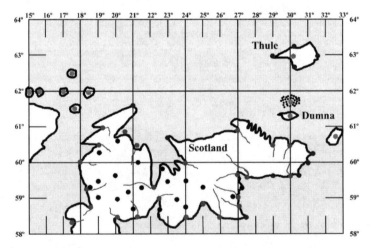

The dots are placed according to Ptolemy's latitude and longitude. The black ones represent his towns/settlements, while the grey ones are other physical features (eg river mouths). What I hope the reader will see is the pattern.

We are now in a position to draw up a map of the distribution of tribes in Scotland. To come to a sensible conclusion will require a subtle interplay of logic and geography. So here I present my conclusions/proposition, followed by its justification.

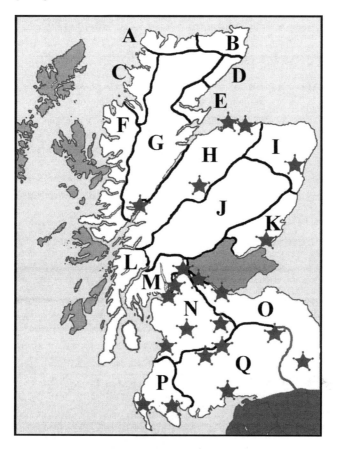

Key to the map

Letter	Tribe	Letter	Tribe	Letter	Tribe
A	Caerini	G	Smaertae	M	Gadini
B	Cornavii	H	Vacomagi	N	Damnonii
C	Carnonacae	I	Taexali	O	Votadini
D	Lugi	J	Caledonii	P	Novantes
E	Decantae	K	Venicones	Q	Selgovae
F	Cerones	L	Epidii		

I hope that the reader will also see how the overall pattern of the settlements broadly corresponds with that on Macbain's map.

Initial observations:

- The islands, Fife, Clackmannan and Strathearn are greyed because Ptolemy failed to identify any tribe living in these areas.

- We see that there is no mention of nor room for the Scots (they are not mentioned in Ireland either).They are under active examination in academic circles at the present time (early 2017). I will discuss them in some detail below.

- There is no mention of the Verturones (who gave their name to 'Fortriu'). For a long time they were supposed to have lived in Fife and Strathearn, but all modern historians follow the work of Alex Woolf, agreeing that the Verturones belong to Moray – thus they must be part of, or emerged from, the Vacomagi.

- There is no mention of the Maeatae and their kingdom of Manau (whence the placenames Dumyat Hill, Clackmannan and Slamannan).

Discussion

* We may start with the Taexali occupying the lowland of Buchan and Aberdeenshire. Their town is recorded as Devona. Here the key to understanding is the line taken by the Roman troops who struck inland from Stonehaven to Kintore (as verified by Marx, agreeing with Rivet & Smith). Strang prefers Normandykes on the basis that the name refers to the River Dee not the Don – but Macbain points out that the "Don" is really a contraction of "Divona" – so Strang's circumspection is unnecessary. Had the Romans been making for Strathspey they might have preferred the Lecht (the A969) or the Cairn o Mount (B964) – but this would have been through enemy territory. So this makes clear in general terms where the boundary between the Taexali and what we now understand to be the Caledonii lay. It also shows the intelligence of the Caledonii in choosing to take the Romans on at the battle of Mons Graupius at a place where their lines of communication and supply were at their most stretched.

* Moving South we come to the Venicones occupying the lowland of Angus and the Mearns. Marx and Strang both identify the town in their area, Orrea (Classis) as Monifieth. This makes good sense and is clearly in the middle of Veniconian territory. The main alternative proposed in the past has been Carpow (Abernethy, Fife) where there was indeed a legionary town. But Monifieth's position is better as it avoids having to navigate some 20 miles of the river Tay and more convenient for resupplying several forts. It was quite a distance from Montrose Basin where the Picts had their fleet.

We may be confident that the fleet based at Montrose was not the sole property of the Venicones and so we may suppose that they had had some sort of client status relationship with the Caledonians. This, I think, is the context for the confusion Ptolemy has between Montrose Basin and Tay Estuary. The Romans will indeed have found it necessary to assert themselves muscularly at Montrose.

*The only other highland tribe with any identified settlements is the Vacomagi (I suspect that the name may refer to a cow-based economy). Two of their four towns are beyond dispute: "Pinnata Castra" is the Roman fort next to the Vacomagi's own Burghead while "Tuesis" – which by its name shows that it is on or very near the Spey is the Roman Camp Bellie. We are left with Bannatia and Tamia. Just how difficult it is to identify Tamia may be judged by the various suggestions variously offered by Macbain, Rivet & Smith and Strang: Inchtuthil, Stracathro and Cardean (Meigle, Angus). Marx has nothing to say. I say that all these are wrong, because we know – now – that the Vacomagi were nowhere in the vicinity. Banatia suffers from the same problem. Marx and Strang both say Dalginross (Comrie) and I have no doubt that this is the location intended by Ptolemy's coordinates. But it cannot be so for the same reason – it is way out of area (or we would know that the Vacomagi crossed Caledonian territory).

So.... I have a new proposition which has the advantage that it fits the pattern on the map for more closely: Banatia is actually Banavie, next to what is now Fort William – meaning that the Vacomagi stretched from shore to shore – Moray Firth to Loch Linnhe. On that basis "Tamia" should be somewhere near Ruthven Barracks in Badenoch. Might the reader be tempted to see a resonance between Tamia and Tromie? This could even be a simple scribal error (many Latin river names have a "tam-" element so it would be easy for a scribe to suppose a mistake). So my working hypothesis is that "Tamia" refers to what we now call Ruthven Barracks.

*In the South West we can see that the Novantes (the "incomers") had made little headway. Rerigonium cannot be sited precisely, but is clearly in the immediate neighbourhood of Stranraer. The many later castle sites demonstrate the range of possibilities beyond the town itself – which remains a strong candidate. Their other town, Lucophibia, is problematic, but a recent (February 2017) news report regarding Trusty's Hill (immediately to the West of Gatehouse of Fleet) has been very helpful. I am grateful to John Williams of the local archaeology society for advising me that the entrance to this fort is from the east. On this basis I think we can dismiss Strang's identification of Lucophibia with Gatehouse of Fleet, preferring Marx who proposes Wigtown. We may next consider the old Wigtownshire/ Kirkcubridghtshire county boundary. This ran up the river Cree (west of

Trusty's Hill) before jinking across to go down the river Doun and Loch Doun. We may reasonably conclude from this line that an earlier boundary between the two lay along the watersheds, so that the Cree was in Novantae territory while the valley of the Doune (at least as far as Dalmellington) lay with the Selgovae. We have seen before that Ptolemy's coordinates often do not match the name which is supposed to go with it. I am sure that readers will have noticed the similarity of the name "Lucophibia" and eg the Water of Luce at the mouth of which stands Glenluce, just 3 miles from the later named Dunragit fort. So I suspect that while Ptolemy's coordinates apply to Wigtown, but the placename probably applies to somewhere near Glenluce.

Now we get to the complicated bit – which is the main point of the exercise!

* In Ptolemy's time the Selgovae occupied the great bulk of the Southern Uplands. Two of their centres are not in dispute: Trimontium (as we have seen) is Newstead east of Melrose; Marx agrees with Macbain that Uxellum is Wardlaw Fort near Dumfries. Marx and Rivet & Smith agree that Corda is Castledykes near Lanark in Clydesdale, while Strang prefers Crawford some 15 miles further south. I have no doubt that the numbers take us to Castledykes, but a careful consideration of the geography demonstrates that this was not a Selgovae stronghold: firstly it is the wrong side of the Medwin Water, secondly it faces south rather than north. Rather Castledykes represented Manau's front line against the Selgovae whose forward positions – with line of sight to Castledykes – at Cairngryfe Hill and Balwaistie Hill. Castledykes came under Damnonii control. The main Selgovae base in this area was probably at Crawford, following Strang's logic. This leaves "Carbantorium". Suggestions range from Moat of Urr (Dalbeattie/Castle Douglas), Easter Happrew (near Peebles) and Raeburnfoot (Eskdalemuir). Marx does not offer anything. For Corda, Macbain suggests modern day Sanquhar – which is a logical site near the head of Nithsdale, but the figures do not fit. We can see that none of the sites offered will impinge on our understanding of the boundaries of the territory of the Selgovae.

* To the east of the Selgovae lay the Gododdin. High Rochester (Bremenium) was in Gododdin territory. Another centre was Curia which Marx says is Borthwick Castle while Strang says Cramond – which does seem more logical, especially given recent finds – but I am loth to disagree with Marx's calculations. [As discussed above I do not think that we need to choose here. We can accept that the coordinates take us to Borthwick while the place name may actually refer to Cramond.]

However we do come to a problem with Alauna. Both the Damnonii and the Gododdin are credited with an Alauna. Marx examines only one. He says that this is Stirling and he allocates this to the Damnonii. He is not alone here – so I suppose it must have been the text he was following – but I think that he has made a mistake here. The Damnonian Alauna on Macbain's map just does not at all look like Stirling. If we look at the other Alauna it looks as if it should be Leven – and Macbain goes so far as to suggest Inchkeith. Everyone seems to be agreed that the name incorporates the idea of a rocky outcrop ("ail"). So I think that Marx is right that Stirling is Alauna – but the Gododdin one, not the Damnonian one.

And so we come to the Damnonii.

- We may dispose of Vandogara: it matters little whether it is in fact Irvine or Ayr. Marx prefers Ayr and I suspect that the "-ara" is from this name. [For ven-/van see Scottish Clans Volume II on placenames, but the middle part ("-do-") evades me.] The fact that it appears well inland led Macbain to suppose Loudon Hill (the "capital" of the Damnonii at the time, which is on the Irvine Water), but for me the combination of Marx's numbers and the name itself are determining.
- It is clear to me that Alauna is Dumbarton Rock.
- Marx and Rivet & Smith agree that Lindum is Drumquassie near Drymen – but for these purposes it matters not even if Strang was right in making it Malling on the Lake of Menteith.
- Marx is silent about Coria while other offerings include Balgair and Barochan Hill – neither of which impact on the understanding of the boundaries.
- To me it looks as if by Coria, Loudon Hill is intended, but the numbers may well refer to Barochan Hill.

This leaves us with Victoria and Colania.

- Marx is silent on Colania which Strang and Rivet & Smith agree to be Camelon. Macbain's map is clear that this cannot be the case and he suggests somewhere near the source of the Clyde (except that it is clear that the Selgovae controlled Crawford if not Carstairs. Colania should be somewhat South and East of Coria – somewhere north of Abington – Carstairs, for example may be in the frame.
- So we come at last to Victoria. Marx says Kinross; while I can accept that this is what the numbers say, I don't believe it. Other offerings are all over the place: Inchtuthil, Fendoch (North of Crieff) and Loch Orr in West Fife. But this site along with Alauna and Lindum are a pattern. Bochastle (Callander) is my opinion on the matter. It lies due east of Kinross and I suppose a scribal error.

g. Interpreting the map (c125 AD)

A clear pattern has emerged: We have three main hill tribes: the Smaertae in the North West Highlands, the Caledonians in the Grampians and the Selgovae in the Southern Uplands. To these we may add the Vacomagi of the Spey/Spean valley. All round them are other tribes – and I suppose that most if not all of these might be described as "incomers" who have forced their way onto one patch of shore or another, establishing themselves and gradually pushing inland – some more than others. However all of these apart from the Damnonii and the Gododdin had become acculturated so that whether or not they were, or had been, ethnically distinct, by Ptolemy's time all these others should be understood as "Picts" – and we can tell that they shared a common name for themselves, for just north of Caithness we have the "Pentland Firth" defining a boundary between "Pent" people and the Orcadians while the Pentland Hills show where the "Pentish" Selgovae faced the "non-Pentish" Gododdin. We should not find it in any way surprising that it is the (coastal) lowlands which were the contested areas – both because of their accessibility and because of the relatively high productivity of the land. Conversely we should not imagine the main tribes as monolithic blocs where law and order prevailed – cattle 'lifting' in the Highlands and rieving in the Borders continued into the 1700s. Rather we should see these areas as fairly loose confederations of like minded people who saw an underlying affinity with each other.

1.4 What happened next (120-140AD and beyond)

When the Romans retreated from their line of Glen Blocker forts they left their allies – the foederati (the Gododdin and the Damnonii) – in charge of as much land as they thought they could cope with. The new front line was the river Teith, but given the huge moss which was the whole area between the Teith and the Forth, this left Bo'castle (otherwise Callander) as an exposed salient. So the Picts were soon able to push the Damnonii back first to Drymen then to the Clyde. Similarly first Stirling and then the Falkirk area fell to the Picts until the Gododdin were forced back behind the Avon gorge. We need to note the ethnic disparity between the Damnonii and those the had been trying to stay in charge of not only north of the Clyde but also in the Clyde valley itself – which, as we can see from Slamannan was Maeatae (ie Pictish) territory. So also with the Gododdin whom we must suppose also not to be ethnically Pictish (see further below) – albeit not of the same ethnicity as the Damnonii.

This gave the Caledonians in particular an easy route south through the lowlands from where they had a free choice – they could turn west to plunder the Damnonii, they could turn east to attack the Gododdin – or they could push south to pillage Britannia proper.

Such was their ferocity that, as we saw in the time line above, it was a mere 20 years before the Romans attempted once again to redress the balance, establishing their new forward positions on the Antonine Wall. Thus Ptolemy's map of Scotland, accurate or not, should be understood as no more than a freeze-frame in an otherwise continual flux.

With vast plains in Northern Europe and in North America – even in Ireland on a smaller scale – it would be easy to think of power creeping incrementally, but in the great majority of Scotland, dominated by hills and glens, the general concept should be that of the quantum leap.

Thus, for example, we can see that in the course of time the Novantes, whom Ptolemy shows controlling no more than Wigtownshire – not even as far East as the Dee or as far North as Ayr – later expanded to include the whole of the Dee valley and Nithsdale at the expense of the Selgovae.

The Selgovae also suffered encroachment from the East by the Brigantes and the Gododdin so that by the time we are considering there was a rump kingdom only covering Annandale and Liddlesdale, with perhaps the headwaters only of the Tweed – and reduced in this way they were essentially a client atate of the Damnonii.

Some of the pressure from the Gododdin would in turn seem to have been a result of their losing ground to the Brigantes of North Yorkshire who spread eventually up the river Tweed. In general it should be expected that pressure would be from South to North if for no other reason than the better climate and soils sustaining a greater population.

The Romans understood the inherent military necessity of ensuring non-fraternisation of its border control troops. So, for example, on Hadrian's wall we find detachments of eg Spanish and even Sarmatian troops being rotated in and out of service. The obvious reason for this is to avoid the danger of the troops "going native" – forming relationships which might compromise their loyalty. One quasi-exception to this seems to have been the Antonine Wall, for even by Ptolemy's time Dumbarton Rock was, as its name implies, controlled by the Britons who were the Damnonii. Rarely and only briefly was the Antonine Wall controlled directly by the Romans, but at other times the "foederati" tribes, particularly the Damnoniae and the Gododdin had exactly the same outlook – they too wanted to be defended from the Picts and Scots.

To understand this better we should consider the status quo ante – ie the position the Damnonii and Gododdin found themselves in before the Romans invaded Britain. Naturally we have no sources for this and so the reader will be aware that this is speculation on my part. But I think that it is at least informed speculation. The only real evidence we can call on is placenames and even here we have to be careful in trying to assess when the names became settled. Nevertheless I think that we may reconstruct something approaching the tribal map for, say, 45 AD in this fashion:

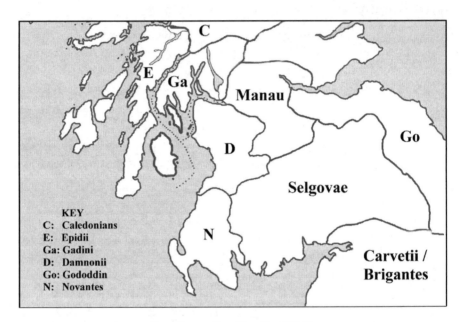

Southern Scotland c45AD

As we can see the Damnonii were bounded in the east by the River Clyde (even in modern Welsh "clwyd" means "hurdle" from which I think we may understand "boundary" by allusion). Further south their boundary lay on the watershed of the upper Clyde and its tributaries, as can be seen by placenames such as Cumberhead. [In this connection we should note also in passing that the name of the Cumbrae Islands in the Firth of Clyde imply that they were Pictish – ie belonging to the Gadini rather than to the Damnonii.] Meanwhile the placename Slamannan shows that it was the kingdom of Manau (whose principal tribe was the Maeatae who held sway west of the Avon gorge) rather than the Gododdin. The border between Manau and the Gododdin would appear to have been along the high ground – so that Cathlawhill near Torphichen was an 'obvious' Gododdin stronghold at or near the border. So, too, it is unlikely that the Gododdin would have penetrated much beyond West Calder. Just South of that the name "Pentland Hills" (marking the boundary between the Pictish Selgovae and the incomer Gododdin) are a bit of a give away – though just where Manau gave way to the realm of the Selgovae is rather more complex.

[NB We have noted already that Ptolemy did not specify the tribes living in Fife and Kinross. In most texts he did not mention the Gadini – but they do appear on Bleau's map apparently based on Ptolemy, so it is on that basis that I have included them on this map.]

208-11
Further persistent raids into England by the Picts led Severus and his son Caracalla to reinforce Hadrian's wall, invade Scotland, refurbish the Antonine Wall and then mount punitive raids into Pictish Territory, temporarily re-occupying several of the Agricolan forts we have considered. [After Severus' death the Romans again withdrew to Hadrian's Wall.] This expedition so weakened the Picts that the Romano-Britons enjoyed some decades of peace. By this time the Picts, as an organised aggressive force attacking Roman Britain, had coalesced into just two groups – the Caledonians and the Maeatae. [The Selgovae were not beyond staging their own raids – but except for times when they might reinforce a Caledonian expedition these were more akin to the later rieving.]

305
Given the references to Constantine scattered throughout this work, we should not allow to go unremarked upon the successful punishment expedition against the Picts undertaken by the Emperor Constantius and his son (who would become the Emperor Constantine the Great the very next year). From this we should understand that the Picts had been raiding at least into the "Old North".

367-8
Another major incursion by Picts and Scots incurred during the so-called "Great Conspiracy" created opportunities for a whole host of neighbours to invade and sack Roman Britannia. It was Theodosius who was dispatched with a large force to restore order. In 368 he recaptured Hadrian's wall.

Discussion

In general, historians have been insouciant of and so casual with the use of the term "Manau Gododdin" – most using it interchangeably with the lands of the Gododdin in general. Not so – and it will help us to understand why not. As shown on the last map, in the middle of Scotland was a kingdom usually called Manau, largely dominated by a tribe called the Maeatae. That these people bestrode the Antonine wall can be seen in the placenames Clackmannan and Slamannan. These people really were caught in the middle – their loyalties necessarily divided. With their territory to the North of the wall it was all too easy for them to fall foul of the Caledonians – to be plundered without recourse. But if they tried to ingratiate themselves with the Caledonians, then retribution could be meted out South of the wall equally easily. Given that the pickings here would have been relatively slim anyway a Pictish raiding party would prefer to drive right through the middle to plunder in England. But if and when frustrated it was very easy for the Caledonians to turn on the foederati tribes.

So Manau was the Poland of the British Isles: no readily defensible borders and so ridden over at will by anyone seeking greater things or even just to extend his territory. Manau was often the "problem" and as often expendable. The very latest date for the final division would be 410 when the Roman Emperor Honorious instructed the Britons to look to their own defence, which may also be the instruction referred to by Gildas (Chapter 15) who is so derisive of the inability of a turf wall to keep assailants out. The solution to that problem lay with the Damnonii and the Gododdin simply conquering and annexing Manau south of the wall. Thus much of Manau south of the Antonine wall came to be "Manau Gododdin"; the portion annexed by the Damnonii eventually became the bulk of Lanarkshire. The reason that there was not a "Manau Damnonii" is that this was not retained as a semi-autonomous state but incorporated into Damnonia proper.

Conclusion

The general strategy of the kings of the Hen Ogled was to maintain Hadrian's Wall as their last line of defence, but to encourage their friends – the foederati, the Damnonii and the Gododdin – to maintain and defend the line of the Antonine Wall. The Damnoniae took sovereignty up to the wall on the west, the Gododdin on the east – with their mutual boundary at the watershed between the rivers Kelvin and the Carron – which can still be found easily at the Auld Inn on the M80 just north of Cumbernauld. The effectiveness of this plan varied!

2. THE KINGDOMS OF SCOTLAND AROUND ARTHURIAN TIMES

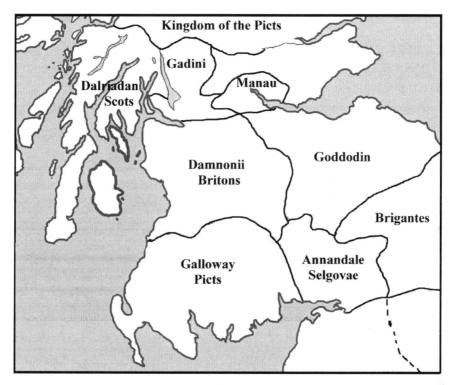

Conjectured kingdoms c490AD

A. The Gododdin

Ruled from the Eastern half of the Antonine Wall and the southern shores of the Firth of Forth to the North the Gododdin controlled the lowlands of the East of Scotland as far south as the river Tyne in Ptolemy's time and still at least as far as Berwick in Arthur's. [With their attention focused on the Picts their southernmost lands were vulnerable to gradual incursion by the Brigantes.] In the time of Old King Cole Cunedda Wledig was the chieftain of Manau Gododdin – which clearly shows the reach of the Gododdin at that epoch (pre-400). But by invitation he took his family (he married Cole's daughter) and a substantial force to north Wales to provide an effective defence against Irish pirates and thereby set up a dynasty. From http://www.earlybritishkingdoms.com/gene/cunedanc.html we can see that he was a grandson of Paternus Pesrut – himself perhaps the son of Tacitus who may well have been a Roman officer put in place (eg by marriage into the local royal family) to take the rulership of the tribe. Unfortunately we do not have a pedigree for Lot (David Nash Ford describes it correctly as "muddled" – it has been interfered with by too many people with prior assumptions about his ancestry). If the Cunedda above was born c 370 and Lot himself about 470 then it is likely that Ceredig's father Edern should be Lot's great-great-great grandfather, but it is very difficult to interpolate any of the individuals named in Harleian MSS and reproduced at

http://www.earlybritishkingdoms.com/gene/lotanc.html except that the idea that his great-great-grandfather was, from a Roman point of view, a decurion may be worthy of follow-up.

As I have suggested both from the general geography and from their general political stance I would propose that the Gododdin were in essence immigrants – albeit long enough before 70AD to be as established (and as acculturated) as they were and to be in a position to be supportive of the Romans. In considering possible origins for the tribe I thought of the Goths; immediately we may note that the Goths described themselves as *Gut-þiuda* (meaning "Gothic people") – which is very close to "Gododdin". The Penguin Atlas of World History has an interesting map reproduced on the Wikipedia page about the Goths showing major exoduses well before 250BC and I see little difficulty with the idea that the Gododdin reached the Berwickshire/Northumberland coast say c300BC, gradually pushing inland and northwards. Although they were acculturated (clearly eg they spoke Brythonnic/Old Welsh) it may be that they retained aspects of their 'own' culture – some personal names, for example. Looked at from a Brythonnic perspective the name "Lot" (after whom Lothian is supposed to take its name) is difficult to translate (notwithstanding that some people suppose that Llew or some such is "obvious"). If, however we go down the Gothic route, we find names such as Ljotr/Leuhta, meaning "shining/bright" becoming available. While I am not going to try to assert this (being so specific is of no consequence to our story) I hope that opening up the possibility may prove interesting and constructive to others in due course.

Although in some senses acculturated (the incomers would have had to learn to live with the natives they ruled over) the Gododdin also maintained their separate identity sufficiently as to be able to see their political path quite differently from their neighbours the Selgovae who tended to side with the Caledonians and even staged some raids of their own into Roman Britannia.

"Orkney"

Some derision has been heaped on Arthurian legend because of the claim that Lot was king of Orkney.

We should start by recognising, as we saw above that the implication of the name "Pentland Firth" is that the Orcadians were ethnically distinct from the "Pent-ish" people and there is no good a priori reason for discounting the possibility of a Gothic invasion and take over – perhaps in the same wave of emigration as the Gododdin – nevertheless this is not the point. I propose that this problem has arisen because of the way that the Gododdin were represented by the Romans *inter alia* as "Otadini" (see Ptolemy). It is not immediately apparent that "Otadini" and "Gododdin" are one and the same. However when we compare "Otadini" and "Orcades" we find:

O RC A D E S
O T AD INI

So if we start with a writer who has failed to understand that "Otadini" (or some variant) is the same as "Gododdin" what should he make of it? [And why would such writers be familiar with the name of a tribe which had vanished centuries before leaving a mark they might well not come across?] I suggest that "Orcades" may well have been the best he could come up with – and hence the confusion.

We should also note that Ptolemy's map shows the names of tribes, NOT the names of territories (which were in any case far from settled). When the legend says that Lot, king of Orkney became king of Lothian, we should be comfortable with translating this as "Lot, king of the Gododdin (people) established his territory and called it "Lothian" after himself."

B. The Damnonii:

As we can see the Damnonii were well established in Ayrshire by Ptolemy's time. They were sufficiently ethnically separate to be characterised as "Britons" in contradistinction to the Picts. There was a tribe of broadly the same name in south west England so, despite most commentators saying "surely not" or putting the similarity of the name down to coincidence, my presumption is that a group of people from England settled in Ayrshire (probably some hundreds of years BC), later consolidating and spreading throughout the county.

Although they had their moments of disagreement with and even of fighting against the Romans, perhaps it was the ethnic distinction which made the Damnonii amenable to federation with the Romans. As we have seen they were supported as part of the front line against the Picts and then also the Scots. This relationship would appear to have included the establishment of a new royal line in the person of Clemens (or possibly his father usually named as Cursalem), probably in the aftermath of the Great Conspiracy.

The Damnonii were not politically stable in the days leading up to Arthur's as this list of their kings (from their Wikipedia page) suggests:

Name	Regnal dates	
	Start	End
Dumnagual/Dyfnwal Hen	450	475
Erbin	475	480
Cinuit	480	485
Gereint	485	490
Tutagual	490	495
Caw (*deposed)	495	501*
Domgal	501	508
Clinoch	508	540

Ambrosius supported Dyfnwal Hen but then there were 6 reigns in just 33 years until Clinoch came to the throne in 508. While some of these short reigns may actually represent the ascendancy of one family member over another in a situation where the "kingdom" had been divided, I suspect that there was three-way rivalry between the "old" royal family, Clemens' own dynasty and the interests of the kings of the Old North who will have preferred Damnonia to be ruled by one of their own. Such a situation is hard to resolve with a simple marriage. Over and above this, of course, there is the matter of whether the individuals concerned are "up to the job".

In "Brewer's British Royalty" David Williamson further muddies the water by claiming that Geraint was married to a sister of the king of the Picts (which is to be expected), that his son Caw went on to be King of the Picts (as Galan, see below) and that later Pictish kings descend from two of Caw's sisters. Given that Caw was the father of Gildas the idea that he would be king of the Picts at all seems a bit unlikely – even more so given the dates (510-522) and the way Gildas wrote – for Gildas was unsparing and unqualified in his references to the Picts as "the enemy". My own hunch is that if Caw had been Galan then Gildas would have been just a little more circumspect – so I am disinclined to the idea that they are one and the same.

It would seem that Arthur's campaign started under Caw and this would accord with Gildas' going on and on about the Picts and Scots as "the enemy". Curiously Caw seems to have been deposed immediately after the securing of the Lennox following the battle on the river Basas (see below). Even if he were not the king of the Picts, Caw's family connections could well have led to his exile amongst them. Could it have been he who was responsible for selecting targets for Pictish counter-attack?

Client Kingdoms of the Damnonii

i. Galloway

After Ptolemy the Novantes appear to have expanded their rule in Galloway as far as Nithsdale – at the expense of the Selgovae. While there is evidence of "Devil's Dykes" defensive works implying hostility between the hill people and the Damnonii below them, my understanding that in broad terms at this time there was peace. During the time we are considering, Urien expanded the Kingdom of Rheged to include Galloway (as evidenced by the fort Dunragit) and some time later the whole area was to fall to the Anglians of Bernicia.

ii. The "Kingdom" of Annandale

Immediately east of Nithsdale lies Annandale and the adjacent Esk/Liddlesdale. Though small it is of huge strategic importance – including the routes of the present M74 and the A7 and the west coast main railway line. There has been dispute about this, but I think we can resolve it.

At http://www.derwas-read.co.uk/old_king_cole_descendants.htm we can see that one Old King Cole faction, which Derek Read rehearses on his site argues that the "kings" here were descended from Cole through St Ceneu, Mor, Einon and Ceidio to Gwendolleu, brother of Caw. Contrarily, Williamson (Brewer's British Royalty) proposes a descent for Caw from Coroticus through Erbin and Geraint. Caw was the king of all the Damnonii, albeit for a short time.

At http://www.earlybritishkingdoms.com/gene/coel.html, David Nash Ford can rescue us, for he shows that Ceidio ap Einion became King North of the Solway as if by magic. His wife is unknown. Gwendolleu and Caw are amongst his children.

The solution is that Ceidio, a younger son of Einon with no real prospects married a daughter of Caw and through her gained the lordship (not really as "kingdom" as such) of Birrens and Annandale. This was also part of the demonstration of friendship between the kings of the Hen Ogled and the Damnonii. Naturally a junior son would be called Caw out of respect for his father-in-law. Thus not only were there two Caws, but the scene was set for Gwendolleu to think that he was worthy of a kingdom – so that in the end Rydderch Hael (the then King of Strathclyde) had no choice but to assert his authority by force of arms – which occurred in 573.

The sources on which Read's site relies unfortunately have the two Caws elided.

If we follow Ford's timescale, Einon's marriage would normally have been c510, but he suggests that Gwendolleu was not born for another 10 years. Not only that, but, as we have seen that Caw himself was deposed in 501 – so it is far from clear that a subsequent king of Strathclyde (as it had become by this time) would want the potential aggravation implied (ie a Caw family member allied to a prince feeling hard done by, in a key strategic position). All in all it is much more likely that the marriage took place in the wake of the peace following Badon Hill and was a deliberate part of the rapprochement following the peace. Thus Ford's date for Gwendolleu looks reasonable, making him early 50s in 573 – still very much young enough to be a boil which needed to be lanced. Actually Gwendolleu was generally recognised as worse than this – so Rydderch had support from elsewhere in the Old North as well. Rydderch's overlordship here is indicated by the village of Carruthers – a reference to Birrens Fort as Caer – Rydderch, at least post 573.

Annandale and Gwendolleu had been the last redoubt of the Selgovae, so if it was, in effect, at the disposal of the Damnonii in 520 how did this come about? Lanarkshire was absorbed by the Damnonii probably some time after 410 whereafter the Selgovae would not have been able to sustain themselves. New strategic alliances would have been necessary so they would have had to calculate with whom to throw in their lot. There was a choice of Galloway Picts, Damnonii Britons or Britons south of the wall. In "Scottish Clans..." I show that St Patrick's father held an estate almost exactly covering the present parish of Gretna – so it looks as if they chose the Britons. With Coel Hen in charge the sense of this choice is evident.

Subsequently the British kingdoms kept squabbling amongst themselves to the point where the king of the North East of England felt the need for Anglic retainers – thereby giving them a free bridgehead for a later take over.

C. The Picts:

For these purposes "The Picts" should be understood to be a confederation of those tribes north of the Maeatae led by the Caledonians which coalesced into a single political unit with an over or high king. Their Southern Boundary would appear to have been the watershed of the river Earn. At this point I should re-emphasise that the vast bulk of the population in the areas controlled by the Gododdin, the Selgovae and the Novantes were also in effect Pictish – but the fact that they were geographically cut off from those north of the Central Belt meant that they were never part of the Pictish kingdom.

The first King of the Picts mentioned in extant king lists is dated to about 350AD. Although one should not suppose a unitary state – operationally the tribes surely remained largely internally self-governing, as did the Mormaerdoms well into the historical period – this seems like quite an appropriate date for a step change in the coalescence of the various tribes.

The core Wikipedia pages about Scottish History are maintained by academics who are broadly reliable, so we may observe this list of kings pertinent to Arthurian times:

456–480	Nechtan	Nechtan son of Uuirp (or Erip), Nechtan the Great, Nechtan Celcamoth
480–510	Drest	Drest Gurthinmoch (or Gocinecht)
510–522	Galan	Galan Erilich or Galany
522–530	Drest	Drest son of Uudrost (or Hudrossig)
522–531	Drest	Drest son of Girom (or Gurum)
531–537	Gartnait	Garthnac son of Girom, Ganat son of Gigurum
537–538	Cailtram	Cailtram son of Girom, Kelturan son of Gigurum

Thus we can see that in so far as the Picts may have been involved, Nechtan was on the receiving end of Ambrosius Aurelianus' attention While Drest (some claim that this name is the same as Tristram) may well have been the motivating force behind the attack on Guinon Fort and so it was he who was the object of the retaliation at the City of the Legion. It was Galan who orchestrated the "one last heave" at Badon Hill and failed.

We have noted already the claim that Galan is identical with Caw, deposed king of Strathclyde. There is no doubt that he was heavily involved with the Pictish royal family, at least by marriage, but this identification seems unlikely.

We may note the coincidence of the death of Gartnait and the battle of Camlann which invites speculation about any possible linkage.

D. The Maeatae

Regrettably we have no information at all directly from them relating to this time window, but they ruled a kingdom usually referred to as Manau, comprising Clackmannanshire, probably some of west Fife (close to the outskirts of Dunfermline), The valley of the Devon as far as Pow Mill and Cult Hill and possibly the catchment of the Allan and extending west along the Braes of Doune nearly to Callander. The existence of such a "buffer state" suited the Caledonians. Manau would have been largely unmanageable by them and it provided an expendable no-man's-land with regard to any attack from the south. Nevertheless throughout the period we are considering Manau remained a client of the Picts.

South of the Antonine Wall, Manau included most of the land between the Avon in the East and the Clyde in the West. But this was a hostage to fortune as the Maeatae were not strong enough to resist a two flank attack by the Damnonii and the Gododdin whenever they so conspired. How they got used to it is hard to fathom, but the placenames Slamannan as well as Clackmannan and Dumyat bear witness that it was indeed so. It is clear that the part of Manau under Gododdin control retained a separate integrity not only because of the name Manau Gododdin but also because it appears that it was ruled by Cunedda Wledig (albeit under his father) before he and his family and men went South to defend North Wales and settle there.

E. The Gadini

We have noted that the Gadini appear in Bleau's interpretation of Ptolemy's map. We know that there were several tribes in Central Scotland left unnamed in most versions of Ptolemy's work. [Fife, for example, was clearly not a desert.] Whether or not they really were called "Gadini" it is, in effect, necessary that there was a tribe in this area sandwiched between the Epidii of Kintyre and Argyll to the west, to the north the Caledonians whose sway, Ptolemy tells us, reached to Loch Long and, to the east, the Maeatae based around Dumyat Hill. With Loch Lomond at its centre the Gadini had what might appear as an idyllic home, but the lie of the land means that it is not easily defended. Between the time of Ptolemy and that of Arthur they were weakened by loss of land to the ever more muscular Dalriada (see below) and, as we shall see, by the end of Arthur's campaign they had ceased to exist as a separate entity altogether.

F. The Scots:

As we have seen, the Scots were not mentioned by Ptolemy in Scotland – he did not recognise them in Ireland either. So who were they? Superficially this may seem to be very simple to answer because their kingdom in Scotland was called Dalriada, a name they shared with an area of Antrim in Ireland – and indeed right up to Arthur's time their overlord was in Ireland. In Ptolemy's time the tribe occupying that area of Ireland was the Robogdii.

We can, however, go further than that because the Robogdii were amongst a small number of tribes regarded by the Irish as "Cruthin" (variously "Cruithni" etc.) – which is otherwise the term they used for the Picts.

In recent times it has been suggested that Cruthin is a Irish version of "Priteni" – ie Briton – and this is asserted without equivocation on the Wikipedia page (~/Cruthin, accessed February 2017) but I do not accept this, for these same people referred to the Britons of Strathclyde as Britons – so Cruthin, whatever its derivation, refers NOT to the Britons in general but specifically to the ancient people of Scotland. Cruithin is more likely a corruption of "Cumbri" (partly by metathesis) which is how the Picts in Southern Scotland as well as Cumbrians and Welsh referred to themselves. Whatever the meaning of the name, what this tells us is that at some time in the past there had been a plantation of this part of Ireland by peoples from Scotland. [This should not come as any surprise. Ireland like Great Britain had been subject to many waves of immigration – the Fir Bolg (Belgae), the Iverni (from Spain) and so on.] However this plantation must have occurred long enough before their first return to Scotland (a) for them to have taken on the Irish Gaelic language and (b) to have adopted a new local name. [I am not aware of any meaningful attempt to explain the name "Robogdii" and have nothing to offer here. Clearly it bears no substantial relationship to any of the tribes identified by Ptolemy.] The Wikipedia page also says 'Professor Kenneth H. Jackson has said that the Cruthin "were not Picts, had no connection with the Picts, linguistic or otherwise, and are never called *Picti* by Irish writers"'. Accepting everything that Jackson says does NOT imply that they were not ethnically what was later called Pictish. This is no problem as the appellation "Picti" (too!) is clearly Roman in origin. The fact that there were no current connections is similarly of no consequence – and it certainly does not in any way stand in the way of the idea that the Irish Cruthin could have settled in Antrim and Down around say 200 BC and then largely acculturated to local circumstances. The nearest point of Scotland to the Cruthin is Kintyre, occupied in Ptolemy's time by the Epidii – so Alex Woolf has suggested an ethnic connection. This is very plausible, but the necessary time gap is such that it is not clear that the people in Kintyre would have identified themselves as Epidii (or their Brythonnic equivalent) at the time.

So how did the Scots acquire their name and what does it mean? We may begin by dismissing the *post hoc* myth of the name deriving from the Egyptian princess Scota – for had there been anything in it then there would have been very prominent Scots in Ireland in Ptolemy's time! The standard explanation currently is that the name is one given to them by the Romans, the suggestion being that it has the general meaning "pirate". There is the Latin word "scatere" meaning "to swarm" – and one can see the allusion of Irish pirates swarming over the coast causing pain and damage like unwelcome wasps. Nevertheless this seems quite unlikely as Irish pirates raided the whole west coast of England and Wales as well as Scotland – and if this were the reason then the same name should applied equally to them.

There is an alternative, for the Latin word "scutulatum" refers to tartan clothing. References to clothing, especially when applied eg in a derogatory tone of voice, remain to this day (eg "towel heads"), so I can well imagine this – indeed it is my preferred explanation. So hereby I propose that the Scots got their name as "the tartan folk".

So the name "Scots" was not their own; it was a derogatory term applied by others – possibly the Romans – which they adopted. This too should not be considered remarkable. We may remember the way Harriet Harman used the term "Ginger Rodent" of MP Danny Alexander, intending it to be derogatory, but gleefully adopted by him. Similarly in the 1970s when teenage gang members were labelled "mental" whether by magistrates or by the press, they adopted this into their gang name! So too it is fashionable amongst today's youth to use the words "sick" and "wicked" as terms of great approbation – these labels initially used against them by the more sanctimonious elements of the establishment in general, and prosecuting lawyers and the press in particular.

The ethnic identity of the Cruthin is further complicated by the false dichotomisation between the Cruthin and the Ulaid – descendants of the tribe Ptolemy called the Voluntii (whom he located in present day Monaghan) and who gained pre-eminence eventually giving their name to "Ulster".

The Annals of the Four Masters also tell us that Conn of the Hundred Battles gained power in Ireland in 123AD, being killed in 157 (see http://www.rootsweb.ancestry.com/~irlkik/ihm/ire100.htm). They go on to say that he was succeeded by his son-in-law Conaire (husband of Saraid and himself a descendant of Conaire Mor). In parentheses it is added that it was one of Conaire's junior sons Cairbre Riada who moved north to settle in what would become Irish Dalriada. We see no reference to war or conquest and so we should suppose that the trigger was marriage. So here we can see that the line of the "kings" of at least a section of the Robogdii must have failed to an heiress who married an Ulsterman. And so it is that later kings of Dalriada could claim descent from both lines – and there is no need to dichotomise them.

[There is a potential problem with the story of the three Cairbres as they bear too great a resemblance to the three Collas of Airgíolla. Mitigating this, it appears that (i) the Three Collas are not given much credence today and (ii) their legend dates them to a time rather over 100 after the Cairbres – so it is feasible that their story was confected on the earlier one of the Cairbres.]

This explanation of the place name Dalriada (from prince Cairbre Riada) is very much at odds with a modern understanding which tries to force "Riada" from the name Robogdii! At http://www.rootsweb.ancestry.com/%7Eirlkik/ihm/ire150.htm we find the suggestion that ".....the Robogdii may be a corruption of Redodii, which would indicate the Dal Reti, or the Dal Riata, who later colonized Scotland....". This is a step too far for me. Interestingly Dwelly has "riatachd" meaning 'illegitimate'. It would make particularly common sense for an illegitimate son to have sought his future and fortune 'out of area'.

No mention is made of when and/or led by whom a further expedition led to the settlement on the Scottish mainland. In 240 Cormac, another grandson (let us say 'descendant') of Conn asserted sovereignty over the colony in Scotland, showing that it was already in existence. No more mention of Scotland is made until 326 – the year when Colla Uais at the head of 300 sought refuge there for a year – only 27 surviving to return.

John O'Hart (1824–1902) *Irish pedigrees; or, The origin and stem of the Irish nation*, first published in 1876, Vol I p622 et seq., tells us that the king of the Scots prior to 498 was called Loarn and that his daughter Earca was married to Eoghan, son of Niall of the Nine Hostages. Skene's Chronicle of The Kings of Scots lists 14 names between Fergus, brother of this Loarn back to Conaire covering a period of 300 years – an intergenerational gap of about 21 years. Thus we should not take it literally as a pedigree – it is probably the case that some of these were brothers of their predecessor – even more so if we allow that during such a long period of time one should expect a grandson to succeed directly. But the number in the list is of a size to be taken seriously.

So all in all it would appear that the Irish Dalriadan expedition to Argyll must have been some time in the period 200x240. Again there is no suggestion of war, so again I suggest that the motivation will have been marriage. If the line of Epidii kings had reached a point of difficulty – or perhaps the Epidii were looking to strengthen their position against eg Caledonian attack, what better than a strategic marriage with an Irish dynasty whose people were in any case somewhat related?

Family Lore

Lore associated with the Clans Forbes and Colquhoun (see the Appendix on The Lennox) may be taken to imply that the regents or vice-roys in Argyll before 495 (whose descendants included the family of Luss) claimed descent from Conchobhar mac Nessa, a legendary king of Ulster. Legends about him make him even older than Cu Chulainn – so he belongs to a time BC. So any supposed pedigree as such is far from complete or accurate. But nevertheless it supports the scenario being developed here.

Summary so far

A descendant of a king of the Voluntii married the daughter of the king of the Robogdii from this emerged the Irish sub-kingdom of Dalriada. Two or three generations later, in the very early 200s AD a scion of this family became king of the Epidii, also by marriage. He took with him a considerable entourage. The result of this is that the lands of the Epidii became, in effect, a vassal state of Irish Dalriada, even taking its name. And then....

Fairly quickly this kingdom expanded. First it gained the Cowal peninsula. From what I can see of the original Gaelic from which "Cowal" is rendered, "Còmhghall" looks as if this was "promised" land – again most likely as a result of a strategic/political marriage. But the Dalriadans expanded further – whether by agreement or, as I suspect, by conquest – for we should note that in the process of this expansion the Caledonians lost their access to Loch Long.

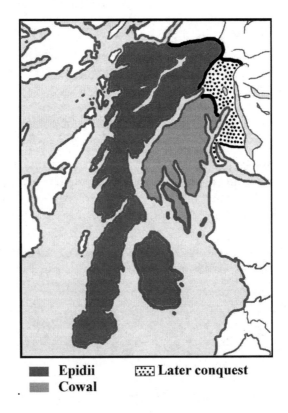

■ Epidii   ▦ Later conquest
■ Cowal

Dalriada/Argyll 200-495

Placenames

In "Scottish Clans..." Volume II I discuss Pictish place names. Based on this we can see readily that Gaelic speakers had encroached onto the West side of Loch Lomond – for "Duglas" is a Gaelic form. "Glas" in Pictish (and indeed, old Irish) means green-grey and so there are water courses called eg "glassie" because of this distinctive hue. In Ireland this became understood as characteristic of water courses in general – hence "glas" came to mean "burn"/"stream". Thus "Duglas" means the Blackburn/Blackwater; the Pictish equivalent would be Lochie/Lochty or even "Dubhie" etc. Normally one finds such Blackburns paired with Whitburns (eg near Bathgate, but widely) so we should not be surprised that just South of this Glen Douglas is Glen Finlas (ie Fin-glas); these two rivers sandwich the water of Luss. So we may be confident that the Gaels had penetrated that far. The next glen South, however is Glen Fruin. My referee on matters of Gaelic Placenames, Neil Macgregor, is fully agreed that "Fruin" is Brythonnic rather than Gaelic, but we disagree as to its meaning. He suggests that the root word means "dripping" – and it is true that Glen Fruin was well known for its extensively boggy ground, but I prefer the modern Welsh "ffrwyn" which means "Bridle". My reason for this is that it is through Glen Fruin which runs the "High Road to Scotland" as immortalised in the song "The Bonnie Banks of Loch Lomond" and I see in this a parallel with "Glen Truim" – the Glen of Avon Truim (at the bottom of which is Invernahavon) – the glen of burdens, ie a packhorse route. So at least two different potential explanations, but no doubt about it being not Gaelic. This explains the placement of the southern boundary of the stippled area on the map above.

So we may construe that for some considerable time the border between the Scots on the one hand and Brythonnic-speaking tribes on the other lay on the watershed between Glenfruin and Glen Finlas. This was the situation confronting Arthur. The Scots were far too close to Dumbarton Rock for comfort; they were growing in strength and threatening to subsume the Gadini altogether. In a world of turmoil in matters of allegiance they would ally with the Picts for raiding expeditions to the south alternating with fighting each other over just where their mutual borders should lie.

"The Jocks"

In "Scottish Clans...." I argued that the use of "Jock" as the generic name for a Scotsman arose in England because the main experience of a Scotsman that ordinary English people would have had was as a horse trader. The Gaelic given name "Eochaid" – which is approximately pronounced "Jocky" – would have been the self-referential description they would have used, whence the word "jockey" was absorbed into the English language. The basis of this name is the Scots Gaelic "each" which means Horse. But I now have to consider an alternative, earlier, explanation.

As we have seen the Pictish tribe essentially taken over by the royal house of Dalriada was called the Epidii – which in essence means "horsemen". We do not know what name they called themselves, but it may well have been based on a now lost Brythonnic equivalent of "each". Whether or not so, given the meaning of Epidii, it would have been natural for an incoming Irish aristocrat to refer to the local population as "Eochaid"s ie Jockeys/Jocks – and this may have spread more generally through Scotland following the triumph of Kenneth MacAlpine in uniting Picts and Scots under his leadership.

Whichever is the correct explanation (and there is not especial need for one to be correct at the expense of the other) in this context I find utterly pathetic some Scots who affect to take umbrage at being called "Jock" (or collectively "Jocks"). There is no more wrong with the nickname Jock than there is with the given name Eochaid – or Eachainn. Indeed in general it is a badge of affection and honour in military circles. Time for the whingers to grow up and take their ignorance-based chips off their shoulders.

2nd dynasty of Kings of Dalriada/the Scots

The Annals say that Fergus Mor mac Erc came to Argyll to rule there in 498. [For a consideration of when the name "Argyll" came to be associated with this area see the part about the battles in Glen Douglas in the next section.]

Fergus Mór	Son of Erc	Annals of Tigernach report his death c. 501	498-501
Domangart Réti	Son of Fergus Mór	The Annals of Innisfallen report the death of Domangart of Cenn Tíre c. 507	501-c507
Comgall	Son of Domangart	Said to have reigned 35 years; death recorded in the Annals of Ulster c540	?505 - c540

There is a clear dispute between those who want to believe that "Fergus Mor" was the son of Erc – ie in the direct line of the existing Dalriadan dynasty (and if so why did he have to "come to" Argyll?) and those who accept O'Hart's clear distinction detailed above – which has convinced me. I hope that the greater detail on Fergus Mor, in the discussion of the battles in Glen Douglas in the next chapter will convince the reader.

Conclusion

In essence what we can say is that the kingdoms of the Old North had no ambitions to rule beyond the Southern Uplands, but because of the Pictish attacks they needed friendly relations with the foederati. The Gododdin and the Damnonii had no ambition beyond the Forth/Clyde line, they were reliable and this was strengthened through dynastic marriages; the Selgovae were no substantial threat and would surely have been subsumed through time in any case. The Maeatae, however, had afforded too easy a passage to the Picts and Scots.

Afterword

I am well aware that this chapter contains a good deal of speculation woven round very little evidence, some of which is in any case not entirely secure. However this speculation is not grosser in quality than that being engaged in by the recognised academics as displayed by their differing opinions (eg on the Wikipedia page). On the contrary I suggest that the scenario I have set out is a good deal more simple and hence elegant and so is to be preferred, other things being equal.

3. Narrative Summary

The Roman conquest of Britain was not like the Norman conquest which followed it. Invading in 1066, King William the Conqueror had subjugated even Scotland just 6 years later (by the Treaty of Abernethy (1072)). The Romans had a far harder time of it. Their initial intention may have been the incorporation of the whole island – even Ireland – into the empire, but it was some 40 years after they arrived that they first set military foot on what is now Scotland.

The Scotland the Romans encountered was a smorgasbord of tribes by no means well disposed to each other. The Caledonians, whose territory's focus was modern day Perthshire had succeeded in dominating all their neighbours to the East and South and had penetrated westward to gain access to the sea at the head of Loch Fyne – from where they threatened the Epidii who held the core of modern day Argyll including Kintyre and Arran.

In time honoured fashion, the Romans' first ploy was to try to play one off against the other. Their most staunch allies were the Gododdin of the south eastern coast, principally because they had had the closest contact over some time. The Gododdin were pleased to have Roman support to allow them to defend themselves against and make further inroads into the territory of the Selgovae – the ancestors of the Border Rievers of mediaeval times.

After some skirmishes the Romans also found good allies in the Damnonii who inhabited Ayrshire and, like the Gododdin had retained an ethnic identity separate from that of their neighbours.

Despite a notable victory and establishing a muscular presence on the Highland line, The Romans lacked the will to provide the resources necessary to complete the job of subjecting Scotland, so they retreated, leaving their allies to hold such territory as they could – almost exactly parallel to the situation in Afghanistan over the recent past and a not incomparable period of time. The locals were not up to the job and had to cede land. Periodically the Romans had to reinforce this effort.

The relationship between the Caledonians and the Epidii was equivocal, for on the one hand they combined together to mount raids to the south but on the other hand this was interrupted by skirmishing between themselves. The Epidii were determined not to come under the Caledonians' sway and decided that the best way to shore themselves up was by seeking assistance from their distant kinsmen in the Antrim and Down area of Ireland. This proved something of a Faustian pact for very quickly their friends came to dominate them, making them a tributary sub-kingdom with even their own language (Irish Gaelic) replacing the Brythonnic of the Epidii. [The reader will notice the parallel with the Anglo-Saxon take-over in what would become England some 250 years later.]

Thus strengthened, the Epidii, now 're-badged' by themselves as Dalriadans, but with some disdain called "Scots" by the Romans and their allies, were able to push back against the Caledonians to a limited extent and they came to dominate their weaker neighbours to the east – the Gadini – taking over a substantial part of their territory in Cowal and then the western shores of Loch Lomond. For the Caledonians (and those they had subsumed – themselves now also re-badged simply as "The Picts") – the effort required to recover their position was beyond their reasonable capacity not so much to prosecute on a one-off basis, but rather to sustain; so it came to be that mostly they found it preferable to combine with the Dalriadans in raiding expeditions to the South.

The strength of this combined force became intolerable to the Southerners, but by this time the Romans had forsaken Britain altogether – the underlying issue being, with Rome itself under attack and resources stretched as a consequence, that the locals were unwilling to pay the taxes necessary to sustain their defence forces. Finally, after Ambrosius Aurelianus had felt that he had no option but to come north to relieve a siege of Dumbarton Rock, the Britons came to realise that they really had no option but to deal with the matter robustly for themselves and this is where, eventually, Arthur became the pivotal and heroic figure.

PART 3
IDENTIFYING
THE BATTLE SITES

IDENTIFYING THE BATTLE SITES

We may now turn our attention to the sites of Arthur's 12 battles. We may begin with a map of the sites that I will argue for in this section.

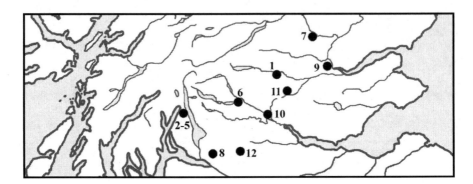

Here are the are the first seven battles with the indicative dates I propose:

Indicative Date	Battle	Location
c495	1	at the mouth of the river called Glein;
497	2	on another river, called the Dubglas, which is in the region of Linnuis; (1)
497	3	on another river, called the Dubglas, which is in the region of Linnuis; (2)
498	4	on another river, called the Dubglas, which is in the region of Linnuis; (3)
498	5	on another river, called the Dubglas, which is in the region of Linnuis; (4)
499x500	6	on the river called Bassas;
502x3	7	in the Caledonian Forest, that is, the Battle of Cat Coit Celidon.

For the second "set" of battles I would guess that someone with an axe to grind could manufacture a basis for siting these battles elsewhere (as indeed, many have throughout history). Indeed the accusation could be laid at my own feet in that I have sought sites that fit what has become my proposition. Nevertheless I believe that with Guinon Fort and Badon Hill I am on very strong ground. Given that the battles took place in Scotland there are very few possible sites which could be called "City of the Legion". This leaves only the River Tribuit and Agned Hill as more problematic. It will be for the reader to judge how far my interpolation is logical and, therefore, at the very least, likely.

Indicative Date	Battle	Location
505x7	8	Guinnon Fort
507x9	9	City of the Legion
509x11	10	On the bank of the river called Tribuit
513x15	11	On the hill called Agned
516x18	12	On Badon Hill

I will not be starting the discussion in strict chronological order, as I would prefer the reader to follow the logic as the sites demonstrate the thesis being put forward here.

A. BATTLES 2, 3, 4 AND 5 – GLEN DOUGLAS.

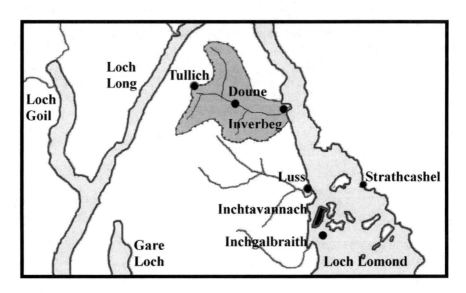

We are told by Nennius that four battles took place here. To anyone without an agenda it is "obvious" that this refers to the river Douglas which runs into Loch Lomond, but lest there be any doubt about this, Geoffrey of Monmouth is specific about it:

> **[Book 9] Chapter VI–Arthur grants a pardon to the Scots and Picts, besieged at the Lake Lumond.**
> Having therefore settled peace here, he directed his march to Alclud, which Arthur had relieved from the oppression of barbarians.... after three several battles.... entering upon the lake Lumond, sought for refuge in the islands that are upon it. This lake contains sixty islands, and receives sixty rivers into it, which empty themselves into the sea by no more than one mouth. There is also an equal number of rocks in these islands..... To these islands therefore, had the enemy fled, thinking the lake would serve them instead of a fortification; but it proved of little advantage to them.
>
> For Arthur, having got together a fleet, sailed round the rivers, and besieged the enemy.... While he was harassing them in this manner Guillamurius, king of Ireland, came up in a fleet with a

very great army of barbarians, in order to relieve the besieged. This obliged Arthur to raise the siege, and turn his arms against the Irish, whom he slew without mercy, and compelled the rest to return back to their country. After this victory, he proceeded in his first attempt, which was to extirpate the whole race of the Scots and Picts. ...... he would allow them the enjoyment of a small part of the country, since they were willing to bear the yoke which he should impose upon them.

[The reader will have noticed already that Geoffrey has conflated Arthur with Ambrosius regarding the earlier siege.] As I mentioned in introducing Geoffrey's work, as it stands it is pretty much nonsense, so the extract I present above is edited to retain just the parts which are relevant – and they will need further examination.

We need to start with the Geography of the area.

(a) Loch Lomond

Geoffrey calls it Lake Lumond, but the river running out of it is called the Leven. The loch was called Loch Leven, but takes its "new" name from Ben Lomond which towers above it on its Eastern shore. the name "Lomond" in turn comes from the Latin and refers to its use as a site for a warning beacon.

(b) Battle sites

If we look in detail at Glen Douglas, there are two locations which stand out as potential sites for battles.

(i) Very near Loch Lomond at Inverbeg there is a "mound" which Canmore (https://canmore.org.uk), the website for Historic Environment Scotland, describes as a natural feature which appears to have been modified by having its top flattened (and, I would add, its sides rather steepened) – which would turn it into a very satisfactory "rath" – a larger and older version of the motte of Norman times.

(ii) Half way up Glen Douglas is Doune Farm (from "Dun" = "Fort"). There is no extant evidence of defensive works here, and I am advised by the farmer that Doune Hill which overlooks it takes its name from the Doune rather than because the hill itself had any defensive significance. The need for a stronghold at this location is clear: control of the river crossing – which was achievable both by ford and by stepping stones.

We should not overlook Geoffrey's claim that one of the encounters may have been at least in part water-based, but the tale about "Guillamurius" could equally apply to the mound at Inverbeg. Not even Geoffrey claims that there was an actual battle on the Loch – but Arthur's prowess has always been supposed to be in cavalry.

We should not move on without considering "Gillamurius". There was, of course, no High King of Ireland by this name, nor can the name be associated correctly with any appropriate antecedents of Fergus Mor mac Erc(a), the first independent king of Argyll. However there is a "Muirchertach mac Muiredaig" who died c534. It seems likely that his reign started in 512, but as he is prominent before that time it is possible that he could have led an expedition of this sort before he was actually High King. While "Gille" means "servant lad" it is sometimes taken as "son" – even if wrongly. In other words I am suggesting that "Gillamurius" is a not unacceptable rendition of "mac Muiredag". So once again we have evidence which is broadly confirming of the general thesis we are developing.

The reader will have noticed that I have identified Tullich, at the head of Glen Douglas, as a likely battle site. This is entirely in connection with Gillamurius. I suspect that the tale has been rather twisted. Yes, Guillamurius arrived with a fleet – but portaging over into Loch Lomond would have been an enormous task – one likely to have been interrupted by Arthur's forces. Instead the logical thing to have done would be to sail the fleet up Loch Long and beach somewhere around Gorten – where the jetty and pier shown on old maps imply a relatively convenient landing opportunity, taking the short (2 miles) but steep route up to the head of Glen Douglas (there is still a track there today). The scene would then be set for the final, decisive encounter on the flat land around Tullich. However one cannot rule out that even if Gillamurius had chosen this route, the ensuing battle could still have been at Doune or even Inverbeg.

[Other sites identified on this map will be considered elsewhere.]

What we would normally infer from Nennius is that these four battles were in short order, near the beginning of the campaign. Of course it would have taken time to send a message to Ireland for reinforcements and still longer to mobilise a fleet of the size implied, so I don't think that the battles were all in the same year, but it is likely that they took place over two or three years. Arthur needed to neutralise the Scots to give him the freedom from the need to defend his new western flank so that he could focus his forces on the full might of the Caledonians.

At the end of Geoffrey's description he makes clear that there was a peace treaty and boundaries were set. This again rings fully true with the geography, for just next to the Cobbler mountain due West of Arrochar is Ben Arthur, while way up Glen Falloch, which feeds the head of Loch Lomond and reaches its watershed just a couple of miles from Crianlarich is Clach nam Breatan – "The stone of the Britons". In other words, Arthur's side took over all the land whose rivers drained into Loch Lomond and the head of Loch Long. By these the eastern border of southern Argyll was defined.

The Wikipedia entry on Fergus Mor mac Erc says "the historian John Morris has suggested.... that Fergus was allowed to settle in Scotland as a federate of Arthur, as a bulwark against the Picts." This is supported by the legend, for Geoffrey of Monmouth (IX, 9) says: "....he restored to Augusel the sovereignty over the Scots....". Particularly bearing in mind that Fergus was usually spelled "Uurguist", could "Augusel" be a mangled representation of this? I think so.

From what we can see the Scots in Argyll threw everything they had at Arthur, they even had support from the man who would become the High King of Ireland. They lost. Not only that, but the kings of Irish Dalriata realised that they could no longer exercise rulership efficiently over their own people in Scotland. So the arrival of Fergus Mor could indeed have been an integral part of the peace treaty agreed and this in turn would date the last of the four battles, if not all four to the year 498 – the year in which the Annals of Ulster record that he went to "Alba".

Time would have been required for a fleet to be mobilised by the Irish, so it seems to me likely that these four battles took place over two years – 497 and 8. The fact that there were four battles means that it was serious last-ditch stuff, but the result, as Geoffrey implies, was indeed a peace that lasted two generations or more.

The Lady of the Lake and Excalibur

The first time in Arthurian Legend that we come across "the Lake" is in connection with "The Lady of the Lake" who gives Arthur the sword Excalibur.

The Lady: Varying editions of Mallory give the Lady's name as "Nimue" and "Nineve", which I suspect are corruptions of the well known Irish name "Naimh". The fact that she was "of the Lake" suggests that the principal residence was on the shore of the Loch. Because the battles took place in Glen Douglas, it is quite likely that the principal residence was on top of the "mound" at Inverbeg.

The Sword: Geoffrey calls the sword "Caliburn", while Mallory tells us that it is "Excalibur" meaning "cut steel". In Welsh "dur" means steel, while "Caled" means "hard" – so we should suppose that Excalibur is a corruption of Calibur, itself a corruption of "Caleddur", ie "hard steel".

Even at the end of the Second World War, the capitulation/surrender of Japanese forces was symbolised by the handing over of a ceremonial sword. [See three examples at https://en.wikipedia.org/wiki/Surrender_of_Japan.] And so – I say – it was in those days. "The Lady of the Lake" was by now the widow of Loarn mac Erc, the last of the original line of the Vice-roys of Dalriada, and so were any of her sons. So it was her duty (it would have been her husband's, of course) to demonstrate the surrender of the Scots to Arthur by the ceremonial handing over of the sword. The surrender would need to have been as public (and hence as humiliating) as possible – so this was probably done at the base of the mound in front of an assembly of both armies as well as such local population as could be brought together.

We should note that Mallory conflates the Lady of the Lake giving Arthur a sword with Arthur pulling the sword out of the stone. He also calls her the Lady of the Isle of Avalon. [We will have more to say about Avalon in due course.] This actually serves to support the proposition I have made – ie that the sword given by the Lady of the Lake had significance in terms of regal authority.

[Regarding the contradictory idea of "pulling the sword out of the stone", I accept the argument proposed by Sir Tony Robinson on the Channel 4 "Time Team" (#54 Series 7 Episode 9, first broadcast in February 2000) and demonstrated by Dave Chapman of the Bronze Age Foundry (http://bronzeagefoundry.com/) in supposing that this idea goes back to a far previous age when (copper and then bronze) swords were cast in stone formers and that religious ritual surrounded this. The sword should also be considered along with the Thirteen Treasures of Britain – which were not quite contemporaneous, but which illustrate the nature of story telling and of the zeitgeist soon thereafter.]

Evidence from Irish sources

It was only when I was considering, very much as an afterthought, the origins of the Buchanans that I stumbled upon this marvellous vindication for this analysis from Irish sources – though we do need to disregard the political spin they put onto the events. An example of the weakness of this source can be seen from the reference to the Buchanans (for which see the appendix on the Lennox)

https://archive.org/stream/irishpedigreesor_01ohar#page/712/mode/2up

89. Muireadach (III.): son of Eoghan; was married to Earca, daughter of Loarn, King of Dalriada in Scotland, and by her had many sons and daughters, two of them are especially mentioned: – Muirceartach Mór, and Fergus Mór, both called "Mac Earca." From this Fergus Mór descended the Kings of Scotland [.....]

In the 20th year of the reign of the Monarch Lughaidh, the son of Laeghaire, with a complete army, Fergus Mór Mac Earca, (with his five brothers....) went into Scotland to assist his grandfather King Loarn, who was much oppressed by his enemies the Picts; who were vanquished by Fergus and his party, who prosecuted the war so vigorously, followed the enemy to their own homes, and reduced them to such extremity, that they were glad to accept peace upon the conqueror's own conditions; whereupon, on the King's death, which happened about the same time, the said Fergus Mór Mac Earca was unanimously elected and chosen king as being of the blood royal by his mother. And the said Fergus, for a good and lucky omen, sent to his brother, who was then Monarch of Ireland, for the Marble Seat called "Saxum Fatale" (in Irish, Liath Fail, and Cloch-na-Cinneamhna, implying in English the Stone of Destiny or Fortune), to be crowned thereon; which happened accordingly; for, as he was the first absolute King of all Scotland of the Milesian Race, so the succession continued in his blood and lineage ever since to this day.

From this, then, we should suppose that what we have here was (sub?) king Loarn with his queen Naoimh. The Irish sources confirm Loarn's death at this time – leaving Naoimh to surrender – not to the Picts but to Arthur. We can see that "Gillamurius", now, in effect, confirmed as Muirceartach, was acting in support of his maternal grandfather Loarn and the selection of Fergus – another grandson of Loarn's – becomes the "obvious" choice to rule Dalriada/Argyll following the peace treaty. [Reading behind the lines we may notice that many sons of Loarn are referred to – so we may suppose that several if not all of them died with their father in the course of the battles.] Meanwhile various "damsels of the Lake" are left to be married off to those who will assume control of the Lennox on behalf of the Strathclyde kings.

We should enter a word of caution, however. The Irish source quoted is John O'Hart's 1892 "Irish Pedigrees" – very much a secondary source. Nevertheless and despite many other mistakes his work contains I think that the way in which the story has been twisted nevertheless now allows the underlying truth to shine through.

Hart adds this footnote: (still p713)

> Fergus Mor mac Earca; According to the Linea Antiqua, Muiredach had only two sons by his wife Earca. But some writers confound this Fergus Mor Mac Earca, the grandson of Loarn (the last King of Dalriada in Scotland) with Ferghus Mor, the son of Earc who is No 96 in the "genealogy of the Kings of Dalraida" and who was therefore, a brother of Loarn, last King of Dalriada.

The first Viceroy of the Lennox

Crétien de Troyes refers to "King Lac" and his son "Erec". I interpret "King Lac" as being the member of the Strathclyde Royal family installed as Viceroy – and his son appears to have been called "Erc". This is quite likely – for as we have seen, Loarn and his brother Fergus were the sons of Erc. Thus it is likely that Loarn's eldest son (O'Hart tells us he had many children) will have been called Erc and this Erc will have had a daughter available for marriage to the incoming viceroy – who would then call one of his sons Erc, quite possibly the eldest son, as part of pacifying the locals as part of an attempt to ingratiate himself with them.

Joseph Duggan ("The Romances of Crétien de Troyes" (2001) p59 &seq) refers also to the name of the kingdom as "Estre-Gales", citing "Bromwich 1991:292n23" as claiming that this may resemble a form used for Strathclyde. I would like to refine this claim. "Estre-Gales" looks to me like "Eastern Gaels" – ie the Lennox – distinguished from the Western Gaels – ie the residual Scots of Dalriada/ Argyll. Crétien also tells us that the chief castle was "Carrant" (variously "Carnant") which is parsed as "Caer nant" – the castle in the pool. I think that this could be a reference to Inchgalbraith – the crannog in Loch Lomond – very much a castle in a pool!

In the list of Strathclyde kings we find that Caw was the king in charge while these battles in Glen Douglas were taking place. But he was deposed in 501 and his surviving sons seem to have left with him. Dyfnwal Hen regained the throne whence it devolved onto his son Clinog Cedig who ruled in the period 508-540. This suggests that Clinog was a contemporary of Arthur's – probably born 470x80. Clinog is known to have had a brother Garwynwyn whose wife is unknown and whose progeny is only known from a grandson Gwddno who married Irb, sister of Drust IV, king of the Picts. Gwddno's father was called Caurdav (this pedigree from Williamson).

I suggest, therefore, that the most likely candidate as "King Lac" – and hence the progenitor of the Galbraiths – was this Garwynwyn. This would make "Erc du Lac" a brother of Caurdav. I have no view as to who may have been the elder of these, but Crétien asserts that "Erec" was installed as "king" following the death of his father.

We should note here that the term "king" is loosely used. At no time was the Lennox an independent kingdom, however much autonomy was devolved upon the Viceroy – or "mor-maer" (great steward).

Postscript 1: Loch Leven becomes Loch Lomond

When we consider the location of Ben Lomond it is hard to see it having been of any value before Arthur's time – after all who was to be warned about what? Ben Lomond does have a clear line of sight to the great majority of the Lennox north of the Southern end of Loch Lomond. So should a beacon have been lit in most of the Lennox, it would have been seen at Ben Lomond from where word could get back quickly eg to Dumbarton Rock. Similarly it would have been of reasonably easy access for any spies in the Callander area. Looking at it the other way round, it is hard to see why anyone eg in Roman times at Callander would have valued a warning signal from Ben Lomond – warning of what? Any attack from the Dalriadan Scots would need to have come either through Crianlarich or up from Drymen – in either event Ben Lomond would have been very largely irrelevant.

In short I would propose that the change of name from Loch Leven to Loch Lomond would have come only once the warning beacon system for the Lennox based on Ben Lomond had become ingrained in people's thinking.

Postscript 2: "Argyll"

The Wikipedia page about Argyll (~/Argyll) shows just how at loggerheads the various academics are at the moment (Spring 2017) there is no meeting of minds and nothing even approaching a consensus (of the various suggestions, that of Alex Woolf seems, as usual, the most plausible).

Too much is read into minor variations in spelling dating from a time when spelling had not in any case been standardised and despite the considerable later mangling of many Irish words. Thus, for example, of Airgíalla (now Oriel) Wikipedia (~/Airgíalla) says:

> "*Airgíalla* may mean "those who give hostages" or "the hostage givers", and refers to both the Irish over-kingdom of Airgíalla, and the confederation of tribes that formed it. It is commonly Anglicised as Oriel; however, archaic Angliciations include: Uriel, Orial, Orgialla, Orgiall, Oryallia, and Ergallia."

So I will lob in another idea: it seems to me most plausible that the root of the Scottish "Argyll" is in essence exactly the same as the Irish one. At what stage hostages may have been demanded – and by whom – is another matter, though my guess would be that the requirement would be by Irish overkings. The persistence of the name might be taken to imply that this stems from post 498, but it is not impossible that it derives from the initial take-over by Dalriada – when one can imagine that Epidian hostages would indeed have been considered a necessary precaution for the security of the new Dalriadan monarchy.

[Even if Woolf is correct on timing, the 'hostage' explanation is still feasible.]

Postscript 3: The Cumbraes

It is likely that The Cumbrae Islands referred to in passing in the previous section were also ceded to Strathclyde as part of the treaty. While they may have been important to the Gadini, they were of no consequence to the Dalriadans who retained Bute.

B. BATTLE 7 – CAT COIT CELIDON

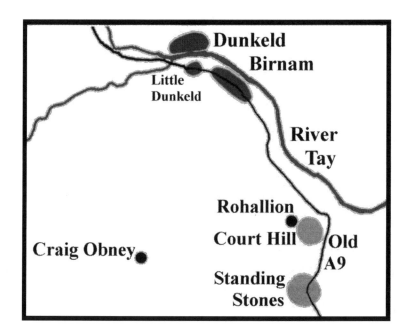

Arthurian enthusiasts have played far too fast and loose with the concept of "Caledonia". To be fair we have seen that they have Ptolemy as a referee in this matter for as we have seen he names the Minch and the Atlantic "Oceanus Duecaledonius" despite, even as he saw it, the Caledones having no direct access to it. Sadly the Picts left no written records which might have been to the contrary. However I hope that the discussion of Ptolemy's geography will have left the reader convinced that the Caledones occupied the great bulk of what we now call the Grampian mountains.

Even today there are only two significant routes into this area from the south. The western one runs up from Gilmerton, near Crieff till it reaches the River Almond at the mouth of the Sma' Glen. To go beyond this point would have been suicidal for Arthur as the cavalry would have had to be close to single file over several miles – and thus totally open to be taken apart by a Highland Charge as was the Picts' wont. Sensibly the Romans had built a(n albeit shortlived) fort (Fendoch) just at the entrance to the Sma' Glen. Just one mile to the North, on a hilltop on the other side of the river, lies Dun Mor ("Big Fort") which would have been in plain view from the Roman one. Essentially we should consider this as impregnable for any other than a huge force – and Arthur's supply lines were already greatly stretched. It would only have been feasible for the battle to have taken place here if the Caledonians had taken leave of their senses and their natural fortress, so I think we should discount this site from our considerations. [There is another fort – at Craig Obney guarding the entrance to The valley of the River Garr from which a path leads into the middle of Strathbra'an – essentially the middle of no-where from Arthur's point of view.]

The other major access into "Caledonia" is up the valley of the river Tay. As we have seen, on the west bank of the Tay the Romans had established themselves some miles south at Bertha, while on the East Bank there was Inchtuthil.

I think it more likely that Arthur chose to follow what is now the route of the old A9. Bankfoot seems a good place for an encounter from Arthur's point of view, but the choice was not his. An even more evocative site just 2 miles further North suggests itself: Rohallion – the "rath" of the Caledonians – now in Birnam Wood and just across the river from Dunkeld. [For a deeper discussion of Raths, see "Scottish Clans....." volume II, but suffice it to say that a rath is a larger precursor of the "motte" of Norman times. A particularly good example is the mound in Badenoch on which Ruthven Barracks sit.] Rohallion would appear now to be named locally as "Duncan's fort" and immediately below it is Court Hill about which the Old Statistical Account says:

> A round mound at the bottom of Birnam hill on the south-east side is worthy of remark. It is faced with steep oaks, except for a few yards where it is fortified by art. This eminence has been known for time immemorial, by the names of Court-hill, and Duncan's hill, and is believed to have been on some occasions occupied by the unfortunate Scottish king of that name. It looks full in the face, at a distance of about 12 miles, the celebrated Dunsinan-Hill, the seat and fortress of Macbeth. Within the range of an arrow from this mound are to be seen a number of tumuli or small heaps of stones, about the length of a human body. It is not unlikely that upon digging, human skeletons would be found under these tumuli.

This is the look and feel of a battle site.

In short Arthur's forces took the line of the old A9 road before making the ascent to take on the Caledonians at their fastness. However, as the reader will have seen that I have identified an alternative. Rohallion provides a wonderful vantage point – even without this it is very likely that scouts will have alerted the Caledonians to Arthur's approach – so it is possible that they descended from the fort to take Arthur on on flatter ground – if so the sites of the standing stones beside the old A9 in the general area of Boglehall could have provided a suitable site. However I consider this to be less likely than Court Hill. From a military point of view why not, after all, allow Arthur's men and horses to tire themselves out in the climb from Myres of Murthly to Court Hill – where they may have supposed also that Arthur's cavalry would have had much less room for manoeuvre?

C. BATTLE 1 – THE MOUTH OF THE RIVER GLEN

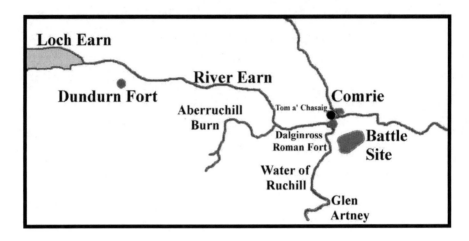

Identifying this site was a breakthrough moment for me and it happened remarkably quickly after I simply started scouring the map.

Just above Comrie to the South is Allt Srath a' Ghlinne – which means "burn of the Strath of the river called Glinne".

This is an apparently silly name for several reasons: the burn is in a glen not a strath – so Strath a' Ghlinne must be further downstream. The river of which it is a tributary (which must, therefore, have been the Glein) is now called the Water of Ruchill, meeting the River Earn at Comrie. But "Water of Ruchill" also is a silly name for this reason: within Aberuchill estate (Aberuchill: "mouth of the Ruchill") there is a burn called the Aberuchill burn (so how silly a name is that???). And there is another problem, for the Water of Ruchill now runs not in Strathglein, nor in Strathruchill, but in Glenartney!

So it is the Aberuchill burn which was originally called the Ruchill – and Aberuchill was its mouth; the Water of Ruchill was called the Artney (because that's how Glenartney got its name) and before that it was called the Glinne – which roughly means the "pure burn" (in Old Welsh/Pictish). [Later, as Christianity got established this word came to imply "holy".]

Where this stream meets the Earn (at Dalginross) there was a Roman Fort. Unfortunately a substantial part of this has now been eroded away by the rivers and much of the remainder is now built over by the likes of Queen's

Road, Glebe Road, Strowan Road etc. It occupied the whole of the area south of the Earn between the Ruchil Water and the Lednock Burn (the Earn has moved somewhat south since those times).

The Romans were long gone when Arthur's battle took place, of course – but it is likely that the Caledonians were making use of the fort site – as an outpost of their main fortress in this area at Dundurn just four miles away. The battle is likely to have taken place immediately to the South of the fort – with the lines drawn up parallel to South Crieff Road.

Some time following Arthur's success the lower stretches of the Glinne came to be known as the Artnie – basically "Arthur's burn" – and so its valley became "Glen Artney".

St Kessog

The observant reader will have noticed "Tom a' Chasaig" on the map. I may say that I had already identified all the battle sites before the significance of this dawned on me – indeed I had published my discovery that Dalginross was the site of Arthur's first battle in the local paper before I was even aware of this site or of its relevance. So I ask the reader to be impressed by how much extra strength this adds to the argument.

The site Tom a' Chasaig is a small mound where, it is claimed, St Kessog preached. It is apposite that at this point we take time out to consider Kessog.

All are agreed that the name "Kessog" comes from the Old Irish "cess"/"ceas" meaning.... spear. Thus "MacKessog" (really Makessog) should be parsed as ma-kess-og – "my little spear", the "ma-" and the "-og" being terms of endearment. This is not a "real" name, it is a nickname.

Kessog's birthdate is usually given as 460; he was one of many sons of Óengus mac Nad Froích whose Wikipedia page describes his ancestry as: Nad Froich mac Cuirc [ie son of Corc]. Oengus and his sons were baptised by St Patrick himself, making him the first Christian king in Munster (at this time Munster was not really a united province, so Oengus is more correctly recognised as the King of Cashel – where his seat was). His reign is given as c453-489. The Annals of Munster for 489 say "Aenghus, son of Nadfraech, King of Munster, fell in the battle of Cell Osnadha fought against him by Muircheartach Mac Earca......"

Thus we can see that it may well have given Kessog some pleasure to have taken on Muircheartach in Glen Douglas.

Corc was also known as Conall Corc; his birthdate is given as c340. To me the numbers do not seem to fit. We might expect Óengus to have been born c430, Nad Froich c405 and so Corc c380. So it looks as if two Corcs, one the grandfather of the other have been elided. But one or more missing generations need not detain us as they are not directly relevant to our story.

Kessog was killed malevolently. The usual date given is 520 – or 520x30. The 520 date would have made Kessog some 60 years old. A cairn was set up at the spot where he died – at Bandry which is about a mile and a half south of Luss. The site is very close to the marina there; sadly the cairn which well-wishers had added to over the centuries (it is an old Gaelic tradition to honour a dead person by adding a stone to their cairn) was taken down more than 200 years ago to make way for road widening. Fortunately no bones were discovered, so we may be confident that in this case it was not his grave, but only a marker. We should note here that "Bandry" is otherwise 'ban-druidh' which Dwelly translates as 'sorceress' – and we can see readily the etymological origins as "female druid". Thus we should interpret this murder as religiously motivated (those holding to Druidry attempting to defend themselves from Kessog's attentions) and so, from a Christian standpoint, he should really be classed as a martyr. So it is reasonable to accept the legend which claims that he was buried where he is supposed to have lived – on the island of Inchtavannach ("monk's island"). Given the animosity towards him which occasioned his death, we might treat this claim with some sympathy – and we can see an immediate parallel in the case of Inchgalbraith – a crannog (ie deliberately constructed for defensive purposes). However we should not suppose from the name Inchtavannach that Kessog lived a monkish lifestyle – the name of the island is more likely to date from a time more than 500 years later when monasteries were being established in Scotland.

When Kessog came to Scotland is a problem. The legend at Luss says that he set up there around the year 510 – and we can see immediately that this is thoroughly consistent with the timeline I have set out for the conquest of the Lennox. But this battle (at Dalginross) probably took place around the year 495 – very close to the death of St Patrick (493). Indeed I suppose that St Patrick may have introduced Kessog to the Damnonii, founding what became Old Kilpatrick in the process. Any time in the period 480x89 is feasible.

Directly across Loch Lomond from Luss is Strathcashel point. It is possible to dismiss any direct connection to Kessog by recognising that "Cashel" simply means castle – and there is a fort on the point. However I think we should not exclude the idea that Kessog – who came from Cashel, after all – may have been based here for some time before settling down at or near Luss. We should add to this the evidence of the Buchanans (see appendix on the Lennox) – for Buchanan was in the parish of Luss well into historical times – and the most likely explanation is a prior common ownership of the two separate estates.

Kessog was no ordinary "missionary". First he is classically thought of as a warrior armed with bow and arrow. The only extant depiction of this is a new one at the very new Catholic Church at Balloch (at the south end of Loch Lomond) – and no-one associated can explain the basis of this characterisation. But as we shall see the depiction is indeed apposite. Kessog did the first Christian preaching at several of the sites of Arthurian battles – so we should understand him to be very important member of Arthur's army as well as a keen proselytiser.

Seven hundred years later, the Earls of Lennox wishing to draw a veil over their true male-line descent sought the assistance of the exiled Irish poet Muiredhach Albanach O'Dailly to whom they had offered a home. O'Dailly wrote a poem about their ancestry (recorded in the book of the Dean of Lismore), tracing it back to Corc a king of Munster. For a full treatment of this see the appendix on the Lennox. Suffice it here to say that the descent from Corc is possible only because Alwin II Earl of Lennox married, as his first wife, the (frustratingly, for us, unnamed) daughter of Maldoven the then head of the family of Luss. Thus we should infer that the family of Luss descended from St Kessog, for we know that St Kessog was active in the area and as we have seen he was indeed of this descent. So far from being a monk as we would understand the term today, St Kessog was a soldier and a father.

As we shall see Kessog is remembered at several of Arthur's battle sites; in later centuries other places have been dedicated to him – but there is one 'erratic' – the area called Kessog just north of Inverness, whence the Kessock Bridge. We should not rule out the possibility of a visit by Kessog to the capital of the Kingdom of the Northern Picts – particularly in the short period available to him after the Battle of Badon Hill – and we should note that this was long before Columba.

St Kessog as the model for Lancelot du Lac

We may begin by observing the spear/lance equivalence which is apparent immediately. Many of those characters who are not wholly made up in the Arthur legend are anachronistic – ie they did not live in the Arthurian epoch – but some clearly did. I had supposed, especially given his name, that Lancelot was a wholly fictitious character. This would appear to be the view of eg Deborah Deliyannis (https://history.indiana.edu/faculty_staff/faculty/deliyannis_deborah.html) who did an excellent job of distilling Arthurian material from Geoffrey of Monmouth. Geoffrey does not mention Lancelot

– Deliyannis suggesting that he was a creation of Chrétian de Troyes. But he does appear in "Le Morte D'Arthur". In Book II, Chapter 4, Mallory refers to "Lanceor" who got involved with an intrigue starring the "great lady Lile of Avelion", later referred to as the Lady of the Lake (also not mentioned by Mallory). Several people, male and female end up killed in this story. Here a king "makes a tomb" over the dead body – which I take to be a (mistaken) reference to the cairn at Bandry.

Mallory distinguishes Lanceor from Lancelot. I rationalise this because the various strands of stories about him as he tells them appear to conflict. But Lancelot was from Ireland and was a son of a king. This is a strange claim – giving it the ring of verisimilitude.

In the legend Lancelot's son was Galahad and this was supposed to be his (ie Lancelot's) real name.

Despite all the experts telling me that it is not possible at the time in question I still like the idea of parsing the name as "giolla-h-aed" – servant boy of Aed (the Celtic god of fire). The objection made to this is that in Ireland at that time people did not use that form in pre-Christian times – and indeed it is clear that names of Celtic gods were given freely to people (Aed/Aidan, Brigid etc.).

Against this, however, we may note

- Gillamurius. This works both ways for on the one hand the king involved was clearly NOT called Gillamurius, (as we saw, I propose Muirchertach mac Muiredaig) but it provides consistency with this parsing of the name.

Then from the Druid Circle website we may note

- Giolla Deacair — an Otherworld champion who owned a horse that could not be ridden.
- Corc mac Luigthig (where Luigthig may be parsed as thig: 'acceptable' and Luig: 'to Lugh')

source: http://www.druidcircle.org/library/index.php?title=Celtic_Names_Glossary#Celtic_Male_Names_of_Ireland

We know that Kessog's father was Oengus

So I am content that the name Galahad bears at least a parallel relationship to Lancelot/Kessog's real name as Gillamurius does to his. If this is, as I have supposed, to the patronymic then Galahad is really "mac Oengus". If, however Gillamurius represents Muirterach then it would seem that Kessog's real name probably referenced the fire god "Aed" somehow.

D. BATTLE 6 – THE RIVER BASSAS

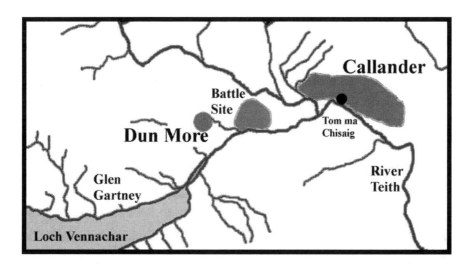

Let me start by making it clear that my analysis of this battle site is an interpolation – but I will set out the logic and it will be for the reader to decide how likely my proposition is. Having examined the battle sites so far we are in a position to begin to identify a pattern and work out some underlying strategy.

Arthur began c495 by heading straight through the Maetae who inhabited central Scotland to hit the Caledonians hard at Comrie – where they had come to meet him from Dundurn and Rohallion. He realised that his campaign would be significantly easier if he were able to prosecute the war against the Picts on one front only. With the Caledonians needing to lick their wounds he had bought enough time to take on (and see off) the Scots of Argyll, which he did after a two year campaign, securing from them what would become the western half of the Lennox for the Southern forces.. He was close to securing his western flank but the eastern shores of Loch Lomond presented a residual weakness he needed to resolve. When considering Ptolemy's map we saw that around Loch Lomond the Pictish tribe in occupation were the Gadini. Since Ptolemy's time the Scots had encroached upon their lands steadily from the west so that by the time of Arthur they were confined to the area between Loch Lomond and the Trossachs. By this time also the residue of the Gadini were a part of an albeit loose Pictish confederation. The best model for thinking about this may be that of NATO, with the Gadini cast as Lithuania. The Picts did not have the resources to maintain a standing army so far away from their heartland; mobilisation took place as and when needed or desired. The territory of the Gadini was like a salient – albeit a salient sticking into notionally friendly Maeatae territory. The Damnonii needed this land also to consolidate their western flank so the Gadini had to be treated as hostile and hence neutralised. Thus Arthur's next task was to secure what would become the eastern part of the Lennox. This then became the purpose of the battle of the River Bassas. Today there is, of course, no such river, but can we find a relevant potential site? I think we can.

I draw the reader's attention to Glen Gartney. Immediately you will be ahead of me, for the name Glen Gartney looks remarkably similar to Glen Artney! Let us now look at this glen. The head of Glen Gyle is just a mile and a half from the banks of Loch Lomond. Glen Gyle, empties into Loch Katrine; this in turn empties into the Achray Water which runs into Loch Achray which feeds the Black Water into Loch Venachar ('the horn-shaped loch'). From Loch Venachar the Eas Gobhain enters the River Teith at Callander.

At the foot of Glen Gartney is a flat flood plain. Standing some 200 ft above it to the North West off it is Dunmore fort, one mile from a Roman fort right next to the Teith also about a mile above the confluence. It is the site of the fort which I propose as the site of the battle.

So we may notice four things straight away:

1. the Locals considered this a key military position (whence the fort called Dunmore);

2. the Romans considered this a key military position (whence their fort now called Bochastle);

3. there is a large area of flat land ideally suited to a military engagement involving cavalry;

4. none of the place names along the glen seem to have any connection to "Gartney".

We have seen that the Damnonii had already occupied Bocastle from time to time, so the site is not such a great surprise, but after I had decided to offer this as the likely location two wonderful extra pieces of evidence came to light:

1. Tom ma Chisaig. Yes, I am sure that the reader, having looked at the map, will be ahead of me again: here is another mound on which St Kessog is said to have preached. We notice that this site is well behind the front line of the battle. In turn what this tells us is that the Gadini had control of the lowlands

here, so their fort at Dunmore was overseeing this land (possibly lived on in subjection to them by others) so that the fort represents the defence behind which they would retreat in bad times. [I remind the reader that the bulk of the Forth/Teith basin at this time was a more or less impenetrable bog.]

2. The name "Bassas" is clearly Pictish rather than Gaelic. This is just as well as there is nothing in Dwelly which could apply even remotely. The Welsh dictionary is not overburdened by suitable offerings – the best I could come up with was "bas" meaning "shallow". Imagine my surprise, then, when I consulted my friend Dr Ian Cameron whose children canoed there several times competitively. The river is so shallow that there is a serious risk of a canoe scraping the river bottom! It is readily fordable. Potentially against this we have to be mindful that at the head of this river is Loch Katrine from which Glasgow takes a substantial amount of water, so in Arthur's time we should expect there to have been a substantially greater flow. But a look on old maps shows the area as "liable to flooding" – apparently more so than today. So my understanding is that the extra flow would not have contributed to significantly extra depth, but rather to greater flooding. We should note that the name "Eas Gobhain" (literally "the smith's waterfall") for the river below Loch Vennachar refers to the weir built to provide for the smith's needs – although there is no extant indication of where and for what this was required.

I conclude therefore that I have identified the correct location for the battle and that the name "Bassas" here refers to the shallowness of the river. Following the battle and the annexation of (at least) the lands between Loch Lomond and the watershed (perhaps all the way to the bog), the valley was renamed Glen Gartney in Arthur's honour.

Endnote

Arthur had made great progress. In chess terms it was the end of the opening and Arthur was as well placed as he could be to prosecute a robust middle game.

E. BATTLE NO. 8: GUINNON FORT

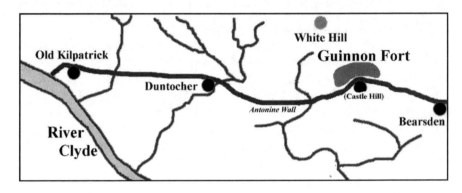

From the Caledonians' point of view, the Scots, as incomers and frequent enough enemies, could be seen as expendable, but Arthur's victory at Callander was serious. By now it was clear that his attack at Comrie was no mere punishment raid, which would in essence imply giving the Caledonians back some of what they had dished out sporadically but too often. The acquisition of the territory of the Lennox was indicative that Arthur meant business. The Caledonians could rely on the Maeatae who were tantamount to a client state. They had dithered too long – a counterattack was imperative. Although I think this quite unlikely they may also have been motivated by the brooding exiled king Caw, previously of Damnonia – who will have wanted at least revenge if not his kingdom back.

The key to locating the site is to keep in mind that the first element "Guin-" should be seen as "gwyn" – which still means "white" even in modern Welsh. Because it is a identified as a fort the first place for us to look is the Antonine Wall. Fortunately a potential solution is not hard to find: Castlehill on the Western outskirts of Bearsden. Just one mile NNW of this site is White Hill. As can be seen from satellite imagery even the topsoil around Castle Hill is light in colour. White Hill is being quarried by the company Tarmac (who call the site "Douglasmuir"). They describe the stone quarried there as "golden quartzite" – the bulk of which they crush to various sizes largely for decorative use. While there is a yellow tinge to the rock making it clearly different from eg the White Cliffs of Dover, it is more than white enough for our purposes. So I suppose that this rock will have been evident in the fortifications sufficiently for the name to have been given – Gwyn-dun the White Fort.

First we should note that the new Lennox border is not straight but actually concave which means that the residual Maeatae territory comes within just 10 miles of Castle Hill at the junction of the A811 and A81 near Balfron Station. With the Damnonii in firm control of the Lennox, the Picts would have given the game away far too early if they had tried to use the Roman road through Callander – indeed it is possible that Callander itself was under Damnonian control. So the most westerly crossing of the Forth which they could have accomplished was at the Fords of Frew. It is more likely, however that they mustered at Stirling – where they could marshal the Maeatae as well and from there took the route of the A811 which would still be in friendly territory. Thus but for any scouts or spies the army could have reached Balfron, only 15 miles away essentially unnoticed. With a surreptitious deposit of stores at Balfron in advance of this, the army could have marched from Stirling in a day and from there the lightning strike on Guinnon Fort, whether taking the route of the A809 or the A81 would not have exceeded 13 miles – again just one long day's march. As the area they were travelling through had been under their control just five years before they may have expected some assistance also from local inhabitants.

The Caledonii had miscalculated. They had been successful in attacking Roman Britannia when they had teamed up with the Scots. For all their squabbling, the longer term strategic interests of the Caledonii lay with cooperation with the intruding Scots, but they left them high and dry. Without them even when they pressganged the Maeatae into assisting they just did not have the strength. By selecting Guinon Fort for their attack they may have supposed that they were so far away from Gododdin territory that they could complete their raid against seriously reduced numbers of troops. But Arthur was just too good and too ready for them.

This is the battle where it is noted that Arthur carried an image of the Virgin Mary on his shoulder. As this is where the shield was normally carried we should have no difficulty with the idea that his shield was painted in this way – and from the two instances we have seen already of St Kessog lecturing the losing troops and their camp followers we should have no doubt as to the intent to Christianise the losers.

An indicative date for this battle is 505x7

F. BATTLE NO. 9: THE CITY OF THE LEGION

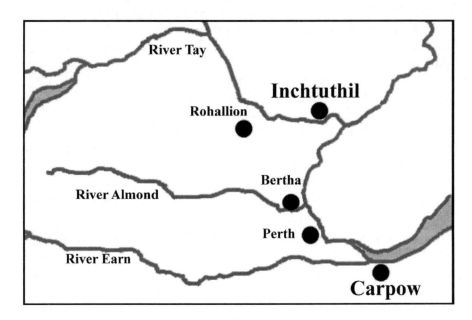

The effrontery of the Caledonians had to be addressed in short order – so Arthur and his army set off to do just that. Earlier we saw that there were four battles in Glen Douglas. This battle at the City of the Legion was very much Cat Coit Celidon Round II.

According to all the authorities I have been able to find there are only two places in Scotland which could be construed as a city "of a legion": Inchtutil and Carpow.

Neither of these sites is wholly satisfactory, nevertheless we are where we are. Inchtuthil was never properly finished – and strictly it is difficult to characterise it as a "city". In the case of Carpow the best of my understanding is that it was a residence for veterans – not that this remained of any significance by the times we are considering. Both these sites make no sense at all if Arthur had been planning to punish the Maeatae and this in turn reinforces the idea that it had been the Caledonians who had led the attack on Guinnon Fort. If he wanted to take on the Maeatae far better to have done this closer to home.

The case for Inchtuthil is that it is on the very edge of the Caledonians' heartland. But Arthur did not cross the Tay when he went for Rohallion and it is very difficult to see why he would lengthen and weaken his supply lines in this way on this occasion. And what would his target be?

Then there is the matter of the route that Arthur would have chosen. The "natural" route would have been up the A9 from Stirling through Auchterarder (which by now was the Caledonian/Manau frontier) reaching Perth from the west. On this basis there would have been no reason to detour south and east to Carpow.

So what is the case for Carpow? Arthur may have chosen to take a route which he hoped might provide an element of surprise. So from Stirling he struck east to Kinross and then on through Glenfarg which, although a narrow defile, would not have been convenient for ambush. At its mouth it opens out suddenly on to flat land at Abernethy where cavalry would be at a substantial advantage.

This stratagem would depend not only upon the Maeatae not alerting the Caledonians, but also upon the attitude of the tribes local to that area of Fife and Kinross. Normally they would be clients of the Caledonians and, far enough away from the Antonine Wall they would be largely oblivious to the politics and manoeuvrings. Arthur's objectives may have included convincing these locals that supporting the Caledonians was not in their interests.

As it played out, the hope was not borne out. The Caledonians were forewarned and had plenty of time to gather a force to confront Arthur as his army emerged from Glenfarg.

Because I can find no basis for supposing Inchtuthil as the site of the battle. If we are to take Nennius' words literally then we must choose Carpow, but I would not rule out the possibility that the battle actually took place at Perth itself.

The indicative date 507x9.

G. BATTLE NO 10: ON THE BANK OF THE RIVER CALLED TRIBUIT

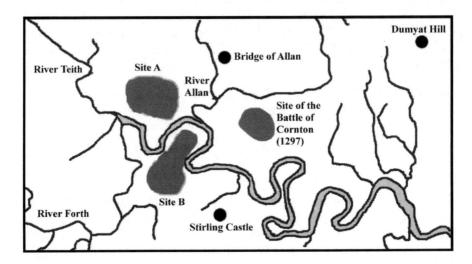

I should start by admitting that this site – and at least partly hence the protagonists – are not at all clear. So what follows really is speculation.

There are two ways of looking at the reason for this battle. On the one hand the Caledonians having been taught their lesson, the role of the Maeatae (a) in alerting them and (b) in the attack on Guinnon Fort needed to be addressed forcibly. Alternatively the Maeatae may have had the idea to attack what they will have seen as the rump of Arthur's forces given that these will have been weakened by casualties and tired by the stringencies of the battle at the City of the Legion.

Currently there is no river called Tribuit and despite extensive searching there is no linkage obvious. So I have fallen back on the "Tri" part of the name to consider where three-ness might be relevant. I am also assuming that Arthur would have made significant use of the existing Roman road system.

A Roman road heads straight for Stirling, just north of which is an area where three rivers meet. The one now called the Forth is the most southerly and by no means the biggest; it joins the far more substantial Teith and less than a mile further downstream these are met by the Allan Water. We should be hesitant to suppose that the courses of these rivers are exactly where they were 1500 years ago, but the crossing of the Forth has been problematic. Even many centuries later the Fords of Frew proved very important. Just below these confluences we can see the site of an old bridge at Kildean; in between the two confluences, at Craigforth Mill there was a salmon weir – suggesting a relatively easy crossing coinciding with the highest reach of spring tides. Close by is the site of a later encounter: the Battle of Cornton (1297). In this area the river meanders greatly – providing large areas of flat land.

So I think that there is a logical case to be made for this site – it is close to the Roman Road; it is close to the fortress rock of Stirling Castle; it is in the middle of Maeatae territory; it is where three rivers meet; it is just 500 yards and across the river from a known battle site.

It is tempting to give an indicative date of 509x11 for this battle, but, as just suggested I could equally imagine it taking place when Arthur was on the way home from the battle of the city of the Legion.

If the Maeatae had, in effect decided to ambush Arthur on his way home, then they may well have started the assault while his army was crossing the river. In that case it would be likely that they would be sallying forth from Stirling Castle hill and the battle would be at Site B. If this battle was a result of a separate incursion/raid by Arthur then there is the question of where he was intending to go – perhaps an expedition further to punish those who had not sided with him on his journey to the City of the Legion. In this case it would still have made sense for the Maeatae to lure him into crossing the river; their forces would have had to be massed above Bridge of Allan and the likely site of the main conflict would have been Site A – or even the Cornton site itself.

H. BATTLE NO 11: ON A HILL CALLED AGNED

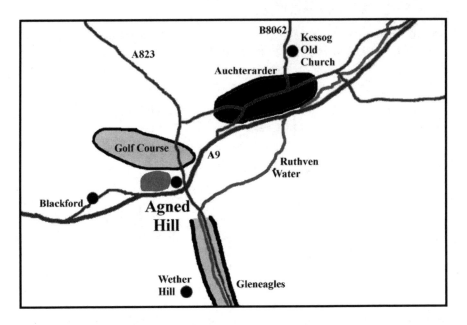

This site eluded me for some time, but I have a fair degree of confidence that I have found it. This is the penultimate battle of the twelve. Because the site is a hill it seems likely to be north of the wall and so one should probably assume some sort of punitive sortie by Arthur into enemy territory.

Fist we must consider the meaning of the name. Two potential explanations for "Agned" commend themselves.

(a) Agnus = Lamb the first choice I would offer is that the name may be cognate with "agnus", the Latin for a lamb. In "Scottish Clans..." I demonstrated how farming practice provides the basis for so many place names and how this shows that while it was the practice to take adult animals up to summer pastures, the young animals – calves, kids, piglets, lambs etc. – were kept behind in more temperate surroundings. There are many "Lamb Hill"s and several are associated, unsurprisingly, with "Wether Hill"s (a wether is a castrated ram). One such Wether Hill is to be found just above the lower Glen Devon reservoir in the Ochils beside Glen Eagles and just South of Blackford in Strathallan.

Just north west of the A9/A823 junction just below the golf course is the site of an old Roman fort. This is one of several low hills in the vicinity which would indeed have been highly suitable for lambs when their wether uncles were up on Wether Hill. This is a good site because it is on the main road north from Stirling to Perth.

Another Wether Hill is to be found at the west end of the Cleish Hills. The A823 half encircles it just three miles south of Crook of Devon. Just across the road is Cult Hill and to the north, across the Pow burn is Keith Hills. The lower slopes of Cult Hill in particular offer not only suitable grazing for lambs but also a site suited to a cavalry engagement. The down side of this site is that, notwithstanding that Arthur may have taken this route on his way to what turned out to be the battle of the city of the Legion, really it leads nowhere interesting; it had been tried before, it is the long way round in what was still in essence enemy territory and so has nothing to recommend it.

(b) Agen = Slot An alternative direction to seek for an understanding of the placename can be found in the modern Welsh word "agen" which means "slot" or "cleft". There are many placenames in Scotland incorporating this idea, including, for example, the island of Eigg and, in Strathspey, the Beum a'Chlaidh. Bizarrely the Roman fort near Blackford already mentioned can be seen to fit this explanation also in so far as it stands directly opposite Glen Eagles which is very much a "slot". In private conversation with the Chief of Haldane who still lives in the area I have been given to understand not only that Gleneagles has no connection with eagles, nor with any church (supposedly from eglis) but is indeed cognate with Eigg and does mean cleft.

And so it was that I found myself drawn to the Roman camp which is strictly between Blackford and Auchterarder. But I was lacking the finally convincing element. It was while I was pondering this that the Kessog connection became apparent to me in general (I was working on several lines of this research in parallel) and Kessog came to the rescue here! The Episcopalian church in Auchterarder is dedicated to St Kessog. This in itself was not necessarily a big thing – but it reflects a far older dedication of a church which can be seen on old maps immediately adjacent to the grounds of Auchterarder House – farms on either side of it being called East and West Kirkton respectively.

This is not proof, of course – especially when the meaning is still equivocal, but it does merit serious consideration.

What, then, should we understand from there having been a battle here? We can notice a pattern in the battle sites from Rohallion to Carpow and then to Gleneagles. The confrontation with the Caledonians was moving South. I interpret this as the Caledonians consolidating their position, absorbing tribes which had been separate and moving their own front line further and further south. They absorbed Strathearn and then Strathallan and North Fife. This left the Maeatae becoming the sole buffer between them and the foederati with their base in Clackmannanshire spreading as far west into the Forth basin bog as was feasible and as far south as the Antonine Wall. Later they too would be absorbed.

So the choice of this battle ground belonged to the Caledonians and once again they were discomfitted.

We should probably suppose a date of 515AD for this.

I. BATTLE NO 12: BADON HILL

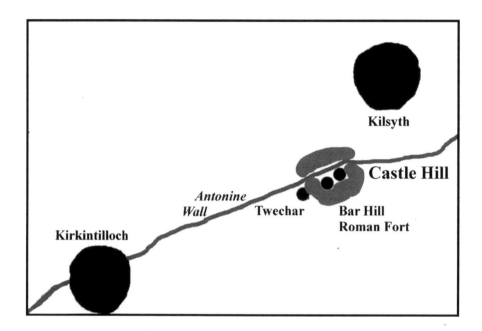

We should start our consideration of this site by discussing pronunciation. I take delight in pointing out to potentially interested parties two places in Scotland (there are others besides) called Balloch. One near Loch Lomond is called BAL-och, the other, near Culloden is called Ba-LOCH. Same spelling, entirely different pronunciation and meanings. Similarly we are confronted by BBC presenters, even SNP MSPs failing to pronounce the names of places correctly (in the case of MSPs places in their own constituencies!). Thus Tomintoul rhymes with towel despite the efforts of those who would rhyme it with tool. So too with Badenoch which is not BAD-enoch, nor even BADE-enoch. So far as I understand it, it is closer to BAY-enoch – with just a hint of a 'd'! And so on!

This is bad enough, but there is great change in pronunciation over time and this can lead to changes in spelling. Thus most people pronounce daughter as "dawter" – but there are still those who show that the spelling is not silly as they stick with the older and very much correct "dochter" (as, too, they say "wecht" for weight etc.) And then there was the vowel shift in the 1700s dividing those who pronounce water "watter" (as in batter) from those who have moved on to wauter (as in daughter).

And so we come to Badon. Is it "Bay"-don or "Bad"-on or "Baa"-don or even "Bar"-don? All we have is the name as represented in writing – giving us precious little clue. I will be offering what I consider the answer, but we should not presume at this stage.

As we have seen, Nennius tells us about the battle "....and on which fell 960 men from one charge by Arthur; and no-one struck them down save Arthur himself". Although, as we have seen, Gildas attempted to erase Arthur from history he did refer to: "....the siege of Badon Hill, and of almost the last great slaughter inflicted upon the rascally crew." we should note that even today in English "bar" can mean "ridge" and shoals in a river. There is the famous "Carter Bar" – the watershed on the A68 road.

Partly from these early records and partly because we have the benefit of hindsight, we may understand that the Picts in general and the Caledonii in particular had been completely exasperated by the way Arthur's army had been riding roughshod over them. Like a poker player staring defeat in the face, they decided to go "all in". This could be no pinprick, it had to be of somewhere seriously important. Moreover it needed to be readily accessible to them – for resupply and reinforcement. So we can be confident that that it was the Picts who had laid siege to a foederati strongpoint.

There is one place which fits all the criteria we have considered: Bar Hill near Twechar between Kilsyth and Kirkintilloch. Bar Hill lies on the Antonine Wall and on it we find not only a Roman Fort, lying some 30 yards behind the wall, but also a "local" castle right on the wall itself. It is this latter site which the Picts besieged. Bar Hill is on the Damnonian side of the wall – 5 miles or so from the boundary point with the Gododdin. So we should understand that it was the Damnonian garrison which was besieged – and it was Arthur's force coming from the east to raise the siege which routed the Pictish forces.

Nennius' hyperbole – written 300 years later – is excusable. Not Arthur by himself, but Arthur at the head of his force of cavalry arriving suddenly may well had killed nearly 1000 Picts in a single charge – particularly if, settled in for the long term, they had relaxed their vigilance somewhat and were therefore caught before they had been able to form up in battle order.

The Annales Cambriae give the date of this battle as 516 and we may be confident of this being correct to within a few years – ie before 520.

Geoffrey of Monmouth specifies that Ambrosius became High King of Britain following Vortigern.

As we have noted already, for the year 473, The Anglo-Saxon Chronicle records Hengist and Aesc wreaking havoc in the south-east of England. I proposed that they chose to do this because Ambrosius had taken the cream of the British Army north to relieve the siege of Dumbarton Rock. This would push Badon Hill very specifically to 517. However, as we have seen, the Anglo-Saxon Chronicle is only reliable to within two or three years. However we may say with considerable confidence that this most definitive of victories took place in the period 515x520, probably 516x518.

CONCLUSION AND THE AFTERMATH

The war was over. The Caledonians and their client neighbours were so thoroughly defeated at this, their last ditch effort, that Arthur had secured a specific peace which would last a generation and more. There was indeed an almost unprecedented 20 years of peace from Badon Hill to the death of Arthur – which the Annales put in 537, Geoffrey of Monmouth at 542. But such were the times on the island of Alba that this by no means implied peace in general.

After the peace treaty with the Scots of Argyll and the assertion of the eastern border of the Lennox, what was left of Manau was a small and neutered shell of its former self. It seems that following the end of the major hostilities (ie after Badon Hill) the foederati were happy to give the Scots free reign to assert whatever hegemony they could and wanted over the Maeatae on the basis that this would offer greater protection – a more effective buffer state – between them and the Picts. This gave rise to considerable intermarriage and, later still, to Scottish assistance to residual Manau in the face of raiding by Angles from Northumberland. Thus I am open to the suggestion made to me that Aedan mac Gabhran was even the king of Manau for some time before gaining the Dalriadan throne.

PART 4:
WHO WAS ARTHUR AND WHAT HE DID NEXT

WHO WAS ARTHUR AND WHAT HE DID NEXT

0. WHO ARTHUR WAS NOT

In the legends Arthur is the next in line as High King of Britain to "Uther Pendragon" – but Pendragon does not mean king! In those days there was a perfectly good title "Bretwalda" which had the specific meaning of "High King" of (Romanised) Britain. With regard to Pendragon, we may parse it into "Pen-" and "-Dragon". "Pen" we recognise as meaning "high" or "top" – and it remains widely part of the name of hill tops etc. (like the Scottish "Ben"). Elsewhere we find "Dragon" being used to refer to an army – white dragon fighting red dragon etc. – and we retain the derivative term "dragoon" for a unit of cavalry. Just where this came from is moot, but I do not demur from the many who propose that it may derive from the Carnyx used to rally the troops and hopefully instil fear in the enemy. Thus we should understand "Pendragon" to mean Commander-in-Chief of the army. It was common right up until the time of George II for a king to lead his troops in battle – so that very often Bretwalda and Pendragon will have been the same person. But it is not necessary. Not only that but at times when "Britain" was not united (as was the case so often) each faction may have had its own "Pendragon".

We are told by Nennius that Ambrosius Aurelianus was the "Bretwalda" – High King of Britain – after Vortigern. He was probably also "Pendragon" – army Commander-in-Chief – as and when a joint army was put together. Some people have tried to suggest that it is Ambrosius who is the model for Arthur.

We know that Vortigern was active in the period around 450 (we should note in passing that this puts him too completely out of the running as "Arthur") and that it was Ambrosius who relieved the siege of Dumbarton Rock c473. Let us assume that he was 33 in 473. Were he "really" Arthur, then, born in 440 he would be 97 when he fought a duel with his "son" Mordred. Even if he were a stripling Pendragon of 23 in 473 he would be 87 by the time he died. This is just not credible.

Similarly the Wikipedia entry for Riothamus (~/Riothamus) gives as much as one needs to know about him. He (or is it both of them?) are anachronistic in relation to the facts that we have to lay out. (At least one of them) active and clearly well established in Brittany in the 470s he is of the same era as Ambrosius. This is not to deny that some of his/their exploits may well have been incorporated into Arthurian legend – and if this is so it is more than time that the deeds are reattributed to their rightful doer.

The worst, but currently the most fashionable, misattibution is to try to make Arthur mac Aedan "the" Arthur. Amongst a plethora of snags with this proposition are that he died c590 and predeceased his father (who only died c609). Aedan was born c535 – so we can see immediately that his son Arthur could only have been born a whole generation after the real Arthur's death. Which having been said, I do not exclude *a priori* the possibility of some of Arthur mac Aedan's exploits later finding their way into Arthurian legend – if only at the behest of those wishing to sow this confusion.

Unfortunately there is a gang of self-defining Scots who cannot cope with the Pictish language, or the influence on and legacy for Scotland of either the Norse or the Angles. They also tend to buy in blindly to the many fabrications I exposed in "Scottish Clans....". I do not expect that this treatise will have any effect on them whose main line is "Don't confuse me with the facts". This is sad, because the truth is far more interesting, exciting and, indeed, fulfilling.

We should not leave this section without dismissing also the idea that Arthur was the son of "Uther Pendragon". "Uther" here is a reference to Rydderch Hael king of Strathclyde who died c614 (so probably born c540).

1. IDENTIFYING ARTHUR

So far we have seen that we have a quite narrow window for Arthur's birth around the date 475; this would put him in his early 40s – perhaps the very peak of his powers – at the battle of Badon Hill and in his early 60s at his death.

Even a thousand years later when a girl went to marry away from her homeland it was normal for a brother or other close relation to go with her and take a senior place at court to look after her interests in all the palace intrigue which is intrinsic to that mode of life. In "Scottish Clans..." I show that precisely this happened when Bera, niece of Siward, Earl of Northumberland, went to Scotland to marry her first cousin Duncan I, son of Crinan and heir to Malcolm II. Her brother, also called Siward, was made Thane of Fife, and his story was presented in a mangled form by Shakespeare in "Macbeth". Even in more recent times a bride might bring a retinue of servants with her – as happened in the case of some women who became the wives of various Chiefs of Clan Grant. Another, nearly parallel comparison may be seen some 100 years later in Kent, when Aethelbert married Bertha, daughter of Charibert, King of the Franks. Bertha was Christian, while Aethelbert was not. A condition of this dynastic marriage was that Bertha was allowed to bring and keep her own chaplains and to continue to practice her religion freely. [Such were her charms that Aethelbert later converted to Christianity and in 597 St Augustine was allowed to get a toehold in Britain for the Roman church.] Thus when we note his sister marrying Lot(h), king of Lothian/The Gododdin there is no inherent surprise to find Arthur as a "spare" junior son appearing in Scotland to fulfil this role.

A dynastic marriage for Arthur's sister was indeed required in these post Roman times as part of a programme to bind together too often quarrelling sub-Roman kingdoms. If this was true in general, how much more true would it be for tribes north and south of Hadrian's wall where, viewed from a Southern perspective, there was the danger that the foederati might throw in their hand with the Scots and Pictish raiders who were making their lives such a misery.

There is, however, a further "political" consideration: given the strategic thinking we considered regarding the sub-Roman kingdoms south of Hadrian's Wall, we should not rule out the idea that Anna was given in marriage to Lot in order to justify sending Arthur North to be the C-in-C of the Gododdin and other foederati forces. Perhaps such an arrangement was a condition of military support for the foederati from the Old North. The military leadership of the foederati may well have been reluctant to accept external command (we need think no further back than World War II and

Montgomery and Eisenhower) – so a position such as brother-in-law to the king may have helped massage what might otherwise be bruised egos. The thinking would be that assuming that Arthur was not actually up to the job, at least he held the titular position and the top brass of the Britannic reinforcing troops could make the decisions which Arthur would promulgate.

Geoffrey of Monmouth (XI, Chapter 1) says that Arthur was only 15 when he was chosen as king – and while we know he was not a "king" and so this assertion is not true, it does suggest that he was mature for his years and that something significant did happen to him at that age. So I suggest here that he was indeed only 15 when he was "chosen" for the role described above and then went North with his sister also to look after her interests in the Lothian – and pinning her birthday down to about 478. Thus we can see that all of Arthur's early key military training was done in what is now England.

It is clear from his phraseology that Geoffrey's audience (more than 600 years after the purported events) would have considered 15 very young - but there is precedent. Consider, for example, the Roman Emperor Constantine II (son of Constantine the Great) whose Wikipedia page (~/Constantine_II_(emperor)) records:

"…. born in February 316….. At age ten, he became commander of Gaul…. His military career continued when Constantine I made him field commander during the 332 campaign against the Goths."

So such an appointment for Arthur at such an age should not be considered too remarkable.

For an examination of the Royal families in Sub-Roman Britain I am indebted to Derek Read who maintains http://www.derwas-read.co.uk. He has compiled lists and tells me that he relied on:

a) http://www.earlybritishkingdoms.com/ maintained by David Nash Ford.

b) Old King Cole – Coel Hen by Geoff Bagley 1998.

c) Family Line of Coel Hen ap Cunedda – Compiled by Barry L Mathews 1987 published under GedcomCoelapCunedda.

Clearly we have a liberal sprinkling of fantasy here but that need not concern us overly as we shall not need to pay attention to most of the more fabulous figures.

Immediately one figure springs out at us – a figure overlooked only because everyone has been looking in the wrong place and the wrong times! The Arthur we are looking for was a younger son of Masgwid Gloff ("The Lame"), King of Elmet. The kingdom of Elmet was centred in what is now West Yorkshire. It appears that the capital was Leeds, but the royal residence may have been in Barwick-in-Elmet, some 7 miles from the city centre.

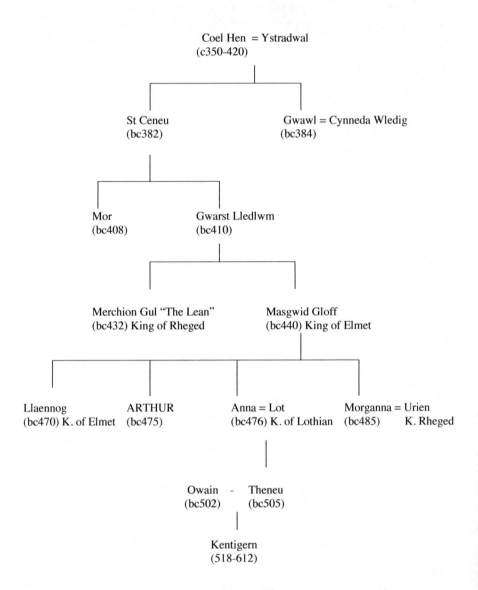

As for Arthur's pedigree, we may note that from Old King Cole came Cole's son St Ceneu and then his grandson Gwarst Lledlwm ("The Ragged"). Masgwid was the son of this Gwarst. Derek Read gives his approximation for Arthur's birth at 479AD but he has told me (in private correspondence) that the dates he offers are intended as indicative only – and we do not know the name of Arthur's mother, so we can be quite relaxed about how specific this date actually is. As will be seen below I think that it is necessary to prefer 475, perhaps 477 at the outside. What we do not have is any indication of any daughters – but sadly such an omission from a family tree remained only too commonplace for another thousand years.

The date 479 would have made Arthur still a teenager for the first 5 battles and while we have seen kings of this age (eg Canute) apparently leading armies, the truth is that they were figureheads because of their status, rather than because they were sufficiently competent or chosen by the officer corps; the actual marshalling of the troops was done by someone else. [Canute seems to have depended on Thorkil the Tall, while another excellent example is that for several years in Norway, the army of Harald Tanglehair (who was still only 10 years old when he inherited the crown) was led by his maternal uncle Guthrum.] But 20 or 21 is a very different matter – particularly given the technology and tactics of the time. The battle of the mouth of the River Glein cannot have been later than 496 and is more likely to have been a year or two earlier.

The title "king"

As we have seen, Arthur was a junior son of a king, the brother of a king and the brother-in-law of a king. Nennius is keen to point out that Arthur was not a king. But what do we mean by "king"?

In "Scottish Clans..." I noted the Viking custom (as exemplified in the sons of Harald Tanglehair) that all sons of kings were entitled to be called "king"; there was a parallel entitlement for Jarls (as exemplified in Orkney). The result of this practice was sometimes the sub-division of the lands of a kingdom (or Jarldom), sometimes a (usually uneasy) joint rule. Seldom was either custom sustainable – usually ending in murder, or at best being overtaken by a determined aggressor.

Nennius is clear that Arthur was the commander in chief of an army for all 12 battles – and in that sense a Pendragon. But he was fully committed to that campaign and so clearly not "the" Pendragon for any or all of post-Roman Britain as such.

As we shall see below I think that there is good reason to suppose that he was also Regent of Lothian after the death of Lot. But still I do not think he was considered a true king in that capacity.

Arthur was never properly invested with a kingdom to rule so if that is your criterion he was not a king. But he was the son of a king, so if that is how you judge the matter then he was. I am with Nennius.

Arthur's Religion

Much has been made of Arthur as a Christian hero battling pagans. In the scenario I have developed here there is no reason to disbelieve this. We know, for example, that St Patrick's parents and even grandparents were Christians and in "Scottish Clans..." I show that Bannavem Taburniae where Patrick says he was born was actually on Hadrian's wall – the vicus associated with the fort Banna (Banna means Wild Boar – which fits with the garrisons some of whom called themselves "Venatores Bannienses" – the boar hunters). [There is more to be said about the life of St Patrick, but that is for another work.] So there is no difficulty with the idea of Elmet being a Christian kingdom. Not only that but we noted above that Arthur's grandfather was "St" Ceneu; he also had a brother "St" Cynllo and many other relatives characterised similarly.

Arthur's sister is variously given the name Morgawse and Anna. Anna is in essence a Hebrew name (from Channah, meaning "grace") and is the name commonly understood to be that of Jesus' maternal grandmother. So although not at all a Brythonnic name, it would be far from out of place in a religious family of a Christian persuasion even at that time. [Compare the current politician and former prime minister of Poland who has no Scottish or Irish blood, but nevertheless has the given name Donald.]

At the time in question while Christianity had been spread by St Ninnian into the lands of the Galloway Picts and, at least notionally, the Damnonii, there is no reason to suppose that it had reached the Gododdin. This meant that Arthur had an even bigger responsibility in looking after his sister Anna – for, married to a pagan, it would have been important to herself and to her family that her religious scruples were given due respect and she had the space and freedom to give expression to them.

Just as Christianity had not reached the Gododdin when Arthur came North, nor had it reached the Scots of Argyll, albeit St Patrick had been busy for many years converting mainland Ireland and St Kessog was biding his time at Old Kilpatrick waiting to take the message into the Lennox. Columba (b. 521) was still more than a decade from being even a twinkle in his father's eye when Arthur was repulsing the Pictish attack at Guinon Fort. So it is quite reasonable to recognise the Christian aspect of his leadership in these battles. Commentators, perhaps put off by the sanctimony of the apologists, have poured scorn on his bearing the image of the virgin Mary on his shoulder, but first of all we can see the connection to his sister "Anna" and then, as the cover to this book illustrates, we may note the way in which this was done.

We should not see Arthur as an ascetic, however, nor that his practice of Christianity was as perfect as the churches may have sought to ordain – as other elements of the legend imply.

Arthur's persona

My view is that Arthur saw the Roman Emperor Constantine as his rôle model and aspired to be like him.

- He was born just 20 miles away from York where Constantine was declared Emperor by his troops;
- As we have seen, albeit with his father, Constantine conducted a successful campaign against the Picts - indeed during the course of his own battles Arthur would have celebrated the 200th anniversary of that campaign.
- Setting aside nuances of our understanding of Constantine's religious beliefs (as I think Arthur too would have done) both could be seen as Christians whose main enemy was Pagan - so the violence of battle was imbued with a particular sense of moral rectitude.
- We have noted above that Constantine was willing to appoint his son to military command at an age even younger than Arthur had been - thus supporting Arthur's view of his own entitlement which may have been scorned by others

So Arthur acquired and assumed a sense of mission to support his self-confidence which together were probably resented and viewed as arrogance by those (and there will have been substantial numbers) who were jealous of him, but were likely to be very much supported by those on his coat tails who were carried along by him and who enjoyed with him a success to which they had contributed. [Modern parallels in British politics are not hard to find!] However the enabling effect of a self-confident and charismatic leader on "ordinary" people should not be underestimated.

2. CAMELOT AND GUINEVERE

Many candidates have been put forward as the place where Arthur held 'court'. This should not be considered at all surprising, given that Camulos was the Brythonnic God of War (recognised by the Romans as Mars-Camulos, just as they equated Sulis (at Bath) with their own Minerva) – so it would be a hostage to fortune for any Briton to fail to invoke the favour of the most relevant tutelary god by not calling any military HQ "Camelot" or something very similar.

Between battles Arthur had a day job – being in overall command of the defence of the territory of the Gododdin from Pictish attack. For that reason he would have needed to be based on the Antonine Wall. The Gododdin half of the wall stretched from near to Castle Cary in the West to Bo'ness in the East – though to be practical it was quite unlikely that an attack would be launched east of the river Avon. [The reason for this is that the Avon Gorge would have hindered both resupply and retreat. Thus any intelligent attack would have been seaborne – and in that event it would make more sense to attack East of the wall itself. Contrast this with the first landing of St Serf in Pictish territory (see the Appendix).]

The ideal location for his headquarters was, therefore at Rough Castle – and so it is no surprise to me that http://www.antoninewall.org says of this site:

> **If you can only visit one location on the Antonine Wall,**
> **Rough Castle fort is clearly the best choice.**
> Although the fort is the second smallest on the wall, it is easily the best-preserved and offers the most spectacular and memorable views of the surviving Roman remains. Here you can see an excellent example of the Antonine Wall ditch, the tallest-surviving portion of rampart, defensive lilia pits to the north of the wall, and easily identifiable fort and annexe defences, including multiple ditches and gateways. This is the best site to gain an impression of how the frontier and its integral forts worked.

If, as I now propose, this was Arthur's headquarters we should be surprised if this were NOT the "best preserved" site.

It is also right next to the village of Camelon (yes, the clue is in the name which has been in clear view all this time, albeit, as we have noted, masked by and hitherto indistinguishable from all the others) now, in effect, a suburb of Falkirk. My understanding is that the village takes its name from various Roman camps, some of very considerable size which were located there – just several tens of yards north of the Antonine Wall. Rough Castle is clearly still in "the Camelon area", but because I think that we must regard the line of the Antonine Wall as marking the border (see for example the life of St Serf in his appendix below), I think it not feasible that Arthur established his court on the exact site of the Roman Camelon forts.

This is also the most likely site for the battle of Camlann (537AD) in which Arthur lost his life. He was about 62 – a classic age for such an event. [It is all too typical for people of that age (55 – 60ish) to see themselves as still virile and capable, but the truth is that they have more than lost their edge. The result is that they make decisions based on their perception of themselves rather than on a realistic view of their capabilities – and they are prey to a younger, fitter, keener opponent. In "Scottish Clans..." I cite other examples of this.]

In 1999 Alastair Moffat ("Arthur and the Lost Kingdoms") tried to make a case for a site where the Teviot meets the Tweed opposite Kelso for Arthur's headquarters – in effect the idea that Roxburgh Castle was Camelot. Troops need to be rotated in and out of the front line, so Arthur certainly did not spend all his time (when he was not actually out campaigning) holed up at Rough Castle. An "R & R" base would be ideal for much of the roistering implied by the legends surrounding Camelot. Indeed if we suppose that it was not Arthur who founded this base and given that the Gododdin were still pagan at the time it is far from impossible that such a base would also have an association with Camulos. But Moffat makes no real case for any association with Arthur at all beyond the lie of the land and the suggestion that "Rox" = "horse" (the more commonly held understanding of the origin of this name is from the Old English *hróc* = "rook" (which would, therefore be anachronistic)). Moreover given that the Selgovae were not really trustworthy, that Trimontium was very close by and definitely under the Selgovae in the time of Ptolemy and that this is the "wrong side" of the Tweed I am not inclined to place any credence on any Arthurian connection to this site.

Setting Arthur to one side for a moment we may note that it is traditionally proposed that kingship of Lothian was exercised from Traprain Law near Haddington.

The place name Camelon is persuasive in identifying Rough Castle as "the" military HQ. We can, however, extend our thinking. We have already noted that some considerable time earlier, Cunneda Wledig was the regulus of Manau Gododdin and that our understanding (if only for reasons of the yoyoing of political control) is that Manau Gododdin was not fully incorporated into greater Lothian as a unitary state.

Two more personages fall to our consideration:

We are told that Arthur married "Guinevere" and that she was the daughter of King "Leodegrance" of "Cameliard". We may begin by noting how close "Camelot" and "Cameliard" are – essentially no more than a suffix – perhaps only scribal misunderstanding. Second we should note how close the "Leod-" of Leodegrance is to Lot and, especially, the Gothic parallels I discussed above (see Part 2 relating to the Gododdin). I will not attempt to understand the "-egrance" part, which looks, in any case, as if it has been Frenchified (as with other characters – see next Part).

We should note the way that junior members of the British Royal family are still given Dukedoms etc today – not just Cornwall, but Cambridge and in recent times Gloucester, Fife etc. Today these titles are entirely honorific and without portfolio, but they echo former days when such a title implied a very serious job (see, for example, in "Scottish Clans...." with the sons of Godwin of Wessex).

The name "Guinevere" is problematic - not only because there are no truly old references to or examples of it, but also because of the various languages through which it has migrated. If we consider it as we see it today then we might parse it as "Guin-" (Welsh, "white/pure") and "vere", perhaps from the Latin "verus", meaning "true". Given the association of the Gododdin and the Romans I see no difficulty in principle with this juxtaposition of word elements from different languages and thus I would see this as a feasible name - with a meaning of the sort a doting father might well give a favourite daughter.

Unfortunately we have no real way of knowing what her real name was. Given that "Gwen" was the name of St David's aunt (see "The Oxford Names Companion") who would have been Guinevere's almost exact contemporary, then her real name may have been (i) simply "Gwen" or (ii) "Gwen-"/"Guin-" with one of a wide variety of possible suffixes (whether as part of her given name or as a pet form), probably implying endearment.

The earliest extant written form is Geoffrey's; he renders the name "Guanhumara". The current fashion is to explain this as coming from a supposedly pre-existing Welsh/Brythonnic name Gwenhwyfar - which is usually translated as "white enchantress". But this is problematic, for if it is, as claimed, a variation of the Gaelic Findabair it is held to carry a negative implication - which I would regard as unacceptable as a given name, particularly in a royal/aristocratic context.

But rather than being her real name, Guinevere/Guanhumara may derive from an ironic form invented by the bards but which contemporary audiences would understand (as with Lancelot for Kessog). Given the sexually precocious way she is portrayed in the legend, one can see the rich irony in the name Guinevere or the cleverness of changng the name to Gwenhwyfar which would not be lost on the contemporaneous audiences. [Later, the negative nuance of Gwenhwyfar would have been overwhelmed by the heroine status she acquired through the legend - whence the popularity of its modern rendering as 'Jennifer'.]

The irony could work one of two opposite ways:

(a) 'Guinevere' may have been the sexually precocious woman as caricatured in the legend - in which case Gwenhwyfar complete with its negative witchlike undertones would be appropriate; alternatively Guinevere as I have offered it would be richly ironic. The difficulty with this scenario is that it is hard to imagine Arthur being relaxed about being cuckolded in this way over a prolonged period of time.

(b) The stories of sexual precocity may have been uproariously funny at all-male gatherings precisely because Guinevere was so utterly beyond reproach in this regard. In this scenario we would have to suppose that Arthur was confident enough in himself and in his relationship with his wife to be able to see the stories as absurd.

There is, however, a potential alternative to the Gwen-/Guin- element of the real name - based not only on the assumption that Guinevere was not the 'correct' name but also - more importantly - on the Gothic origins I have proposed for the Gododdin. [Compare this with my discussion of the name "Lot" in Part 2 Section 2a.] The real name behind Guinevere may be a variation of the ancient Germanic "Genovefa" - which has given us the modern day Genevieve. This is my preferred explanation.

3. "KARDOEL"/"CARDUEL"

In the discussion of the sources we noted that it was generally understood that, especially on the continent, "Camelot" was rendered "Carduel" or some such (as we have seen in the work of Marie de France) and that I did not accept this. There is no real connection between the two names – and it is hard to imagine even the most incompetent scribe misunderstanding one for the other. In the discussion of Marie's poem "Lanval", I suggested, therefore, that we should be open to the idea that there were two quite separate places which had become conflated and that one possible rendering of Carduel was Blackrock Castle or, more simply, Blackcastle.

In the Lothians there are three locations which come to attention immediately. There are two earthworks, both called Blackcastle, in East Lothian. They are less than 9 miles apart. One is about a mile and a half SSW of Innerwick (just off the A1); Historic Scotland describes this as "unfinished". The other is about 3 miles ESE of Gifford just south of the A635 road. Historic Scotland says that this was occupied in the 200s AD or later. Another curious thing about this site is that it is just 600 yards from another earthwork called Greencastle (cf the Green Knight).

My clear favourite, however is Blackness Castle, close (about 2 miles) to Bo'ness and the end of the Antonine Wall and 13 miles from Camelot/Rough Castle – an hour away for a horse or a fast runner. Although the buildings here date to the fifteenth century and later, there is evidence that there has been occupation here since the Bronze Age – so a lacuna during Arthur's time would have been strange. Not only that, but the castle gets its name from the black colour of the rock of the headland on which it sits which is particularly evident whenever it is wet. So Blackness Castle really is Caer Dubh Ail – the castle on the black rock. Not only that, but it would make an excellent Central Command headquarters for Arthur – close enough for immediate mobilisation, with the fantastic line of sight across and up the Forth estuary allowing for continual watchfulness, while being far enough away from the front line to avoid surprise attack and to offer proper opportunities for R&R – rest and recuperation.

Lazy assumptions that the two were one should be set to one side. However it is clear that this distinction has been lost for 1000 years and that the two places may have been confused/conflated by later writers – as indeed the lazy minds referred to above demonstrate. So when we hear stories relating to one place or the other we should be somewhat circumspect in supposing that the story teller had the correct place in mind.

What this leaves open, however, is the location of his "capital" of Manau Gododdin. Looking at the map I would guess at somewhere in the Slamannan area; but the history of the area seems pretty well non-existent. Next to the church to the north east of the village is a motte but the informed local guess seems to be that this is mediaeval. To the south west of the village is Balcastle house – but even at the time of the 1st Statistical account there were no remains of this castle nor any story about it recorded. I have been assuming that "Manau Gododdin" would not have been given any 'core' Gododdin territory. If this assumption is incorrect, then it is quite possible that the 'capital' may be been in the region of Cathlawhill or Cairnpapple Hill near Torphichen, but I think that the Avon Gorge makes this quite unlikely. Bearing in mind also that I have proposed that in Arthurian legend Manau Gododdin is also referenced as "Cameliard", I fall back on the idea, therefore, that Rough Castle/Camelot was the headquarters/capital of that sub-realm.

Conclusion: For the army of the Gododdin Camelot/Rough Castle was the Forward Operating Base, while Kardoel/Carduel/Blackness was the Central Command HQ.

4. "NORWAY"

In Part 2 we saw how references in Arthurian legend to "Orkney" have been used a pretext to heap derision on the whole corpus. So it has been too with Norway. But wait......

In volume 2 of "Scottish Clans...." I demonstrated that far from it being the 10-year campaign lauded in the sagas, it took the whole of the life of Harald Tanglehair to begin to create anything approaching a kingdom of Norway. The land was a patchwork of fiefdoms much more often fighting each other than acting together – and the epoch for this was round the year 900, some 400 years after the events we have been discussing. So we may begin by acknowledging the term "Norway" as an anachronism.

So what (and where) was it to which the legend might be referring when claiming that Arthur had made himself king of "Norway"? I suggest that the proper meaning, which the mediaeval romantic writers did not understand, was none other than that part of Scotland north of the Antonine Wall and excluding Dalriada – the "North lands". We use the term "Pictland" or "Pictavia" because we do not know of any term by which these people identified their homeland. As suggested above I think that the people referred to themselves somehow through the term "Pent" (though that included Galwegians and the Selgovae); otherwise we have seen "Cumbri" (although that refers also to Welsh and Cumbrians) and they were referred to by the Irish as "Cruithni". But all these are references to the people rather than to the land.

So when the legend says that Arthur made himself King of Norway, I say that we should understand that the peace treaty concluded following Badon Hill recognised Arthur as overlord of the Picts. I think that this is supported by the placenames Glenartney and Glengartney. It is difficult to see why the losers should celebrate their routs – in this way or any other – if they had a serious choice in the matter. But the naming of these two glens would be a way in which the Picts could demonstrate to Arthur that they were paying homage to him without feeling that they had lost too much face.

Arthur's O'on: This in turn offers an interesting proposition for the people of Stenhousemuir. For many years the Roman temple which stood there was referred to as "Arthur's O'on". As we can see from the Wikipedia page (~/ Arthur's_O'On) the Arthurian connection was firmly part of the lore even in 1293. If Arthur was the overlord of the Picts then it would be important for there to be at least a token presence in Pictland. So I offer the suggestion that Arthur may well have had his own equivalent of Balmoral at Stenhousemuir in the immediate vicinity of the temple – whence its attribution to him.

[Caution dictates, however, that it is quite possible to construe the reference to Arthur here as being to Prince Arthur mac Aedan – but I am not inclined in that direction.]

5. WHAT ARTHUR DID NEXT

We are told that King Lot was killed by a foreign king – "Pelinore"/"Pellanor"; we are told that when Arthur "went away" he left "the kingdom" in Mordred (variously Medraut)'s hands.

Everyone has assumed – perhaps 'obviously', ie unthinkingly – that given that Arthur was supposed to be the High King of all Britain then Mordred should have become the regent of it – and yet we have no records supportive of this. But actually there is a logical solution which can be found. We have an approximate marriage date for Anna and Lot around 490 – so we may reasonably work with the idea that Mordred would have been born c492/3. Immediately a prolonged war was prosecuted – no time for playing with boy kings. Even in the worst circumstances Mordred would not be fit to rule until c510. Unfortunately we do not know when Lot died, but given that he was a king killed by a king we should safely suppose that it was in battle. Because we hear of no interruption in the rulership (notwithstanding the rapid turnover in kings amongst the Damnonii) and given that Lot had many children (with wet nurses one pregnancy a year is feasible) we should be looking to the period after 505 but before 510 for this event. The most likely occasion would seem to be the battle at Guinnon Fort.

This was no time for political instability caused by inexperience. My conclusion is that Arthur took over as Regent of Lothian – at least notionally "for" Mordred. Did that make him a king? We are back to a matter of definitions. He was the Pendragon for the forces of the Federation, he was the effective ruler of the Lothian and possibly, again because we do not hear about 'Leodegrance' otherwise, he may also have inherited through his wife the viceroy position for Manau Gododdin. But no... technically he was not a king.

He enjoyed the power thus gained and managed to retain it even after Mordred was of an age when he could have taken on his rightful role. The way in which Arthur and his sister ruled the realm gave rise to tittle-tattle. What did they think they were doing usurping the natural/proper order of things? They looked very comfortable ruling and keeping Mordred subordinate. Did they know something everyone else did not? Perhaps they did not give Mordred his rightful place because it was not rightfully his..... Perhaps Arthur himself was Mordred's father.... All nonsense of course, but such is the way that rumour can grow and circulate.

After the peace treaty of 517 relations with the Maeatae improved. If I am right about Pelinore then here is (if there is actually any truth in this story at all) whence Pelinore's son Lamerock fancied his chances of marrying Anna.

Perhaps she too was so bent on this that one of her sons did indeed kill her to prevent any such marriage – with its implications for the succession – from taking place. Or was this just one more lampoon entertainment with a dark streak?

In the scenario I have set out there is a huge gap in Arthur's story after 517 (by which time Mordred would have been about 25 years old). As we saw at the beginning, the Anglo-Saxon Chronicle is remarkably sparing in its entries for this period. Would a cavalry general at the peak of his powers decide to hang up his saddle to spend the rest of his life drinking and wenching? The Old King Cole of nursery rhyme notwithstanding, I think not, especially given that his own homeland (West Yorkshire) which was coming under increasing pressure. So once he was sure that there was stability along the Antonine Wall, probably he did decide to see what he could do, especially in England. So he left Mordred "in charge" of Lothian. This was problematic for he, Arthur, took it that on any return he would re-assume control. But Mordred was the rightful king and now he was in place.

As for what Arthur may actually have done in England in the period 520-535 I will leave to enthusiasts of the period in England – even Wales and Brittany as well. And we cannot rule out the idea that he spent some time as Pendragon of all Britannia south of Hadrian's Wall.

The Battle of Camlann and Arthur's death

When Arthur did finally return it was many years later. The job in England was very far from over – indeed with the benefit of hindsight we can see that the real task was only just beginning and all too soon would end in abject failure. But Arthur was now over 60 years old and the future belonged to a new generation.

Meanwhile Mordred was at the peak of his powers – 45 years old with 15 and more years of kingship of the Lothians under his belt. Nether man was willing to give way – so battle was the only solution. The action took place at Camlann – Camelon – right next to Rough Castle fort. Despite his age, Arthur got the better of Mordred, killing him, but not without himself receiving wounds from which he would not recover. Here again I really do not believe that things would have come to this pass if they really had been father and son. And I think that if Anna had still been alive then surely she would have knocked their heads together before it had come to this.

Arthur was taken to Luss where the best medical treatment possible at the time was given – but to no avail. He was buried on Inchtavannach under the doubly safe control of two families both of whom owed their positions entirely to him – the Galbraith cadets of the Strathclyde royal family as rulers, the family of Luss, with 'Lancelot''s son by his damsel du lac now 27 years old, as the chiefs of the estate.

No doubt Arthur had kept Excalibur as a trophy. No doubt it came back to Loch Lomond with him. No doubt it then came into the possession of the relevant Lady of the Lake – probably Kessog's (2nd) widow, possibly the wife of the Galbraith progenitor. Whether it was then cast into the lake is another thing altogether......

APPENDICES

APPENDIX 1:
AN ARTHURIAN WHO'S WHO

INTRODUCTION

It is very tempting to go all out to try to identify many if not all of the characters in Arthurian legend. But (i) having skimmed one such recent attempt, (ii) giving due weight to how lacking in confidence I am regarding some of the characters and (iii) bearing in mind my conclusion, explicitly supported in the tale of Sir Gawain and the Green Knight, that these stories were, in the first place, satire – an entertainment – I will resist the temptation, and consider only a few of the outstanding names. In "Sir Gawain and the Green Knight" there is the explicit reflexive reference to itself as the sort of fantastic story Arthur would have required at a feast. And all this resonates with the concept of the Court Jester. From this we should conclude that the stories were not intended to be understood as true.

Some of the characters can be identified as historical and of these several can be placed "at the scene", while others can be seen as anachronistic – pointing to the development of the stories and the continuation of the prevalent culture for some time after Arthur's death. There are other characters which we may guess to be entirely fictional, but in most cases I would caution anyone against this, for I just don't know enough about enough of the principal players to be sure – even more so if the name in the legend is part of the parody (compare for example "The Grocer" for Edward Heath, "Jammy Fishpaste" for Sir James Goldsmith and "Dirty Digger" for Rupert Murdoch in the satirical magazine *Private Eye* – you have to be "in" to get the joke). However it is also the case that some "real" characters are involved in unreal situations (eg the search for the Grail). So I cannot tell, at the margins, which characters are meant to be "real" and which are wholly fictitious. I will leave that to long-term aficionados of Arthuriana and look forward to their considerations.

We can tell that the tales are unreal in several ways: places such as "Castle Terrible", "Joyous Gard" and the "Siege Perilous" are clearly at least not correctly named, while "Erec du Lac" – mentioned by Chrétien de Troyes – never did become "king" – either of Dalraida or of Strathclyde. Not only that, but there are several characters who are not named as such (eg Damsel Meledysaunt, Sir La Cote Male Tale etc.), but whose names are intended to denote their character as, eg, in "The Pilgrim's Progress". And then, of course, there is Evelake/Mordrayns, the 400-year-old knight. However I suspect that when he was being talked about all the contemporaries knew exactly to whom the bard was referring!

We might compare these tales to television series such as "The New Statesman", "Yes, Minister", "The West Wing" and "House of Cards" – but these are parody rather than satire. The Arthurian tales, with their specific and often critical references to people alive at the time - sometimes even present in the audience - are more in the tradition of the Greek playwright Aristophanes (5th Century BC) and of the Romans Horace and Juvenal with whose works the contemporary audiences are likely to have been familiar. Not only that, but the nursery rhyme about Old King Cole suggests that this tradition was already alive and well in Britannia. So these tales should not be considered novel. In "Sir Gawain and the Green Knight" we are told specifically that such tales were fantastic and would have been told mostly at a feast, with mead, wine and ale flowing freely.

This intermingling of fact and fiction is commonplace in historical writing – indeed a friend of mine has just completed a series of historical novels all the facts of which are minutely researched and reported accurately, but into which he has introduced a wholly fictional hero/narrator character – and naturally he has invented associated dialogue – to weave all the historical events into a coherent and gripping story.

In these respects, the difference between then and now is that today we have the rule of law and laws regarding libel and slander.

As will be seen, I have also included some characters who do not appear in the normal corpus of Arthurian tales, but who are, nevertheless, helpful in providing depth and colour to the overall picture.

As with almost all the material in this book it is impossible to lay it all out in a simple sequence, so I apologise in advance if and when the text seems to make assumptions which are not supported immediately, or for duplication of explanation at different points.

1. THE FAMILY "DU LAC"

(a) The "King du Lac" was probably Garwynwyn – and if not he then a brother or other close relation of a similar age – the viceroy of the Lennox and progenitor of the Galbraiths;

(b) "The Lady of the Lake" was King Loarn's widow, probably by the name of Naimh – but there may be a conflation with subsequent wives of viceroys

(c) I propose that "Erec du Lac" was Erc, successor in the Galbraith line

(d) Lancelot du Lac aka Lanceor aka Bertilak du Haut Desert aka The Green Knight was St Kessog. We saw earlier that his death is given variously as 520 and 530. Such are the tales told about him and so central is he to Arthurian legend that I am inclined to favour the latter end of this decade. He married (as his second wife) one of....

(e) two "Damsels du Lac".

(i) One such damsel is identified as "Nineve" (variously also Vivaine) – which also looks like "Naimh". This Naimh is likely to have been a daughter or granddaughter of the Lady of the Lake. [One would expect that Queen Naimh's eldest daughter would have been given her mother's name, but such a lady would be considerably too old to be normally characterised as a "damsel". However given Kessog's own age, then provided that Loarn and Naimh's daughter Naimh was available (eg widowed) and still of child bearing age then the daughter is possible.] We are told that she learns magical secrets from Merlin – and we can discount this (see below). However she moved from the mouth of Glen Douglas to live right next to the Bandruidh – and will not have been brought up Christian. So all in all there is a potential basis for the lore surrounding her.

(ii) Another "damsel" du Lac (in this case almost certainly a granddaughter of Loarn) who will have married the male ancestor of the Galbraiths.

(f) Galahad we have discussed, particularly because the name is meant to represent Lancelot's real name. We have noted that Kessog was born c460 – as such it is very unlikely that he remained unmarried until after 498 – so Galahad is likely to be the product of an earlier marriage in Ireland. If Kessog followed a normal timeframe we might expect Galahad to be born c485 – too young to take part in the battles for the Lennox, but well able to be part of the relief of Badon Hill. He is old enough to have accompanied his father from the start – indeed we have no reason to discount the idea that Kessog brought his first wife with him.

(g) Mark and Bodwyne are identified as relatives of Lanceor (I am eliding him with Lancelot) – King Mark wanting revenge for Lanceor's death. We know that King Oengus mac NadFroich had many children and the element "marc-" (= horse) is a common element in Irish names – so there is a potential basis for these characters. "King Mark" sounds like a successor to (a grandson of?) Oengus – whose arrival would come after 520.

(h) We have also identified Excalibur as the ceremonial sword handed over by Queen Naimh du Lac to Arthur as a token of the surrender of the Dalriadan (and other Irish) forces.

2. AVALON

We should begin by noting references variously to Avalon and to the Isle of Avalon. Thus it is not necessary to suppose that the island itself was **called** Avalon, only that it 'belonged to' Avalon somehow. So let us, for the moment, keep an open mind here. Secondly we should consider the meaning. Nowhere can I find anyone or anything to counter the general understanding that "Avalon" means "the place of apples" (Welsh "Afal", Gaelic "abhall" means "apple"). However we do need to extrapolate a bit – by understanding the implications – for in ancient times apples were held to have healing properties. See for example http://www.sacredearth.com/ethnobotany/plantprofiles/apple.php

So where more natural would there be for Arthur to go to have his wounds tended to and where more natural would there be for him to be buried but on an island immediately adjacent?

There is one place which commends itself immediately: Luss on Loch Lomond. There are in fact several places in the west of Scotland with the "luss" element within them. Dwelly says that the Gaelic word 'lus' means "herb, plant, weed, flower" and takes up 6 pages to illustrate various plants. Looked at superficially, from the perspective of today, one might be tempted to scratch the head in bemusement – but no... for we should appreciate that in those days (as elsewhere in the world even today) a multitude of herbs are grown for their medicinal/healing qualities. Thus I say that when Arthur was (as it turns out, mortally) wounded it was to Luss (as a general location) that he was taken for treatment and when this failed he was buried nearby.

I see 'Avalon' as a poetic name (compare this with Castle Terrible and the Siege Perilous) and so I think that it is not actually important whether or not there were apple trees in the immediate vicinity, however it is likely that there were. As for the exact location of the treatment centre a case might be made for Bandry (see above) as well as for Luss itself.

As we have seen the main power centre had been at the mouth of Glen Douglas, but surely as part of the peace treaty and new regime, the Galbraiths took over Inchgalbraith (see Appendix below on the Lennox), while St Kessog's part of the family was moved to Luss. If not before, then following Kessog's martyrdom the Galbraiths took direct control of Bandry.

So which was the "Isle of Avalon"? A case can be made for several islands:

- Inchlonaig (the yew tree island) is directly offshore from Luss;
- Inchtavannach (the monks' island) commends itself because of the religious connection – we have noted the crusading element of Arthur's activities – and because it is directly opposite Bandry;
- Inchmoan (the peat island) commends itself mainly on the basis of interesting herbs (still?) growing there;
- Inchconnachan (the Colquhouns' island).

We may dismiss Inchlonaig and Inchconnachan straight away. These belonged to the Galbraiths of Bandry in historical times and hence could not have been left with the Lady of Avalon at the time in question. Inchtavannach becomes the overwhelming favourite – especially given the tradition that it was Kessog's home. Whether or not it was used as a burial place before the arrival of Christianity, surely Arthur would have been buried on sacred ground.

3. KENTIGERN, THENEU AND OWAIN

As we saw in the introduction, The Catholic Encyclopaedia gives St Kentigern's dates as c518-603, but the modern view regarding his death is more in conformity with the Annales Cambriae (612) offering c614. We know that Kentigern was "old" when he died – but commentators have recoiled from attributing too great an age to him. So it is normal to settle on c85 years (as with the encyclopaedia), which would make his birth epoch c528. On the one hand had he reached 100 years surely this would have been remarked upon, but on the other hand I argue here that other dating constraints mean that he was well into his 90s. In essence I hope to show that we should accept the Catholic assessment for his birth date and the Annales for his death – making Kentigern 95 years old when he died.

The problem is that King Lot died while Mordred was still too young to take the throne – and I have suggested c508 for this (see Part 4 above). In turn this means that Kentigern's mother, Theneu, must have been born by this time – or in the very few months thereafter. As it was normal for girls to be married by 14 and from Roman Law the minimum acceptable age for a girl to have sex then as until 130 years ago (and still in some countries) was 12 (St Augustine of Hippo was required to wait until his girlfriend reached that age), I propose that she was at most 13 when she conceived, implying a date for her own birth at 505.

It was the common practice for visiting dignitaries to be given a girl to sleep with (sometimes a daughter, sometimes a servant depending on the qualities of the visitor); sex would be a normal part of this. I should add to that the history of the Clan Grant amongst others shows that this remained a not uncommon practice for another thousand years and we fell into the grip of Calvinism.

When the 14/15 year old Owain mab Urien of Rheged was visiting the Gododdin court, Lot(h) was already dead, but it was very soon after the peace treaty following Badon Hill – so we should assume that Anna was still very much alive. The scenario we should probably imagine is of 25 year old Mordred as the "man of the house" even though it is his mother and his uncle who are ruling the country. Mead-fuelled "Locker Room Talk" turns into more boisterousness and Owain ends up in bed with Theneu (his first cousin). Because this sort of thing in general was customary there should be few surprises yet – but, imbued with the idea of chastity from her mother inculcating in her a "Christian" attitude to shame, she was not ready for – and objected to – sex. In later more sanctimonious times the sex was characterised as rape, but it is only within our lifetime in the UK that the concept of rape within marriage has been recognised. Before that, the marriage vows had been taken to imply that the wife should submit to her husband at any time as a wifely duty. Nevertheless we may suppose two things: (a) the sex was not wanted and (b) Owain did not follow through by marrying Theneu once he learned that she was pregnant. There is, of course, an alternative scenario: that Theneu was a willing party, but cried rape when Owain spurned her when he learned she was pregnant.

I am sure that critics will argue that I have amended the facts to suit my argument. I say that I have amended the basis upon which sensible but nevertheless quite ill informed estimates have been made – and I have stuck with the "fact" such as "it" is!

Dismissing the objection to this timescale

So the timescale can be made to fit Kentigern and Theneu. But what of Owain? Again I can sense objectors sharpening their pencils....

The family tree from Old King Cole to Owain is shown opposite.

In short if the birth era for Coel was 350, then a date for Owain in the period 500x505 is perfectly feasible.

The crunch issue – which many historians have regarded as a "killer fact" is that, according to Taliesin, Owain took part in the battle of Alt Clud Ford where the leader of the attacking Anglian forces was "king Ulf". This is hard to interpret, resulting in academics giving the event a wide time window 574x90.

The real problem is the identity of "king Ulf". Considerable gymnastics are required to make him a son of Ida, first Anglian king of Bernicia (from 547). The argument they propose is that "king Ulf" refers to "Frithuwulf" who is really "Frithuwald". This is too many twists for me, especially without other justification. We may add to this the problem of whether sons of kings (in this case Anglian kings) bore the dignity of "king".

Morcant, the previous king of Bernicia, was living in exile in Strathclyde. Given that Anglian forces were involved we can actually start any time after 547. We also need to consider the purpose for the raid: I suggest that this was to catch and kill Morcant so that he could no longer be a figurehead for the local Bernician population to rally behind. Indeed given that what we have is all the work of scribes, is it possible that "Ulf" is a misrepresentation of "Ida"? Alternatively, ironically, it could easily be the case at this time that Frithwald was the leader of the Anglian forces on behalf of his father.

Owain's Pedigree
(selected individuals only)

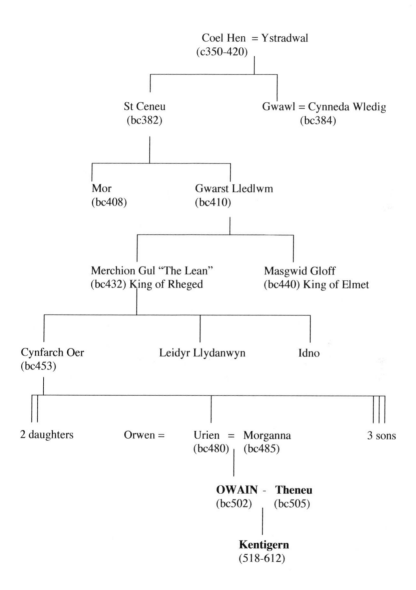

In other words I propose that the raid on Alt Clut Ford was not in 590 or 580 or even in 574 – but much earlier – not long after 547, so that there is no problem with Owain having been involved in the battle even on my timescale.

St Kentigern's birth

The legend surrounding St Kentigern's birth – for which we have to thank (if that is the word) the oleaginous cleric Jocelyn of Furness is garbage.

First: The idea that Theneu would be blamed for obeying her father is ridiculous, not least because he was long dead and because under any interpretation she was not in any way at fault. The story of what is supposed to have happened to her was lifted by Jocelyn from the supposed life of St Dubricious from 100 years and more earlier (and this should not be taken to imply that I believe that story either – in that case I have no opinion).

Second: Kentigern could not have been brought up by St Serf (for whom see his own appendix below) – for his *floruit* in Scotland was in the period 690x710 – over 150 years later than the time in question.

Third: Even under Jocelyn's ridiculous proposition there is no explanation as to how Kentigern and his mother (now commemorated as "St Enoch") reached Glasgow.

The problem of what did happen has been at least half solved by James E Fraser ("From Caledonia to Pictland" p. 256) for he has identified a "Serguan" as a younger son of Clinoch, king (508-540) of Strathclyde. I had been reluctant to accept the idea that someone other than a monk would have the name "Serf" – but Alex Woolf has reassured me by explaining the evolution of the name. Nowadays we think of a "serf" as a menial – a peasant tied to the land. But the original meaning carried the idea of someone in a position of trust who took care of and watched out for someone or something – so perhaps analogous to "Gregory". [A parallel process took place with the word Banna – which clearly meant Wild Boar when Roman Legionnaires were hunting them from Hadrians Wall, but now the Welsh "banu" has degenerated to mean suckling piglet.] So I do now accept that a king might well give this name to a son of his.

So Mordred and, to a lesser extent, Anna had a problem – Owain had refused to marry Theneu and with a baby she was "damaged goods". What appears to have happened is that she was married off to Serguan, moving to the Glasgow area with her son. We can see that Serguan's brother was old enough to be King of Strathclyde in 508, making a likely birth epoch for him c480 – ie broadly a contemporary of Arthur and, therefore a generation older than Theneu herself. So we should not be surprised that Serguan died leaving her a potentially long widowhood. However we will not examine that here.

With Kentigern not even 20 years old when Arthur was killed, we should not take up space here to provide a full biography – but suffice it to say that

(a) the story about the salmon and the ring is also drivel. Jocelyn lifted this from one of the tales about Freuch mac Fidach – who belongs to the period BC – ie over 500 years before the time in question. The proof that this is a cut-and-paste job is evidenced by the same story being told about Kentigern in Wales with different *dramatis personae*. That really would be a coincidence!

(b) He was not called "Mungo" – the association came about because he was for a considerable time based at the church at Hoddom (Dumfriesshire) already dedicated to Mungo. No one had taken an interest in Kentigern until King David I wanted to have what he regarded as a suitable patron saint for Scotland – so Kentigern was alighted upon and a hagiography had to be cobbled together as quickly as possible; this nuance was missed.

(c) Theneu did not say "Mochoi, Mochoi" when Kentigern was born – this story too was lifted from elsewhere

(d) As a prince we may be confident that Kentigern was not left in charge of a fire – but rubbing sticks together is a well known – and not miraculous – method of fire raising.

(e) We may treat the story of the robin with the disrespect it is due.

This focus on Kentigern is relevant not only in supporting the general timescale proposed but also in identifying

(a) "king Uriens" as Urien of Rheged and

(b) Ywain as his son and heir Owain.

(c) there is no inherent problem with Urien's wife being another of Arthur's sisters. Morgan seems unlikely as a name as it contains the idea of "sea" – but I have nothing else to offer. "Le Fay", being clearly French is anachronistic as it stands.

We should note, however, that Owen would not have figured in the 12 battles.

The earliest extant rendition of Theneu's name is "Thaney". Given the Goddodins' Gothic origins I suggest that this name is a variant of the Ancient Scandinavian "Dagný" meaning "New Day". So we might call her 'Dawn' or 'Aurora'.

4. MERLIN

I accept the idea that "Merlin" is a bowdlerisation by French writers of "Myrddin".

Merlin 1: One proposal for the identity of Merlin is – Myrddin Emrys of North Wales. Geoffrey claims that he was old enough to give advice to Vortigern – putting his birthdate back to around 400 and so making him anachronistic to Arthur. [However he is also supposed to be the heir to Morfyn (variously Merfyn) Frych ap Gwriad, King of Gwynneth in the middle 800s!]

We should note in passing that the attempted connection of this Myrddin to Carmarthen is wholly spurious. Before the Romans arrived there was already a stronghold called "Moridunon" – 'the sea fortress' (for all that the town is well inland) – noted as such by Ptolemy. In the middle ages (so well after the time of either Myrddin) the settlement was known as Llanteulyddog, but castles were built – so Caer Moridunum became Carmarthen. As such, the name Carmarthen does not mean Myrddin's fort. "The Dictionary of Placenames of Wales" (pp71/2) proposes that "-Myrddin" was later reinterpreted as a personal name. At http://www.arthuriana.co.uk/n&q/myrddin.htm we find:

> Jarman holds that, when writing his *Historia c*. 1138 Geoffrey was only slightly acquainted with the Myrddin legends and this acquaintance merely amounted to knowledge of the belief at Carmarthen in an eponymous prophetic founder-figure named Myrddin/Merddin. However, at some time subsequent to the publication of the *Historia* he encountered pre-existing legends of Myrddin the prophetic Wild Man and thus set about composing a new 'life' of Merlin, which showed indebtedness to both the Welsh poems and the Lailoken tales. On the other hand, Padel has recently suggested that the reverse is true – rather than believing that the *Vita Merlini* was influenced by the Welsh poems in which Myrddin appears as a Wild Man, he suggests that the *Vita* was in fact the first text to conflate the Dyfed prophetic Myrddin with tales of a northern Wild Man that originally belonged to Lailoken. As such the Welsh poems which name Myrddin as this figure would, in his opinion, date from after the *Vita Merlini* and be derivative of it.

It goes on to say:

> In fact, the only one of the Welsh poems which can be credibly considered pre-Galfridian and in which a concept of Myrddin as the Wild Man does definitely appear is the *Cyfoesi Myrddin a Gwenddydd ei Chwaer*, where Myrddin refers to his madness after the battle of Arfderydd. Both Jarman and Jackson consider that the *Cyfoesi* had its origins before the *Vita Merlini* was written, perhaps even as early as the tenth century; on the other hand, Padel notes that the earliest manuscript of the poem dates to *c*. 1300 and he expresses doubts over whether we can be entirely certain that this poem's composition must have occurred before *c*. 1150.

Merlin 2: Reinterpreting (correctly, with the benefit of being able to cross-reference with other sources) the Vita Merlini Silvestris (which casts the whole story in 'Wales') we may understand that "Merlin" was the brother-in-law of Rhydderch Hael, King of Strathclyde. Merlin served as bard to Gwendollau, king of 'Segontium", broadly Annandale and Eskdale – the residual kingdom of the Selgovae and by now a client kingdom of Strathclyde. Unfortunately Gwendollau mishandled affairs and was defeated and killed at the battle of Ardderydd (now misnamed as 'Arthuret') in 573. Rhydderch then offered the kingdom to Merlin, but the Welsh Annals record that he "went mad".

It is unlikely that this offer would have been made to anyone over 60, more likely he would still have been significantly under 50 years old. Thus it is likely that he was still a child, or only just into adulthood – and surely not of an age to counsel anyone or to be a 'magician' – by the time Arthur died (c537). He is more of the period of Kentigern and Rhydderch. And this is reinforced by the suggestion that Merlin and Rhydderch were brothers-in-law.

Thus I am confident that as a "magician" (druid?) he does not belong with any contemporaneous Arthurian tale.

So who was this second Merlin? The Vita Merlini Sylvestris has been misinterpreted recently to suggest that there was a "kingdom of Cadzow". There was not, but it does seem that the exiled British kings of Bernicia (discussed above) had taken refuge under the protection of Strathclyde – and my guess is that Cadzow was where they were allowed to make their principal home. If so, this would make Languoreth (Rhydderch's wife) a princess of this family – and so 'Merlin' a prince. [If David Nash Ford's proposed birthdate for Rhydderch (c532) is correct, then these are likely the children of Coledog, himself the son of the ousted Morcant Fwlch.]

Further problems are heaped on any Arthur/Merlin connection by the general recognition that this Scottish 'Merlin' was really called Lailoken rather than Myrddin.

The name Merlin/Myrddin

We are left with the problem of whether the personal name Myrddin was real and, if so, what it might mean. Anyone looking on the internet will see that those maintaining relevant sites tend to have swallowed the Carmarthen proposition and so propose that "Myrddin" means "Sea Fortress" Interestingly the Welsh dictionary does offer us "mŷr" meaning "seas" and "dyn" meaning "man". In this case Myrddin might be a direct equivalent of the Gaelic "Murdoch", in essence meaning "seafarer".

The name Lailoken

This is the only instance I am aware of of the name Lailoken. Try the internet and you will quickly find that Lailoken is held to mean "fool". However (a) those advancing this proposition offer no explanation/justification and (b) it is a ridiculous proposition that a noble would name his infant son "fool" – so if that were its meaning then clearly it is a later nickname rather than a given name.

In seeking a meaning for Lailoken we should turn to Welsh; we probably need to parse the name in three parts – Lai-Lo-Ken. I am fairly confident that Lai is represented in modern Welsh by Llai, meaning brown (cf the 'Dun-' element in Scottish given names). "-Ken" (as in St Kentigern) is probably represented in modern Welsh by "Cun" – which can be a noun meaning "chief", but can also be an adjective meaning "dear"- and in this context, both have potential. This leaves us with the "-lo-" element. Here we see that Llo also means 'calf', which is inherently unlikely at least in this context. But Welsh "llu" means "army"/"host" – so "Brown (haired) General" is a feasible interpretation (ie it is not out of place with other names of the period).

[There is a certain resonance between Lulach (the name of Macbeth's son) and Lailoken – who also was clearly far from being a fool. We do know that he called his son Maelsnectan and that his father was Gillechomghain, so we should assume this to be an avowedly Christian family, but I do not have a certain interpretation of Lulach. It might be reflective of eg albinism, with the "lu" representing "laogh" (albeit Gaelic) = 'calf', ('lulaic' is the milk of a newly calved cow) but this is unconvincing. Modern day Gaels render his name as 'Lughlagh'. If this is a fair representation then Lu/Lugh is a reference to the Celtic God Lugh. But 'Lagh' remains problematic. Dwelly offers "renown" and "mould" (so 'in the mould of Lugh' or 'moulded by Lugh' perhaps) – but this does not feel right either. If "lach" is actually a contraction of the adjective 'Laghach' then we may render it 'Lugh is kind' or some such – which parallels several Hebrew names, if of 'Laghadh' then 'Lugh is forgiving', but these are still not Christian.

If, however, we seek a Welsh-based explanation for the name, then 'Lu-" should represent the Welsh "Llu" – army or host – and immediately we are back in business, whether or not the second element is Welsh or Gaelic (eg W. 'llachar' means 'brilliant').]

Summary: Tales told about Arthur and Merlin are no more out of place (after, say, 573) than are tales today involving time travel and 'real' characters such as we find in entertainments such as Star Trek and Dr Who – and should be seen in that context.

5. OTHER CHARACTERS

a. Uther Pendragon

We have already separated the title "Pendragon" as a title meaning "army C-in-C". "Uther" is a corruption of Rhydderch (whose name remains represented at Birrens as "Carruthers" (= "Caer – uther"/ Rhydderch). His dates (he died c614) mean that he is anachronistic in the Arthurian Cycle.

c. Royns of North Wales

Really the only feasible identification is Rhun Hir ap Maelgun whose dates are given as 547-586. We can see that this is not contemporary with Arthur, but does fit with Rhydderch etc.

d. Pellam The Maimed King

There is one "obvious" connection: Masgwid Gloff ("The Lame") – Arthur's father. Clearly there is no immediate connection of names as such, to this, together with other related characters: Garlon, his brother, Pellas, his son with whom young Naimh is supposed to live happily ever after.

e. Dynadin

This is simply a knight – but his name is very like "Dun Eidin" – the name for Edinburgh current at the time (NB long before the Anglian King Edwin of Northumbria)

f. Peredur

There is a Pereddyr, great great great grandson of Cole and son of the king North of the Solway whose approximate dates are c510x80. This makes him clearly too young to have been involved with the 12 battles, but old enough to have been at Arthur's court as a young man.

g. The sons of Lot

i. Mordred

There is no good reason for supposing that Mordred was any other than the eldest son of Anna and Lot. But see previous part.

ii Gawain

So much difficulty has there been with this name that some have taken to suggesting that Sir Gawain is a corruption of Serguan. Nice try – but we are beginning to get overloaded with Serguans and it is based on the idea that the name had to be "real". Actually in Gaelic Gavin/Gamhainn means "a young bull" – and this would surely be an affectionate nickname. Bear in mind also that names like "Mack" in Scotland, "Sweyn" in Scandinavia, "Vaughan" in Wales and "Antony" in Etruria are all personal names meaning, in effect, "Sonny" or "Junior". However, given the time and the context, this is more likely to be a nickname than a given one.

iii Gareth Gaheris and Aggravain

The Arthurian proposition is that Gaheris killed his mother and that one way and another Lancelot kills them all – Gareth being entirely innocent of anything. I don't think these (separate) stories were intended to be taken seriously – but they may point to a some genuine and serious intra-family dispute.

h. King Pelinore (variously Pellanor)

We are told that Lot is killed by King Pellanor. This, of necessity, should make Pellinore one of the Pictish kings – but the only potential names we have to choose from are Drest Gurthinmoch or Galan Erilich, which makes no obvious sense. The matter is complicated by Pellanor being claimed to be Welsh. [There is a King Beli in Wales dating to the middle 600s and the legendary Beli Mawr from centuries earlier.]

There is a potential solution – the relevant king of Manau – but we have no information about this dynasty at this time. In other versions he is king of nameless islands. We could think immediately of the Orkneys or the Hebrides – but because this is where the Grail is supposed to be found, perhaps the fabled Isles of the Blessed (as mentioned in discussion of Ptolemy above) are at least half intended. Pellanor is supposed to have two sons Lamerock and Percival. They are clearly understood not to be Christian – which rules out Phyllis Ann Carr's attempt to link him to Cumberland; I am tempted by the Orkneys on the basis that Arthurian Lore makes Lot king of them – but there seems no reason for him to kill Lot – and so I revert to Manau, islands notwithstanding.

The geographical closeness would provide the context for close family interactions in the years following Badon Hill.

i. Sir Kay Simon Keegan ("Pennine Dragon", New Haven Publishing 2016 – otherwise not at all recommended) describes him as known alternatively as Cai Hir, suggesting him also as Arthur's second in command. This leads us neatly to suppose that we may identify him as Caw, king of Strathclyde until he was deposed in 501. Mallory suggests that Kay was Arthur's foster brother, but the timeframe makes this impossible; we should not, however, overlook the possibility that Arthur may have been fostered by Caw.

k. Hoel In the fictions Hoel is presented as a King of Brittany. He is also cited as a close relative of Arthur's. I have the suspicion that this was a misattribution by later writers for entertainment purposes – that early stories including "Hoel" really refer to Hywel or to Huaill mab Caw – brother(s) of Gildas – and hence, if Arthur was indeed fostered by Caw, Arthur's foster brother(s). As we have seen, Huaill was killed by Arthur – which is why, according to Geraldus Cambrensis, Gildas did his best to destroy the name of Arthur. Courts south of Hadrian's Wall would not recall Huaill – whence the reattribution to Brittany and the creation of new stories in that context.

APPENDIX 2:
THE EARLDOM OF LENNOX

with notes on the clans

Galbraith, MacAulay, Colquhoun, Haldane, Forbes and Buchanan

1. BACKGROUND: LENNOX 515 – 1178

Many aristocrats in Scotland have found a need to fabricate their ancestry. The best lies are those which contain at least a kernel of truth. This applies to the Earls of Lennox and here this kernel is a connection to the family of Luss.

In general terms, as we have seen, The Lennox may be described geographically as the lands draining into Loch Lomond and, further inland, into the Clyde north of The Antonine Wall. With regard to the name Lennox there is no dispute that it is a contraction of the name "Levenach". The river which drains Loch Lomond is still called the Leven, Loch Lomond used to be called Loch Leven.

As we have seen also the Damnonii annexed the Lennox in the period 495-510AD thereby establishing the kingdom of Strathclyde. The Damnonii were ethnically distinguishable from their neighbours. To the North West were the Scots of Dalriada, the aristocracy now of Irish (albeit Cruithin) descent who were already established in Argyll and had spread to the shores of Loch Lomond; to the North East were the Maeatae, a tribe of Picts. South of the Damnonii were two other Pictish tribes the Novantes and the Selgovae. Thus the Damnonii came to be known as the "Britons of Strathclyde".

[One of the many ironies is that when the Britons took political control of the Lennox they thereby gave the Gaelic-speaking Scots living under them the freedom to spread further into those parts of the Lennox that they had not reached before. Thus for example, the original base of the Colquhouns on the Clyde (at Bowling) was called Dunglass ("The River Fort") – a Gaelic rather than a Pictish name.]

By the standards of the day the kingdom of Strathclyde had now become a large territory – too large and too diverse to be managed on a centralised basis and so it is likely that what we might otherwise call a High Steward or High Reeve would have been appointed to take day-to-day charge of the Lennox as one of the principal sub-divisions. Anyone (in particular, the bulk of the Gaelic speaking population west of Loch Lomond) trying to translate "High Steward" is likely to come up with "Mor Maer" and this has led many naive historians to promulgate the ridiculous idea that there was an ancient Pictish Mormaerdom in the Lennox. Nothing could be further from the truth. The Pictish Mormaerdoms followed and were integral to what was really the voluntary coalescence of the various tribes identified by Ptolemy into the two Pictish Kingdoms (North and South of Drumochter).

It seems most likely that the person first appointed as High Steward of the Lennox was an immediate member of the Royal Family of the Damnonii – and as such the job may have been hereditary. It is of great regret that no names have come down to us, But in the section of Part 3 dealing with the Battles of Glen Douglas, the reader will have noted that I proposed Garwynwyn, younger brother of Clinog, king of Strathclyde as the likely first viceroy, followed by his son Erc. The predominantly Gaelic speaking Scots locals gave their overlords managing the Lennox the generic soubriquet "Galbraith"- "British Stranger" – and, despite the way they described themselves as *"Mac a' Bhreatnnaich"* this nickname stuck and they accepted it (see also the commentary on their arms below).

The kingdom of Strathclyde (including the Lennox) was an independent "country" until the middle 900s (so the Galbraiths were responsible directly to their crown) when it was absorbed by the nascent Scottish kingdom. After this time it remained as a separate under-kingdom, often as an appannage of the chosen heir, just as the Duchy of Cornwall is today with our own Royal Family. This arrangement survived right through to and beyond 1098. Despite this, the Lennox was still managed on a day to day basis by the Galbraiths. But we should note that now the Galbraiths had been, in effect, demoted – with the crown prince an intermediary between them and the king.

ILLUSTRATIONS OF COATS OF ARMS

As with "Scottish Clans....." I am extremely grateful to Eddie Geoghegan for his wonderful heraldic artistry. Please visit his website:

www.araltas.com

to see what else he has on offer and for any heraldic needs of your own.

(a) Galbraith and Forbes

Galbraith Arms

Galbraith Crest

Forbes Arms

Forbes Crest

(b) Lennox and Dunbar and MacAulay

Dunbar Arms — Dunbar Crest

Lennox Arms — Lennox Crest

MacAulay Arms — MacAulay Crest

(c) Colquhoun and Haldane

Colquhoun Arms

Colquhoun Crest

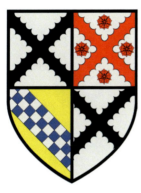

Haldane of Gleneagles Arms

Haldane of Gleneagles Crest

Haldane Arms

(d) Buchanan and MacAulsan

Buchanan Arms

Buchanan Crest

MacAuslan (1)

MacAuslan (2)

MacCasland

It was the crown-usurping younger MacMalcolm kings – Edgar, Alexander I and then David I who foisted Norman-English feudalism on Scotland, breaking up the old landholdings and tenure system piecemeal whether by force, when such was deemed necessary, or as and when the opportunities arose.

And so it was that "The Lennox" having been a High Stewardry first within the kingdom of Strathclyde and then under the heirs to the kings of Scotland became a discrete Earldom. We should note also that, as time went by, the territory of the Lennox was reduced, particularly (but not exclusively) to create an opportunity for more feudal incomers to be given land which would be absorbed later into Stirlingshire.

2. THE FIRST RULERS: THE CLAN GALBRAITH

First we should note the Arms of the Galbraiths:

Galbraith Arms

Galbraith Crest

There is no doubt in my mind that the bear is a reference to Arthur – and it is interesting to note, that even at that time, Arthur was a frequently chosen given name amongst Galbraiths. As we can see, the crest, like the motto, features a muzzled bear. Second we should note the Motto: "Ab Obice Suavior", meaning "gentler because of obstruction". This motto illustrates perfectly the way the Galbraiths chose to respond to their systematic demotion – and a very intelligent and mature response it was. It is interesting to note that the motto is also a demonstration of erudition, for it is a pun on a phrase in Ovid's Metamorphoses *ab obice saevior* ("fiercer because of obstruction"). It could be argued that the muzzling of the bear is a representation of the increasing constraints within which the Galbraiths had to operate.

The Old Statistical Account (Vol XV pp271/2) for Baldernock, County of Stirling, says:

> "In the beginning of the reign of Alexander II the lands of Cartonbenach were conveyed to Maurice Galbraith by Malduin Earl of Lennox. Soon after in the year 1238 we find the same barony granted by a new charter under the name Bathernock to Arthur, son of Maurice Galbraith..... From the Galbraiths of Bathernock, chiefs of the name descend....."

[Maurice appears to have been the 3rd chief. Alexander II's reign was 1214-49]

In "An Ordinary of Arms..." by J&E Malden and WG Scott (2016) many Galbraith blazons are listed – those illustrated above being for the original chiefs. Moreover the Galbraiths occupy a great deal of land over many centuries, which is anomalous in the sense that it is well nigh impossible to explain any of this by descent and acquisition from the first currently acknowledged/recognised chief, apparently called Gilchrist, whose *floruit* is likely to have been of the general timescale 1130-90. [This fits well with the introduction of the adoption of surnames.] One example of this would be the Galbraiths of Bandry who also held the crannog Inchgalbraith. I believe that this holding, so close to the family of Luss, was the original base for the new vice-roys.

The conclusion I draw from this is that the family was already well spread out with their own landholdings and that they adopted the surname in parallel with each other. It is likely that they adopted their arms around the same time. An indicative date for this may well be 1178 (see below – the infeftment of David Earl of Huntingdon as Earl of Lennox) – when they may have felt a particularly overwhelming need to assert their identity and to adopt a style in conformity with royal taste.

Conclusion: Everything we know about the Galbraiths is consistent with – indeed it supports – the general proposition about Arthur.

3. THE EARLDOM OF LENNOX

The earliest extant record of any earldom of Lennox was its gift by William the Lyon to his brother David, Earl of Huntingdon in 1178. The terms of the charter (specifically David's duty to provide knights) would imply that this was a regular feuing arrangement. There is no actual evidence that there ever was an Earl of Lennox prior to this, but under this arrangement the need for a Steward (who may have retained the title "High Steward") would have continued as David had a disparate collection of lands each of which would have needed managing (in 1160 he had been given the Lordship of the Garioch in North East Scotland, for example, and the management of this is discussed in Volume I of "Scottish Clans..."). So the change here was that of the status of the land-holder. An appanage might have been a privilege (and provided a considerable income) with no counterbalancing responsibilities – but now the area was a part of the nascent feudal system.

What is not precisely clear, however, is just when David Earl of Huntingdon resigned the Lennox back to the crown – but we may be certain that it was significantly before 1200, the year of the death of the Alwyn I universally accepted as the first of the first line of hereditary Earls of Lennox. Thus were the Galbraiths, originally in effect viceroys, further reduced, in effect, to the rank of baron.

The Hereditary Earls of Lennox, first creation

The Ancestry of the line of the first Earls of Lennox has been a matter of confusion and dispute for some 800 years already. It has never been resolved during that time because no-one bothered to enquire into the question of why there should be any confusion in the first place. At last this matter can be uncovered and set out once and for all. Even from the early 1200s there were rival propositions regarding the earls' ancestry – and bearing in mind that they were only in place as earls from the later 1100s this is pretty amazing. We should, therefore, look for an equally big reason for it.

Far too much of the history of what is now Scotland is attributed to the invading Gaelic speaking Scots of Dalriada – albeit they exercised excessive influence from 840 onwards. Perhaps it has been their *parvenu* immigrant status which led them to overcompensate – laying claim to many things for which they had no responsibility. The contortions which many "historians" have put themselves though to try to promote the idea of a line of "native" "Mormaers" of Lennox and, for that reason, to dismiss the idea that eg an Englishman could have become Earl of Lennox would fit into any circus act or freak show.

The principle protagonist here is Professor Cynthia Neville ("Native Lordship in Medieval Scotland: The Earldoms of Strathearn and Lennox, c.1140 – 1365" 2005). I will not attempt to *précis* or reproduce her acrobatics here: rather anyone who wants to see them can consider either her book or the relevant Wikipedia page, but I do not recommend such a waste of the reader's time. Amongst other problems a wholly false dichotomy between Anglo-Saxon and Viking names is the basis of much irrelevant and unneeded angst. One need only consider the history of Northumberland over the preceding 300 years (and include also the way in which different religions held sway) to see that both in principle and in practice this is of no consequence. Why, moreover, link Strathearn and Lennox in the first place? She proposes that the early (imagined by her) earls "kept their heads down" – which is code for an admission that she has not got a clue. In one sense (but not meaningfully) it would have to be true given that they are not known to us – but on what basis can she suggest an earl before 1178? The whole concept "earl" depends upon feudalisation and that means post 1100 – so even on her own terms she is dealing with a very narrow time window.

Proposition 1: The words of Murdoch Albanach O'Daily

The Annals of the Four Masters tell us that Murdoch "Albanach" was the poet of Domhnall O'Domhnaill in what is now County Sligo around the year 1213, but had to flee into exile after killing a tax collector. He went on the 5th crusade (which took place in the period 1213-21) but otherwise found refuge at the court of the Earls of Lennox until he was permitted to return to Ireland in 1228.

During this time the family of the Earls of Lennox were:

Alwyn I	b.c1145	
Alwyn II	b.c1170	d by1217
Maldoven	b.c1195	d 1250

Thus we can see that it was most likely in the period 1221x8 that Murdoch Albanach, wrote what purported to be a praise poem in which he seemed to claim that "Alwyn" was really a corruption of "Ailin" and that they descended from the Irish king of Cashel/hero (Conall) Corc mac Luigaid. Skene swallowed this proposition which also found currency in that greatest of all fabrications of this type MS1467 (for a discussion of which see "Scottish Clans...." Volume 2). [Only later did I work out that Skene's proposed date for the creation of this lie was broadly correct – the occasion being the impending hand-over of Orkney and Shetland to the Scottish crown on the betrothal of King James III to Margaret of Denmark.]

The argument of the poem has been demolished very well and systematically by Canadian Peter Anthony Kincaid in 2011. Peter's paper takes apart any idea that "Ailin" and "Alwyn" are interchangeable (see http://www.kyncades.org/Alwin_not_Ailín.pdf). Kincaid amplifies his argument, *inter alia*, by questioning O'Daily's claim that the river Leven takes its name from an Irish person called Leamhan. Peter could have added that O'Daily cannot, for example, account for other rivers of the same name – including one in Fife!

It is clear that O'Dailly was not attempting a full lineage – for Corc himself belongs to the 300sAD and O'Dailly only identifies four generations up to "Ailin" in the later 1100s – a span of 800 years!

William Fraser to the rescue

Sir William Fraser earned a fair crust by writing histories of important families. He was excellently assiduous in collating materials, but unfortunately he was not so skilled at drawing intelligent conclusions. In extrapolation he was severely constrained by his own worldview as well as that of his clients. In "Scottish Clans...." I have had cause to examine closely what he had to say about the Grants and (separately) the Balfours. In the case of the Grants it is impossible to know what he really believed – for he peddled the line that his masters required. In the case of the Balfours we have only a manuscript copy – and in that he was in one sense commendably humble in not being tempted to speculate about the origins of the progenitor whom he named (doubtless from the information provided by the Balfours) as "Siward, a Northumbrian". Actually Siward was not and could not have been a Northumbrian, albeit he came to Scotland from Northumberland.

In 1874, before he was knighted, Sir William produced his work "The Lennox" (See https://archive.org/details/lennoxvol1memov100fras)

Care must be taken with this early work of Fraser. For example he proposes that Walter whom he identifies as a grandson of Aulay born c1200 (so born c1250) became the husband of the heiress Margaret born c1364. On this basis Walter would have been nearly 130 years of age on marriage! Clearly there are several (probably 4) missing generations here.

So too there is a problem when Fraser recognises only one wife for Alwin II: Eva, daughter of Gilchrist of Menteith. However we may show easily that she cannot have been his only wife. We may conclude this – and more – by looking at the naming pattern of his children:

1. Maldoven 2. Dugald 3. Malcolm 4. Aulay
5. Gilchrist 6. Christinus 7. Corc 8. Duncan
9. Henry 10. Eva

- We may discount the placement of **Eva**, for girls were normally only listed after all the boys. However it is "obviously" likely that she was the daughter of Eva of Mentieth.

- We may overlook the names **Henry** and **Malcolm** for the connection of these names to the Royal family.

- The "crunch" name is **Gilchrist**. Normally Alwyn should have named his second son after his father-in-law. To put this name so far down the birth order is little short of an insult. However the likelihood is that Gilchrist was actually Alwyn's first son by Eva.

- We see that even Alwyn II took the Irish line seriously in the use of the name **Corc**. Given this, it may well be that he chose deliberately not to name his first son Alwyn

- We can find the name **Maldoven** as the name of the chieftain of Luss at that time (Fraser p65 refers to *"... a charter granted by Maldouen, Earl of Lennox to Gillemore, son of Maldouen, of the lands of Luss"*). On this occasion Earl Maldouen was infefting his own uncle.

- And then there is **Aulay**. At first glance this is completely out of context – random!

Here is what I think happened:

- Alwyn II had as his first wife the daughter of Maldoven, the laird of Luss. They had three sons, perhaps four (if an Alwyn (or even an Ailin) did not survive to adulthood) and then she died.

- Alwyn then married the daughter of Aulay of the proto-MacAulays (see below in this appendix) and had a son whom he naturally called Aulay. [Aulay was to become the father of Walter; they were infefted with Faslane and from them the second line of Earls was to come.]

- She then died and at last he married Eva who bore him a further five sons and a daughter.

Because Alwyn gave a younger son the name Corc, we may be sure that already he was celebrating and adopting the Irish lineage to Corc, via St Kessog, of his first wife. After her death he may even have claimed it. But was only effected by Maldoven – which was more natural because, he really was a descendant of this line. So what Maldoven commissioned O'Dailly to insinuate was that what was in fact a maternal ancestor was his male line ancestor – and broadly this fabrication stuck for several centuries. For the sake of completeness we need therefore to go back to establish the true male lineage of these earls.

Fraser's attempt to identify the true line

Fraser rightly identifies the Scottish progenitor of the line as Alwyn mac Archil and makes the correct observation that Archil and Alwyn are not Scottish names. Alwyn is Anglo-Saxon (a contraction: from Aelf-wine: "Elf-Friend") while Archil is a variant of "Arn ketil" (it means "vessel of the spirit of the eagle") – essentially Old Norse.

Whether he worked out whom he thought the eponymous Archil to be, or whether he was following a lead offered by his sponsors is not clear to me, but he offers the following generational line:

Aykfrith/Egfrith	c1065	
Arkill/Archill	c1064-1100	
Arkill	1100 – 1130	
Alwin MacArchill	c1130-1155	1st earl
Alwin	1155-1217	2nd earl

We can see immediately that this line is not in accord with the facts – not only is 62 years a remarkably long time for Alwin II to have been earl, but it makes no allowance for David Earl of Huntingdon's infeftment (1178). With the best will in the world you don't go about taking an earldom from someone and later reinstating it for no good reason and with no comment surviving.

Even more serious websites can overlook intelligent chronology. Thus the Foundation for Mediaeval Genealogy (FMG) falls into the trap of accepting O'Dailly's poem at face value http://fmg.ac/Projects/MedLands/SCOTTISH%20NOBILITY%20LATER.htm#_Toc359672175:

1. **ECGFRITH** . **m** —. One child:

a) **ARKIL** . Orderic Vitalis records that "*Archillus potentissimus Nordanhymbrorum*" made peace with William I King of England and granted "*filium suum*" as a hostage, dated to 1068[128]. Orderic Vitalis records that "*Marius Suenus, Gaius Patricius, Edgarus Adelinus, Archillus et quatuor filii Karoli*" joined the Danish fleet which sailed up the river Humber, dated to 1069[129]. **m** —. The name of Arkil's wife is not known. Arkil & his wife had one child:

i) **ALWYN** (-after 1153). "...*Alwino mac Archil*..." witnessed the undated charter, dated to before [1136], under which David I King of Scotland donated "*decimam meam de meo Chan*" to the church of Glasgow[130]. Assuming that Alwyn was a member of the same family as the later earls of Lennox, the chronology suggests that he belonged to the generation earlier than that of the first earl. "...*Alwyno mac Arkil*" witnessed the undated charter under which Malcolm IV King of Scotland donated "*piscium...Crespeis*" to Dunfermline monastery[131]. **m** —. The name of Alwyn's wife is not known. Alwyn & his wife had [two] children:

(a) [**GILLANDERS** (-after 1153). "...*Gillandres filio Alwini*..." witnessed the undated charter under which Malcolm IV King of Scotland confirmed the donation of land "*in... Melchrethre*" to St Andrew's priory[132]. It is not known whether the father of Gillanders was the same Alwyn who is named above.]

(b) daughter . Her parentage and marriage are confirmed by a Celtic poem which is addressed to "*O Leamhan Alun oge, the son of Muireadhach...descendant of "Lughaidh of Liathmhuine*" and "*the Mormaer of Leamhan...son of Ailin's daughter*"[133]. **m** **MURDOCH**, son of —.

We can begin by dismissing FMG's "(b) daughter" (see above). It is because the FMG author has taken O'Dailly's poem too literally that (i) there is a need for the daughter and (ii) that he puts Gillanders in brackets. So let us retain Gillanders in our thinking.

Next we may discard Arkil the son of Egfrith as being the key ancestor, for his mother was Uchtred's discarded wife Sigrida – so his birthdate was surely around the 1020s (Eadulf, his older half-brother, was born c1015) putting him out of the frame. [See, for example https://thewildpeak.wordpress.com/2013/04/01/who-was-the-cumbrian-earl-gospatric/]

Even were we to set this aside we can see that FMG thinks Arkil was old enough to have been an adult in 1068. Let us be generous and estimate him at a mere 24 (so b1045), while Fraser appears to suppose him only to have been born around 1064 – ie to have become a hostage as an infant. Working with the 1045 date and given that his son is said to have died c1155 we have 110 years to be accounted for – and that is basically a minimum. [If I am correct we have 130 years to cope with!] Of course it is technically possible (given that we do not know the date of his death) for Arkil at age 40 to have had a son who went on to live to 70. But it is very rare for someone so important to delay parenthood for so long – and I think that we in turn may set this idea to one side. Moreover although his name has been rendered Arkil and Archillus (from Latin texts) this man is actually Arnkel. Although Archil and Arnkel both derive from Arn-ketil, it is not acceptable to treat them as interchangeable.

Even this, however, is not the point – for Orderic actually says that Archil gave his own son as a hostage in 1068. Now let us be generous and suggest that this unnamed son was as young as 18 – making his birthdate 1050. This takes Archill back to before 1030 at the very latest – and more likely a further decade earlier – and the time window problem is exacerbated still more.

So we need to look elsewhere.

Lessons from Heraldry

That it is possible to try to claim that there is "no evidence" is based, *inter alia*, on the exclusion of heraldry (this exclusion based on prejudice – not on evidence) and is a prime example of unscientific thinking – we all know that "absence of evidence is not evidence of absence"!

In "Scottish Clans...." I show how historians have consistently failed to take account of heraldry and sadly this remains the case. Of course one must take care – some blazons are quite new, some self-consciously referential. Nevertheless a lot can be gleaned. The case of Lennox is almost a copy-book example of why heraldry should not be excluded from evidence.

Consider the Arms of Lennox and then compare them to the Arms of Dunbar.

Dunbar Arms   **Lennox Arms**

The colour combination, the use of the rose and the use variously of the Lion Rampant (Dunbar) and the Saltire (Lennox) show a clear connection. There is no doubt in my mind that whoever designed the Lennox arms intended to demonstrate not only his commitment to the Scottish crown but also his appreciation of the Earls of Dunbar. There is no dispute that the Earls of Dunbar descend from Gospatric, Earl of Northumberland who fled to Scotland after crossing William the Conqueror too often.

Dunbar Crest   **Lennox Crest**

As we can see, there is even a resonance between the crests. This concurs with and makes sense of Jackson's claim that there was a Lothian connection – indeed there was, but not the one that he supposed. [See https://en.wikipedia.org/wiki/Alwyn_MacArchill]

My new proposition: Alwyn was the son of Archil Morel.

At this stage I draw the reader's attention to the character in history known as Arkil Morel. He it was, castellan of Bamburgh, who killed Malcolm III in 1093. The Internet is bulging with misinformation about him – mainly by would-be genealogists over keen to force connections where none exists and I hope that you the reader will not come to the view that I am merely adding to this!

So let us try to pin down Arkil Morel.

- **First**, as mentioned, he was an adult in 1093 capable of killing Malcolm III
- **Second** his son Alwyn mac Archill is a signatory on many Scottish charters during the reigns of Kings David and Malcolm IV (d1165) but not later. Thus Alwyn is likely to have been born shortly before 1100.

- **Third** his daughter Sybilla married Gospatrick, 2nd Earl of Dunbar. I have a guide date of 1082 for this Gospatrick's birth and 1104 for the birth of his son (also Gosparick) – so it is likely that Sybilla was born some time shortly before 1090, possibly as early as 1084 (see "Scottish Clans....").

What we have, therefore, is a pattern consistent with Arkil being born sometime around or rather before 1065 (we have no reason to suppose that either of these children was his eldest).

Arkil is variously described as High Sheriff (or Reeve: Sheriff = Shire Reeve) of Northumbria and as having charge of Bamburgh Castle – so it seems likely that he was in fact the son of Osulf II, Earl of Northumbria who was killed in 1067. Arkil would thus have been taken in and fostered by Gospatick mac Maldred, the next Earl (and a relative). Arkil will have had the support both of Gospatric and of Waltheof in sustaining his hereditary position at Bamburgh (ie through to 1075) by which time, though not an adult, he would have been old enough to be not just discarded with disdain. On the contrary he was a person of such importance to have been a "godsib" of Malcolm III.

[Osulf was the son of Eadulf (d.1041), Lord of Bamburgh, himself a younger son of Uchtred also based in Bamburgh (k. 1018).]

Supporting evidence from Robert de Mowbray, Earl (1086-95) of Northumbria

We must now turn our attention to Robert de Mowbray, who was appointed Earl of Northumbria in 1086. Robert is cited as having married Matilda, daughter of Richard l'Aigle in 1095, but it is also claimed (by Orderic Vitalis) that Arkil Morel was Robert's nephew! It is highly unlikely that an Earl of Northumbria would have remained single for a decade. And so it is that we must conclude that Matilda was his second wife and that Robert had married a Northumbrian girl around the time of his appointment (if not slightly before – the Earldom had been vacant since 1080).

In order for him to be infeofed with Northumbria, Robert de Mowbray might have been born as late as 1065. But Northumbria was a major job – too big, surely, for a 21-year-old – so a more likely date would be around 1055x60. The date of his death is unknown, estimates varying from 1106 to 1125 (the 1125 date accompanied by the description of him "growing old", by which we should understand at least 70 making 1055 more likely than 1060). A man intending to found a dynasty is not going to wait into his forties to marry and produce an heir and, taking over Northumbria would be eased (as was so often the case throughout England and Scotland) by marrying into the previous ruling family.

All in all then, it would be quite reasonable for us to suppose that Robert would have married a sister of Osulf (ie an aunt of Arkil) as part of a plan of securing his position in Northumbria – and this could have been any time after 1080. In the case of such a dynastic marriage it is more than possible that she was older than he. All that is required in this scenario is that by 1095 Robert's Northumbrian wife had died without providing him with a living son – and he was free to marry Matilda.

And so it is that there is every reason to accept the idea that as a result of Robert's first marriage, Arkil was indeed Robert's nephew.

Conclusion: The line of the Earls of Lennox

All in all then, there is no room left but to allow that the Earls of Lennox did indeed descend from Alwyn mac Arkil and that he was (or would have been), in effect, the hereditary High Reeve of Northumbria.

Here then is my proposal for the generational table for the early male line of the earls of Lennox

Dates	Name	Title
971 – 1018	Uchtred	Bamburgh Castellan
c1015 – 1041	Eadulf	Bamburgh Castellan
c1040 – 1067	Osulf	Bamburgh Castellan
c1065 – c1130	Arkil Morel	Bamburgh Castellan
c1095 – c1155	Alwyn mac Archil	Lennox: 1st High Steward
c1120 – c1180	Gillanders	Lennox: 2nd High Steward
c1145 – c1200	Alwyn	Lennox: 1st Earl
c1170 – bef.1217	Alwyn	Lennox: 2nd Earl
c1195 – 1270	Maldoven	Lennox: 3rd Earl

We have seen that David Earl of Huntingdon was appointed Earl of Lennox in 1178, but this may have been a reappointment. David was born c1144. The practice of entitling very young princes was already established practice in Scotland (with Duncan I for example) and continues to this day with titles, and all that go with them, such as Duke of Cornwall – this would have given him a decent income. So it is far from impossible that David was given the Lennox any time after 1149. Alternative potential occasions include the death of his father, Prince Henry of Huntingdon, in 1152, or his grandfather, King David I, in 1153.

Accession to Lennox

While 1178 is well after the death of Alwyn mac Archill and not long before the death of Gillanders, it is quite feasible that it was Alwyn mac Archil who gained the position of High Steward of the Lennox. It is now generally recognised that Alwyn mac Archill was "rannair" to Scottish kings – specifically David I, so my hunch is that it was he, king David I, who entrusted the running of the Lennox to Alwyn on behalf of his (David's) namesake grandson, with an indicative date around 1150. He probably expected Alwyn to survive into David's full adulthood – but it is clear that Gillanders was also well known and well liked at court and was more than old enough to take on the responsibility. So there was no reason for Malcolm IV to seek a replacement. Indeed we have seen elsewhere (eg with the Grants in Urquhart and Glenmoriston) that it is quite a normal procedure to give a noble a salaried position to see how he copes, allowing the job to become feudalised and hereditary if he proves effective. This appointment did, however, imply a downgrading in rank for the Galbraiths.

4. THE CLAN MACAULAY

Because it has been supposed for too long that the MacAulays of Ardincapel are cadets of the Earls of Lennox then it seems only fair, having corrected the matter of the Lennox ancestry to complete the job by considering the MacAulays.

A. MacAulays as part of the Siol Alpin

First we should note that the MacAulays are and have always acknowledged their place within the Siol Alpin, but notwithstanding the bond of friendship which they signed with the MacGregors in 1591 acknowledging that through their co-descent from two brothers, the nature of their shared ancestry has not been understood properly for several hundreds of years. This confusion (*inter alia*) has allowed conflicting and erroneous conclusions to be drawn and legends to find currency.

In Volume I of "Scottish Clans:....." I show for the first time in extant history (*inter alia*) the exact nature of the interrelationship between each of the Clans which constitute the Siol Alpin (including the way the MacGregors put one over on the MacAulays by persuading them to acknowledge the MacGregors as senior to them!) [The Macgregors tried this on with the Grants also – so MacAulays should not feel as if they were singled out for this sort of treatment!]

In short the clans of the Siol Alpin have as their common male-line ancestor the Viking princeling Olav Hemingsson who found his *métier* as one of Malcolm III's most trusted and senior lieutenants but who was written out of history in 1098 having been executed at the behest of the usurping king Edgar – at a price (in today's terms) of some £100 million. In my work I document Olav's male line ancestry back to Heming the Great king of Denmark (*fl.*810). His wife's line is also taken back – both to Alpin, father of Kenneth (whence the soubriquet "The Siol Apin" adopted in subsequent generations) and to the ancestors of Coroticus, kings of the Damnonii in late and immediately post-Roman times.

The specific progenitor (ie of the MacAulays and of no other clan) was Aulay, eldest son of Gregory, son of Olav Hemingsson. The most likely scenario is that Aulay was born on Fraoch Eilean on Loch Awe around the year 1090. Gregory himself was not landed – so his sons had to acquire their lands, whether by preferment or by marriage.

And so it was that while Gregory's younger sons gave rise to the clans Macnab and Macgregor, Aulay found his future on the land between Loch Lomond and the Loch Long. If he moved there on reaching adulthood we should be expecting this to be around 1110x15 – during the Reign of Alexander I when the future king David I was Regulus of the South of Scotland (including the old kingdom of Strathclyde). It would seem likely that Aulay had been prepared for this by spending time as a house carl in the court either of Alexander I or of David I, perhaps even of Edgar.

It is likely that his own initial holding was at Shandon – for two farms (High and Laigh) still bear the name "Balernock" (on the OS map 1st edition it is spelled "Ballernick", ("Bullernok" in 1351)). I believe these to be corruptions of *Baile Chernach*" (cf Balchearnoch in Stratherrick and Balerno,. previously "Balhernoch" in Midlothian) which means "Victor's farmstead". This is a reference to the angel Victorius who appeared to St Patrick in a dream telling him to evangelise Ireland (see "Scottish Clans....." for a more detailed explanation of all this). This place name element is one of several found on Siol Alpin lands (thus eg Glencarnaig of the Macgregors and Glenchernick in Strathspey).

B. Muddied Waters

While the original purpose of "Scottish Clans...." had been to identify the true origins of the Clan Grant and later widened to examine the Siol Alpin as a whole, I found it necessary in the end to deconstruct the many lies told about the origins of so many different clans. At different times in different areas it became politically inconvenient to admit to one's true origins – and so confections, some more elaborate than others, came to substitute for the truth. The applied not only to Grants and Macgregors, but to Campbells, Camerons, MacDuffs, Macdonalds, Mackintoshes, Stewarts and other clans of substance.

The MacAulays of Ardincapel found it at least desirable, if not exactly necessary, to pretend to a more direct relationship with the Earls of Lennox (of the first creation) than was the case.

C. Ancestors of the MacAulay line

We see Aulay mac Gregory born c 1090, looking to better himself perhaps from as early as 1105 (eg as a house carl). Given his connection to Malcolm mac Malcolm III it would be very easy to imagine him as an integral part of the court of David I as regulus of the South of Scotland from 1107 – not impossible to see the same with Alexander I a year or two before. Alwyn mac Archill, sponsored by Gospatrick (1st earl of Dunbar) would also have been seeking preferment only a few years later.

There seems to have been no hurry in feuing Lennox out. Above I have proposed a family of hereditary stewards (who would become the Galbraiths) already in place – in which case one is left with the supposition that Alwyn would have married into it. With Malcolm mac Malcolm in Argyll, Lennox was not a dangerous place – far from it – and it would be a foolhardy Norwegian or Manxman who would venture so far up the Clyde to attack by sea. Once Somerled had full rein, however (pretending to full reign!), in the period c1150 until his death in 1164 the Lennox became, albeit briefly, the front line.

Aulay will have needed a wife – and she will likely have been from the existing Ardincaple minor aristocracy – so probably a proto-Galbraith or a Luss girl. In subsequent generations it is almost impossible to believe that some proto-MacAulays will not have married some spare Lennox girls. Elsewhere, attempts to maintain friendly relations with powerful neighbours and superiors through intermarriage was more or less *de rigueur* – so there is no reason to suppose it was not here also. It may even be that in due course MacAulay enthusiasts will be able to identify several such, now that there is a clear framework within which to conduct further research.

D. Identifying the First Chief

A clan chief is defined as being the head of a "name" – thus we cannot identify correctly someone as a Clan Chief who has not adopted the style of using a surname. It is well known amongst MacAulays that it was the 12th chief who sold up in 1767.

The full list of chiefs may be deduced quite easily from "Ardincaple Castle and its Lairds" by Edward Randolph Wells (1930)

Chiefly number	Dates	Name	Relationship to predecessor
1	?1450 – ?1510	Alexander	Son of Aulay of Ardincapel
2	?1480 – 1514	John	Son of Alexander
3	?1480 – 1529	Aulay	Cousin of John
4	?1525 – 1583	Walter	Son (2nd mar.) of Aulay
5	1557x60 – 1617	Sir Aulay	Son of Walter
6	?1560 – ?1620	Alexander	Cousin of Sir Aulay
7	?1585 – 1645x8	Walter	Son of Alexander
8	1620x3 – 1675	Aulay	Son of Walter
9	?1650 – ?1729	Archibald	Son of Aulay
10	?1675 – ?1730	Aulay	Son of Archibald
11	?1680 – ?1745	Walter	Brother of Aulay
12	?1705 – 1767	Aulay	Son of Walter

The first thing we should note here is that the MacAulays took their name from their immediate progenitor – Aulay of Ardincaple. It is fortuitous and no more than that, that this was also the name of their distant ancestor, Aulay mac Gregory (this is true also of the MacGregors). This Aulay of Ardincapel must have been born c1425. Thus we may date the adoption of the surname to the period 1471 – 1488

Second we may note that this is quite late for the adoption of the surname style by a chief (by contrast I argue that the first Macgregor *qua* Macgregor dates to c1250, the first Grant to 1175) but it does correspond both with the widespread (often forced) adoption by the peasantry elsewhere in Scotland in general and, locally, with the second creation of the Earldom of Lennox in 1488 (in a cadet Stewart line).

In passing we may note also that this table conforms very well to the 25 year inter-generational estimate which I have found useful in other contexts (I see that others use this too, although in some cultures 30 can be appropriate).

Ancestors of the MacAulay Chiefs

1. From Wells

We may take a line of ancestors of the first chief from the same source (my generation numbers):

Generation	Dates	Name	Notes
8	?1265 -	Maurice I	
9	?1290 – ?1333	Arthur I	?killed at Halidon Hill
10	?1325 – 1406<	Maurice II	tutored by his uncle Duncan
11	?1350 -	Arthur II	
12	?1375 -	Duncan	
13	?1400 -	XX	
14	?1425 -	Aulay	Eponymous of the chiefs

As we can see there is a missing generation – and it is most likely that this is a case of Duncan's son pre-deceasing him some time before 1445, so that he was succeeded by his grandson. Because of the break in the naming pattern we might suppose also that Duncan was a younger son of Arthur II.

[In the context of the major subject of this book being "king" Arthur who is claimed to have had an image of the Virgin Mary on his shield, it is interesting to note the repeated use both of "Arthur" and of "Maurice" (used as an Anglicised rendition of Gillemhuire – "servant of the Virgin Mary").]

2. Interpolating to Olav Hemingsson

In this table Olav, Gregory and Aulay are fully accounted for in "Scottish Clans....".We may deduce 3. Aulay (capitalised) from the marriage of Alwyn II of Lennox.

Generation	Name	Dates
0	Olav	1038 – 1098
0	Gregory	1065 – ?
1	Aulay	c1090-1150
2	"Gregory"	
3	AULAY	c1140-1200
4	"Arthur"	
5	"Aulay"	c1190-1250
6	"Arthur"	
7	"Aulay"	c1240-1300

The other names – in quotation marks – are arbitrary. We have seen the names Aulay, Gregory, Arthur and Gillemhuire – all are likely candidates.

MacAulay Arms

MacAulay Arms   MacAulay Crest

Unlike most of the others, the MacAulay Arms have nothing to tell us about the Siol Alpin connection. The main elements belong to a time much later than 1090. The Fesse chequy on a gold ground is clearly the Stewart arms differenced only by the colour of the check (and hence dating to post 1488 and the take over of the Lennox by the Darnley Stewarts).The crossed arrows appear to echo the Saltire in the Lennox arms and/or the crossed swords in their crest.

It is often in the crest that we find relics of previous coats of arms – and in the case of the MacAulays we find a boot and a spur, which link well with the place names Ardincaple and Portincaple ("Capel" meaning horse – specifically mare) – as do the buckles on the shield. From all this we may hazard that one of Aulay's day-to-day tasks included horse breeding (a key role) for their Lennox superiors (first the Earls themselves and then their Faslane cadets). But this is not more than speculation.

Implications of the timeframe

Aulay mac Gregory was posted to Lennox about 1115 – well before Alwyn mac Archill had had a chance to impress the royal court. The lands of Ardincapel are outside Luss territory, so it would seem likely that his initial patron was a Galbraith. However we should note also that the later-to-be-king David I was already Regulus of Southern Scotland (after the death of Edgar in 1107). We should note also that the lands of Ardincapel are to the west of Dumbarton rock, so they are the "soft underbelly" of the Lennox – the likely front line against any attack from any Viking (including especially Western Islander) with pretentions. So it looks as if the underlying task was to fend off such attacks – and in this regard the motto ("Duce Periculum" – Danger is Sweet) is especially apt – however late it may have been adopted, it references an important echo from the MacAulay past.

Aulay's family continued as loyal and valuable lieutenants of the Earls of Lennox and at least to begin with ranked alongside the Galbraiths and the family of Luss. But later they lost out primarily because their landholding was so small and, hemmed in by the sea, geography dictated that there was no scope for expansion. On the contrary their lands were further constrained when their very close relative, the Aulay of the Lennox line was given not only Faslane, diminishing what they had, but also Glen Fruin to which they might have had reasonable aspirations. [Although this was after Somerled's time, it was before the battle of Largs (1263) – so we might suppose that that Maldoven may have taken the view that he needed greater family control over the defences.]

The Ardencapel family had no pretensions to earldom or other preferment – even only formally adopting a surname when it became vital after the original line of their Lords had ended.

5. THE COLQHOUNS OF LUSS

with notes on the Haldane

It is necessary and in any case apposite to understand the Colquhouns not only with regard to the Forbes (see below) but also because of their long association with a key spot in our tale as the Lairds of Luss.

In "Scottish Clans..." I made fairly cursory mention of the Colquhouns of Luss. The male-line origins are not in doubt as far back as we may trace them. It was Umfridus (otherwise Humphrey) de Kirkpatrick who was infeft by Maldouen, Earl of Lennox, with the lands of Colqhoun and others in the reign of Alexander II (specifically before 1246). The Humphrey's strongpoint was Dunglass Castle on the Clyde – and the site of the old chapel of Colqhoun can be seen on old maps just over one mile to the North East of it.

The history of the Colquhouns was written by William Fraser ("The Chiefs of Colqhoun and their country" 1869). He notes an attempt by the Colquhouns to embroider their ancestry and to obscure their Norman ancestry in these words (Vol I pp 2&3):

> "Not content, however, with such a satisfactory foundation, several writers on the family of Colquhoun have attempted to find their origin in the younger son of Conoch, a king of Ireland, who, it is said, came to Scotland in the reign of Gregory the Great, King of Scotland, that is, between the years 882 and 893, and obtained from King Gregory a grant of lands in the shire of Dumbarton, to which he gave the name of Conochan, a name which gradually became corrupted into Cochon, which afterwards became Colquhoun."

Unfortunately Fraser gives no indication of any date for the first proposition of this attempted fabulisation. The Colquhoun Arms indicate to me an acknowledgement of Humphrey's vassalage to the Earls of Lennox, adopting the same Saltire, engrailed, but in the black and white "Border Drab" of his immediate ancestors. The high position he gained more or less immediately suggests that it is not impossible that he may have married a daughter of the Earl of Lennox – Fraser's disavowal of this claim notwithstanding (in any case the marriage may have been later than (or even followed upon) the charter whose words, Fraser claims, imply no such connection).

Colquhoun Arms **Colquhoun Crest**

We should note that the crest is "a hart's head attired argent" and the motto "Si Je Puis" – "If I can".

The Colquhouns did not acquire the Luss holdings until 1368 when Sir Robert Colquhoun married the heiress daughter of Godfridus, whom Fraser (p10) calls the 6th Laird of Luss.

The **supporters** of the Colquhoun arms are two rach hounds argent, collared sable (note that they have the same colour scheme as the arms. Our problem is that we have no idea whether or not these were the supporters before the Colquhouns gained Luss.

Addendum on the Haldanes of Gleneagles

From http://www.electricscotland.com/history/nation/haldane.htm we read

> **HALDANE**, a surname derived from Haldenus, a Dane, who first possessed the lands on the borders called from him, Halden-rig. "In old charters," says Mr. Alexander Haldane, in his Memoirs of Robert and James A. Haldane, (London, 1852), "in the rolls of parliament, and in other public documents, the name is variously written Halden, Haldane, Hadden, or Hauden. There is no doubt that it is of Norse origin." In the 12th century a younger son of the border Haldens of that ilk became possessed of the estate of Gleneagles, Perthshire, by marrying the heiress of that family, and assumed the arms but not the name of Gleneagles.

Objections to this story from the current chief (to me in private conversation) notwithstanding, it seems to me that it stands up but for the timescale. Alexander Nisbet ("System of Heraldry" first published in 1722) tells us that the Arms of Haldane of that Ilk (to which arms I suppose the current chief to be entitled notwithstanding that the chiefship has descended upon the Gleneagles line) are: Gules two leopards in pale passant guardant Argent.

The arms of Haldane of Gleneagles are entirely different, described (eg by Lindsay of the Mount (1542)) in this way: Quarterly: 1st and 4th Argent, a saltire engrailed Sable (Haldane) 2nd Argent, a saltire engrailed between four roses Gules (Earldom of Lennox) 3rd Or, a bend chequy Argent and Azure (Menteith). There are several other Haldane armigers bearing very similar arms.

Haldane of Gleneagles Arms **Haldane of Gleneagles Crest** **Arms of Haldane**

Notice that "Argent a saltire engrailed sable" is described as the arms of Haldane! This is bizarre because we have just seen that these are the arms of Colquhoun. Until the recent even more bizarre decision by a former Lord Lyon to grant MacArthur *Azure three ancient crowns Or* (discussed in "Scottish Clans...") this is the only example I can think of where two different names have appeared to have the same coat of arms. And that this should be so is also attested by the Lennox and Menteith references in the other quarters. There is an explanation – and that is that a son of Humphrey de Colqhoun must have been given the Gleneagles estate and that he only had a daughter – who married the junior Haldane son. The timescales involved barely leave any room for intervening generations. The subsequent quartering reflects later marriages which need not concern us here.

As we have seen, Humphrey (Colquoun) arrived in the Lennox and adopted his arms only after the death of William the Lyon. Let us be as generous as we can and suppose that Humphrey got his lands and married in 1215, a younger son would not be ready to be infefted with Gleneagles before 1240 and so an eldest daughter of his would not be marriageable before 1255.

This becomes the earliest possible date for the Haldane move to Gleneagles. However this ceases to be a problem if by "12th century" the writer means the 1200s – and this is a convention I have seen commonly used elsewhere. Alexander II married Marie de Coucy in 1239 and it is assumed that the regulation of heraldry followed soon thereafter (Alexander died in 1249) – so it appears that there is not a great deal of latitude before it would not have been possible for the Gleneagles arms to be those of Colqhoun undifferenced. Indeed this timescale seems to be the only one possible and limited at most to +/- 5 years.

The confusion which would result in any armed situation (battle, jousting etc.) demonstrates so very clearly why Alexander II found it necessary to organise and codify the granting of arms, instead of the mere assumption which must have been the case there-before, but it seems that Alexander stopped short of stripping Haldane of Gleneagles of the Colquhoun blazon.

The Haldane Crest, "An eagle's headed Erased, Or" is a pun based on misunderstanding – for it is clearly a reference to "Gleneagles". However, as discussed in relationship to the Battle of Agned Hill, the etymology of "eagles" lies not with the bird, nor with "eglis" (ie church – for which the clue lies in the fact that there is not and has not been one in the glen) but is, rather, cognate with the Isle of Eigg – where the root meaning is "notch" (source: private conversation with the Chief of Haldane). I cannot account for the motto.

6. THE CLAN BUCHANAN

A Survey of the way the Lennox developed would not be complete without a consideration of the Buchanans – not so much because of their influence on it but rather because of some excessive claims made by them which need to be corrected and put in the right context.

Buchanan Arms

Before reconstructing the Buchanan family's origins, let us consider the arms

Buchanan Arms   **Buchanan Crest**

The arms of the last chief (d1682) are described as: *"Or, a lion rampant Sable, armed and langued Gules, within a double tressure flory counterflory of the Second"*. In this regard we should note that the double tressure came to Scotland only with the marriage of Alexander II to Marie de Coucy (1239); in "Scottish Clans...." I set out the rationale of my claim that the Lion Rampant, the first arms in Scotland, came with Malcolm III after 1054. Any alternative view makes this date later not sooner.

The Crest is described as: *"A hand coupee holding a ducal cap, or duke's cornet, proper, with two laurel branches wreathed surrounding the crest, disposed orleways proper"* The style "Duke" came to Scotland only with the Albanys in the 1300s – so we may be confident that this crest post dates that. However in Nisbet's "System of Heraldry" two Buchanan blazons feature for a crest a hand grasping a sword of one sort or another. This may well represent an earlier Buchanan crest.

The War cry is *"Clar Innes"* – an island in Loch Lomond which Buchanan progenitors acquired in 1225.

So we may begin by recognising that the Buchanans reinvented themselves first in the middle 1200s and then again in the 1400s

Buchanan Origins

Discussing the Buchanans is made more difficult by two factors.

(a) Their last chief died in 1680 – leaving the clan so rudderless that the clan worthies who did remain founded the oldest clan society of all – what is now The Buchanan Society – in 1725 with the admirable purpose of filling in for the lack of a chief by trying to help Buchanans who fell on hard times (see their website at http://www.buchanansociety.com/)

(b) The excessive claims of William Buchanan of Auchmar, writing in 1793 (see online at https://books.google.co.uk/books?id=Ht5EAAAAYAAJ&pg=PP9&redir_esc=y#v=onepage&q&f=false) with no-one in a position to challenge him. Nevertheless by picking these claims apart we may be able to arrive at something near to the truth. [Henceforward I shall refer to him as "Auchmar" to distinguish him from any other Buchanan.]

We may set the scene by noting some of Auchmar's claims that:

- (p.8) in 1010 "Ollaus" was "Viceroy of Norway" – when we know that throughout the period 1000-1015 Norway was run by Eric Haakonson and his brother Swein;
- (p.9) in the same period a Danish general was defeated by "a gentleman called Keith, ancestor of that honourable family" which does not even accord with the Keiths' own version of this fable (the Battle of Barrie is in any case now held to be entirely fictitious) in that they claim that the name Keith derives from the lands given to this champion and not from his name;
- the Keith arms derive from this time – which we can see to be impossible from the comments above;
- the Buchanan progenitor was "Anselan Okyan";
- in 1010 Malcolm II also rewarded this Anselan with the Buchanan arms as we recognise them above;
- Alwyn I earl of Lennox (c1180-1200) was a contemporary of Macolm III (k1093);
- they acquired the Leny Estate in 1363 – although he claimed earlier that The Buchanans had land in Strathyre from 1016(!).

So let us treat Auchmar's work with great circumspection – and more than a pinch of salt.

We can begin to get a good handle on the relevant dates from Gilbert – who had a charter in 1231 and was still alive in 1274. This needs to put his birthdate around 1210 (any later and he would be too young to be infeft, much earlier and he would be unfeasibly old). We can then consider putative dates for the other generations. According to Buchanan, the first nine Buchanan chiefs (with dates which I say must be inferred) are these:

1.	Anselan Okyan	1035	1100
2.	John	1060	1125
3.	Anselan II	1085	1150
4.	Walter	1110	1175
5.	Gerald (or Bernard)	1135	1200
6.	Macbeath	1160	1225
7.	Anselan III	1185	1250
8.	Gilbert	1210	1274<
9.	Sir Maurice	1235	

We need to accommodate these relationships/time pegs:

- Anselan III got a charter for Clar Inch in 1225 – which fits;
- John flourished in the time of Alwyn I Earl of Lennox – so 1180x1200, which does NOT fit!
- Anselan III is reported as witness to a charter at the beginning of the reign of Alexander II (1214-1249), which does fit;
- Anselan III is specified as the son of Macbeath;
- Macbeath is surnamed "Macauslan";
- it was Anselan III who adopted the surname Buchanan;
- Anselan III was described by Malduin of Lennox as "clericus meus".

We can see another problem that the name Anselan is repeated for the third time after 3 intervening generations.

So we need to recast these generations. Given that Surnames were not yet in fashion and given that this family became the Buchanans in the next generation, we should consider "Macbeath Macauslan" here not as a surname, but rather as a patronymic. Thus Macbeath is definitely the son of Anselan II. Thus we may dismiss Walter, Gerald (and Bernard?) as brothers (Auchmar mentions them as co-signatories of a charter by an Alwyn of Lennox), whether of Anselan II or Macbeath and the generational table can be redrawn like this:

1. Anselan "Okyan"	1100	1166
2. John	1122	1188
3. Anselan II	1144	1210
4. Macbeath	1166	1232
5. Anselan III	1188	1254
6. Gilbert	1210	1276
7. Sir Maurice	1235	

In this scenario Anselam Okyan could have been "recompensed" by Malcolm IV (1153-1165), rather than the Malcolm II as claimed. One might presume that the fighting would have been against Somerled.

"Okyan" is generally supposed to be O'Kane, variously O'Cathain. Of this ancestry J Scott Porter, (Belfast, 1856) in "Some Account of the Sept of the O'Cathains of Ciannachta Glinne-Geimhin, now the Okanes of the County of Londonderry (concluded from Vol 3 p272)" says this

> p147 "This last peerage [Dunseverin] is of Mr Buchanan's own creation; no patent for it ever passed the great seal of Ireland; and not one of his other statements is a jot more applicable to the o'Cathains of Ciannachta. Their name is different from that which he assigns to his progenitor; the region they rules does not lie in the southern part of Ulster..... If it were worth while to frame an hypothesis,,,,, I would conjecture that Anselan Okyan (if there ever was such a man) was perhaps a member of the race of Cian, from whom the region of Ciannachta derives its name; and that his proper designation was not O'Cathain.... but O'Cian.... But the whole story appears to me to rest on no tangible foundation."
> (see https://www.jstor.org/stable/20608799)

Yet another explanation of Buchanan origins – presumably aimed at supporting the Auchmar claim, but actually contradicting it is made by John O'Hart (1824–1902) in *Irish pedigrees; or, The origin and stem of the Irish nation*, first published in 1876, Vol I

on p623: regarding O'Cathain/O'Cahan – princes of Limavady, County Londonderry we find

(https://archive.org/stream/irishpedigreesor_01ohar#page/622/mode/2up)

> 102 Conn Cionntach O'Cahan: son of Demod; first assumed this sirname; had a brother named Annselan who was the ancestor of O'Bocainain ("bocain": Irish fairies; "an" one who) anglicised as Buchanan. This Annselan was the first of the family who settled in Scotland.

What is most unfortunate is that it is very difficult to put a date to the adoption of this story by the Buchanans.

http://wc.rootsweb.ancestry.com/cgi-bin/igm.cgi?op=GET&db=ryk_brown&id=I7119

> The late Watson Buchanan (author of "History of Clan Buchanan and Its Septs: A Millenial Update" and a fluent Gaelic speaker), following William Buchanan of Auchmar (1723), cites Anselan as the progenitor of the Scottish family of Buchanan. They suggest that Anselan's surname was Buidh O'Kyan (O'Cathan), meaning "the yellow-haired O'Kyan". The Buchanan surname would be somewhat of an elision of Buidhe O'Cathainan, meaning "one of the yellow O'Cathans", from "buidhe" = "yellow", plus the family name O'Cathan, with the suffix "an" meaning "one of". The name would have been pronounced something like "bwee-oh-cay-an-an", and in that form it is easy to see how it would morph into Buchanan.
>
> Watson Buchanan goes on to note that Anselan is definitely not a Gaelic name. It is derived from the name Anselm (a Norman name meaning "divinely protected" or, literally, "helmet of God"). The name became popular after St. Anselm became Archbishop of Canterbury in 1093......

No Gaelic speaker would give any credence to the attempt to force an origin of the name Buchanan from "Buie o'Cathain". Moreover there is no doubt that Buchanan is geographical for (i) it means "the house of the Canon" and (ii) because early chiefs of that name styled themselves "de Buchanan". [There were no canons in Scotland before the arrival of the Catholic church with St Margaret.]

According to https://en.wikipedia.org/wiki/%C3%93_Cath%C3%A1 Auchmar has shot himself in the foot by anachronism on the basis that the O'Cathains do not make a notable appearance in Irish history before 1138 – well over 100 years after Auchmar claimed they were "Princes". The fact that this timescale is just about feasible with mine can be put down to coincidence!

However O'Hart (I p.623) says of the O'Cahans/O'Cathains, Princes of Limavady Co Londonderry that 96. Conchobhar younger brother of Nial Frasach (718-778) was the ancestor through his son Gruagan and Dungan to Cathan (making his birth still just before 800). But the more interesting point is that this pedigree traces directly back to Muirtertach mac Muiredag whence to Niall of the Nine Hostages. In "Scottish Clans...." I did cite several examples where the surnames quoted (eg in the Monymusk Text) were anachronistic – ie applying to the correct family – but only some generations after the time being discussed.

Auchmar claims (p.23) that Sir Walter Buchanan was described by Robert II (1371-90) as "consanguinous", but in reality this was only by marriage (his wife was Isabella Stuart, daughter of Murdoch Stuart, Duke of Albany and Isabel, Countess of Lennox). But it would be quite bizarre to use this (in subsequent generations) as a basis for association with O'Cahain.

The matter is confused further by an entirely separate line of O'Cathains in Ireland – this one based of Hy-Fodhladha – a district on the Tipperary/Waterford border. [The name Hy-Fodhladha seems really to be a personal/tribal name O'Foley (albeit with geographic implications) – so it would appear that it was a group of people whom the O'Cathain/Keanes ruled over.] These O'Cathains, now generally Keanes appear to descend from the same line as Corc – though from my sources I cannot say that they are direct descendants of Oengus (see O'Hart p803).

So my guess here is that the Buchanans were able to claim an Irish descent truthfully from a marriage to a Luss girl. One way or another they learned of the descent both of the Luss descent and that of the Keane/O'Cathains from the kings of Cashell and decided that to formulate their ancestry in this way would be relatively uncontentious. Auchmar, however, misunderstood the claim, knowing only of the far more famous O'Cathains of Limavady – so when he wrote up the Buchanan ancestry he grafted the line in as best he could.

The moral of this story is that if you are going to lie, you really do have to know your stuff!

The adoption of an Irish origin legend was consistent both in general with the local Gaelic speaking population they came to live amongst and, specifically, with the Earls of Lennox as we have just seen. While it is likely that there was, through marriage, some connection of the general sort alluded to, I can find nothing to link the Buchanans with the line of the O'Cahains even by way of any common ancestor upon whom such a claim could stand up. However the claim could have been invented on the basis of some general acquired knowledge of Irish history without there being a real basis for it.

As we can see my timescale regarding Anselan fits perfectly with Archbishop Anselm – so it looks as if Anselm, as we should now call at least the original "Anselan", came up from England, almost certainly during the time of king David I (so after 1107) – and this would tie in with Auchmar's assertion that there should have been an earlier charter arising from about this time.

Before moving on we should note that until 1621 the Buchanan lands were part of the parish of Luss (NSA VIII p89) – which is pretty surprising on the face of it given the distance and water between – but as noted in "Scottish Clans...." parishes were largely set up on the basis of pre-existing land holdings. Buchanan is close to Cashel. These connections do add strength, therefore, to the idea that Kessog was based at Cashel with a substantial estate comprising also Buchanan and then brought these landholdings to the Luss family when he married into it – the parish connection being a faint echo of this arrangement.

Second we should note that it seems generally agreed that the MacAuslans (in various spellings) form a sept of the Buchanans, nevertheless it is suggested that somehow "McAuslan" is the original surname of the Buchanans (and we can see this in connection with the Auselans mentioned above) – so it appears as if at an early stage while the chiefly family adopted the name Buchanan, other parallel branches took or retained MacAuslan. It is also interesting to note that MacAuslans were to be found in Glen Douglas from very early days.

It is, therefore interesting to consider various MacAuslan arms

MacCasland   **MacAuslan (1)**   **MacAuslan (2)**

Immediately we note the lack of any double tressure. Secondly we note the consistency of the rowel "label" – implying a junior son. Third we note a pheon on two if them. Of the pheon, http://mistholme.com/dictionary/pheon-broad-arrow/ says:

> *The pheon and broad-arrow have the point to chief by Continental default, and point to base by English default; the Society follows the English usage.*

Referring to England it goes on to say:

> As an heraldic charge, the pheon dates from c.1295, in the arms of Egerton [ANA2 416]; but it is more famous as the arms of Sydney, Earl of Leicester, d.1586 [Wagner 70].

Finally we note the scimitar in the MacCasland variant (with a more regular sword in the MacAuslan variant). Auchmar (p.18) asserts that it is the McCasland variation without the labels which is the "original" coat of arms.

I think that the only logical way in which a scimitar would find its way onto a coat of arms would be on the basis that the owner had been on crusade. Bearing in mind the label of juniority we may note that the "raw" arms (Or, a lion rampant sable) are those of the Counts of Flanders. So it looks as if MacAuslan is varied from McCasland by altering the pheon and the sword to be less continental.

I am now, therefore, in a position to propose a wholly new origin for the Buchanans and MacAuslans which has been covered up for over 800 years: a Flemish one.

A Flemish Origin for the Buchanans?

The Wikipedia page for Robert I (c1035-1093) Count of Flanders, son of Baldwin V, lists several children:

- Robert II, Count of Flanders, married Clementia of Burgundy;
- Adela of Flanders († 1115); married firstly King Canute IV of Denmkark, and was the mother of Charles the Good, later Count of Flanders; married secondly Roger Borsa d'Hauteville, Duke of Apulia;
- Gertrude; married firstly Henry III, Count of Leuven and had four children; and secondly Thierry II, Duke of Lorraine, by whom she was the mother of Thierry of Alsace, also later Count of Flanders;
- Philip of Loo, whose illegitimate son William of Ypres was also a claimant to the county of Flanders;
- Ogiva, Abbess of Messines;
- Baldwin († bef. 1080).

while Brian Thompsett who maintains the Royal Genealogy database (frustratingly – and hopefully temporarily – offline late 2017) recognises only three:

Born: ABT 1033, Flanders, Acceded: 1071   Died: 3 OCT 1093
Married 1063 to Gertrude of Saxony,

- Child 1: Robert II of Jerusalem, Count of Flanders
- Child 2: Adela of Flanders, b. ABT 1026
- Child 3: Gertrude of Flanders

I am sceptical of the idea that Count Robert would name his first son after himself and then, almost as an afterthought, name his third son after his own father.

I am tempted, therefore, by the idea that Robert's son Baldwin was actually illegitimate and sired before his marriage (so born say c1055). By the time of young Baldwin's death, which we are told was before 1080 – let us say 1078 – he would have been 27 and well able to have sired children of his own – legitimately or otherwise. Any such son (probably called Robert and born say bc1070) left fatherless and without immediate prospects, even if maintained by his grandfather, would face problems. As a young knight he could well have taken part in the first crusade (1095-1098).

Later-to-be-Archbishop Anselm was born in Italy (c1033); he became a monk in 1060 rising quickly to be elected Prior of Bec in 1063, then Abbot in 1078. According to the Encyclopedia Britannica "Under Anselm's direction, Bec became the foremost seat of learning in Europe..." attracting a wide range of students. [He became Archbishop of Canterbury in 1093, holding the post until his death in 1109. He also travelled widely.]

So it is far from impossible that the "Robert" I am proposing could have come under Anselm's influence (eg studying at Bec as a teenager) sufficient for him to name a son after him. The child, Anselm, would probably have been born soon after the return from the Crusade – so around 1100.

Of course this is only one scenario (which I hope the reader will find feasible) to give the general idea. What is left out is any evidence (beyond the heraldry) and any idea as to how "Robert" or Anselm would come to the attention of King David I.

Conclusions

- The time scale suggests that the original Anselm settled in Scotland at the behest of David I
- The name suggests sponsorship by Anselm, quondam Archbishop of Canterbury
- The arms suggest a continental origin, probably connected to the Counts of Flanders
- The arms suggest participation in the crusades
- The "O'Kyan" claim is parallel to that if the Lennoxes, the Colquhouns and the Forbeses (see below). As for a male line ancestry it is false. But it would be vindicated in part if there were a marriage into the Scottish Royal family, co-descended as it is with the O'Cathains from Eoghan, son of Niall of the Nine Hostages.
- Marriage into the family of Luss would confer a lineage back (i) to Corc, whence eventually to Heber via St Kessog and (ii) to Connaire Mor via Loarn and Cairbre Riada – but no evidence is offered.

7. THE CLAN FORBES

This appendix would not be complete without a discussion about the true origins of the Clan Forbes. As we shall see their connections with the Lennox and the families we have discussed should not be overlooked any longer.

Meaning of the Name.

We should begin also by understanding how to say the name. Most people today say "FORBs", but properly the "e" should be sounded, so that it is more like "FORB-uss" (the stress is still on the first part).

There is no satisfactory Pictish explanation, but if one assumes a Gaelic origin then it is possible to parse the word to *forb-* and *-ais*. "Ais" we can understand as an overnight stopping place for cattle or pack-horse drovers etc. and "Forb" means a glebe (land belonging to a church) or proprietor's land (ie not let out). Thus it means "The Church land where drovers (cattle, pack horses etc.) could stop overnight" and so the name is in essence geographical (like Colquhoun).

The fact that we have this Gaelic placename in a very Pictish setting is potentially troubling. However not only were many of the missionaries Gaelic, but this place may only have acquired its religious status well after the end of the separate kingdoms of the Picts. So while I cannot give a definitive justification for the apparent anomaly, I do not regard it as too problematic. Readers must make up their own minds.

The Arms

Forbes Arms

Forbes Crest

The arms are defined as Azure, three Bears heads couped two and one Argent, muzzled Gules. As we can see immediately this is the same as the Galbraith Arms with the colours reversed.

The Crest is a Stag's head attired with ten tines proper. There are 12 other clans featuring deer's heads of one sort or another. The Forbes's is exactly the same as that of Rollo and close to that of Gordon (which is head-on rather than in profile). As we can see it is close to that of Colquhoun.

The Motto is: "Grace Me Guide"; it is interesting that it is in English (not Gaelic or Latin or French). There is nothing really close, but it is interesting in its apparent passivity, which I think makes it somewhat resonant of the Galbraiths' and very much unlike many others.

The fact that the Forbes' arms have the inverse colours of Galbraith suggest vassalage rather than cadetship; on the other hand several Galbraith cadets show far greater variance. So we should conclude that the progenitor of the Forbes was either a younger son or a son-in-law of the Galbraith chief.

The supporters of the Forbes Arms are two bloodhounds in the same colours as the bears on the arms. This is a two-way parallel with the Colqhouns. Regrettably we have no idea what the Galbraiths may have had.

Original Land

The Forbeses spread quite widely over the highlands, but they take their name from the Parish of Forbes – shown as the relatively small dotted part on the map below. This is the first bit of land they were able to call their own (and hence the name). Although the chief would have lived in this bit (probably close to the church) I am pretty sure that they also got the bit of land up to the dotted line – roughly half of the area outlined on the map and it may have comprised the whole of that area.

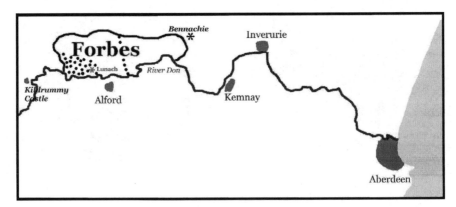

Original Forbes Territory

The area is about 10 miles across, maybe half that north to south. But this very much the "core" territory only. Later the clan was to be heavily represented twice as far to the west and considerably further to the north and west also. Unfortunately there is nothing left of any original "big house", but this may be because it was not long before they had built a castle at (old) Druminnor, 7 miles to the North just over the hill on extra land they had acquired.

The Tryst (where the clan met to prepare for battle) was at Culquhonnie Castle just East of the village of Strathdon and close to Invernochty Castle, but I think that this was later because....

The War Cry is 'Lunach!' and so I think that this was the original tryst (marked with an Asterisk on the map) and confirming the place of the original "seat".

I am grateful to Alex Forbes of Druminnor (Old Druminnor was the original Castle Forbes) for advising me that the area called Forbes is adjacent to but definitely not part of "the Garioch".

When they started:

According to http://forbesclan.com/main.html

> "The Forbeses are Celtic and have held the duthus of Forbes from the time when O'Conochar "killed the bear" which had made the Braes of Forbes uninhabitable. John of Forbes, first of the name, figured in the reign of King William the Lion (1143-1214) when the duthus of Forbes was feudalized."

Unfortunately bears were extinct in Scotland by about 1000 AD. One source puts the date of the bear back to 775, but this is when there were no Scots in the area and, as we have seen the name cannot be parsed except in Gaelic. Also there were no surnames in Scotland before about 1100. So this does not work at all.

The reader will have spotted immediately the similarity between "O'Conochar" and the "Conoch" of Colquhoun myth – further tying the Forbeses to a Lennox origin. In practice the only person this could be a reference to is Conchobar mac Nessa, king of Ulster. The snag here is that he was older than Cu Chulainn who belongs to the period BC (Cu Chulain's death is given as 1AD in the Ulster Annals). For this to be relevant the Forbes (and hence, I suppose, the Colquhouns) would need to be able to claim a decent from Conchobar. It is, of course, possible that the family of Luss from before the time of Arthur might be descended from him – and whether or not they were actually so descended it is more than possible that they may have laid claim to such an ancestry. One must assume some intermarriage between the Luss family and the Galbraiths – indeed it would be very surprising had there not been such a liaison immediately following the installation of the Galbraiths as viceroys of the Lennox. As we know already the male line of Luss following the annexation was through St Kessog and his father Oengus mac Nad Froich to Corc – Munster rather than Ulster. But we need to beare in mind also the ancestry of the original Luss family through Cairbre Riada to Connaire. So for the Forbeses as for the Colquhouns this would be a very tortuous line (ie far from the direct male line they were trying to persuade people to infer) – and nothing to do with a bear.

However we can indeed see a great need for this legend. The Forbes were right in the heart of Caledonian territory. Had they gone around boasting about how his ancestors had thrashed the Caledonians 500 years earlier, they would not have lasted long!

King Alexander III gave Duncan Forbes a charter in 1271 – which is early (significantly before eg the Gordons). From this is clear that the surname had already been adopted and, therefore, that the family was already established there. There are claims for an earlier date – from the reign of William the Lion (so pre-1214). This would be too early for a Colquhoun connection (and in the case of the Colquhouns we see that there is no reference to bears), but if we assume that the Colquhoun legends stem from a date after their acquisition of Luss and that there had indeed been an early Luss/Galbraith marriage then the claim is feasible. It would also be consistent with the history of the Garioch referred to above.

Why they were there

I find the coincidence of David Earl of Huntingdon being Earl of Lennox and Lord of the Garioch too much to pass over. I am confident that it was through his agency that the Forbes progenitor moved to Donside from the Lennox. This would put the move into the period 1190-1214 (assuming it was during the reign of William the Lion as claimed – 1219 otherwise). The timescale would suggest that the Forbes progenitor was a son or son-on-law of Gillescop Galbraith, son of Gillechrist, the first chief of the name. We should note that Gillescop's wife was a daughter of Alwyn I, Earl of Lennox – for whom, as we have seen, pedigree fabrication was already an issue. We cannot specify an immediate relationship with the Luss family – except that we have seen that Alwyn II's first wife was from it. It is possible to argue for an earlier generation, but I think that unlikely because of the Arms. It is unlikely that Galbraiths would have adopted arms more than say two generations earlier – indeed it is quite possible that several Galbraith families were yet to adopt them at all.

So the land of Forbes lay within the Earldom of Mar. Earl Morgrund, who, it seems did not enjoy a good relationship with the crown had died in 1183. His successor was Gillechrist (who died in 1203) so it is most likely that the move occurred in his lifetime, but the next Earl was Duncan, son of Morgrund. Duncan seems to have had a good relationship with King William the Lyon.

We should also note, however, that David Earl of Huntingdon was also a great benefactor of the church and insofar as this was or may have been church land we should not exclude the possibility that the first Forbes' job was to defend the church's rights (and income!) from the Earls of Mar.

So the reader can see that while I feel confident in providing reasonably accurate trails for all the elements in the back-story and memorabilia, leaving also quite small windows of doubt about the precise details of the move of the Forbes' progenitor (apparently John of Forbes) to Donside.

CONCLUSION

The way in which so many families have felt the need to fabricate their family trees reflects the difficulties they had as incomers and foreigners in exercising control over the local population. At least in broad terms the nature of the fabrications, once understood, support the general thesis advanced in this book.

APPENDIX 3: ST SERF AND OTHERS

1. LIFE OF ST SERF

Introduction

In order to understand Arthur's life and times it has been necessary to place St Kentigern. While we have identified the Serf/Serguan who served as Kentigern's stepfather we should not pass up the opportunity to dismiss the idea that Kentigern could have been linked to St Serf/Servanus. So in this appendix we will examine the life of St Serf and what has been said about him and then add some depth and context.

[Throughout this work I have made many references to Wikipedia. I understand how dangerous a game this is to play – but it has improved and knowing some of the people so largely responsible for writing some of the pages, I have been judicious. We should observe an extreme example of the need for great caution with regard to Wikipedia whose page about St Serf (as of March 2017) is unreconstructed nonsense. After this book is published I will try to make an attempt to modify it, but there is a cadre of wilful idiots who undo changes of this sort!]

We can start by noting that one opportunity for confusion has been two Pictish kings called Nechtan – one with a reign 595-616 and the other reigning 706-724 and again in 728-9. Further down we shall note the confusion wrought by there having been two Pictish kings both called Angus mac Fergus, the first reigning 729x761, the second 820x34.

In "Scottish Clans....." and elsewhere in this volume I identified many circumstances in which major players in Scottish History found it politic to fabricate their history – the truth being inconvenient for one reason or another. After the younger MacMalcolms had come to the throne it was not clever to admit that your ancestor had killed Duncan II – or Malcolm III; once Orkney and Shetland were Scottish it was not a good idea to celebrate a Viking ancestry; if you had a right by primogeniture to the Scottish throne but you did not want to be king, then it made sense to invent an alternative ancestry; if you were an immigrant, no matter how illustrious, it made a great deal of sense to create a "bona fide" Scottish ancestry. And so on.

All this is understandable; the problem is that the lies have stuck and today, hundreds of years later, they have continued to be believed. So also within Scottish academia generally: there is a wholly irrational desire to attribute Gaelic explanations where Pictish/Welsh, Brythonnic and Anglo-Saxon explanations represent reality. This leads to fictions being perpetuated – whether by naive wish and resultant myopia or by wilful lying.

The story of the spread of Christianity into Scotland has been subject to the very same pressures. Over time it was variously in several people's interests to invent, promulgate and maintain fictions – lies – to bolster their own position.

- The Catholic Church wanted to diminish the importance of anyone who was not "one of them"; often true stories were mangled to suit ITS narrative.

- Especially from the time of David I the nascent Scottish Nation badly wanted home-grown explanations, especially those which excluded English ones.

- Especially post-Reformation the established church did not want to credit Rome with anything more than it had to.

Such is the political climate today that there is still little appetite for the truth.

In this context so strong is the continuing desire to believe the absurd stories about St Kentigern promulgated by the monk Jocelyn of Furness at the behest of Bishop Jocelyn of Glasgow in the 1100s that all over the internet it is still possible to find a credulity about the life of St Serf which defies rationality. The matter of the life of St Kentigern has been dealt with already, but setting matters straight with regard to St Serf is a task worthy enough in itself and represents a useful bit of further ground clearing in unravelling the truth about Kentigern. The opportunity thus afforded will be taken to place various other characters who appear in and around the associated legends into a more rational context.

His Life before his arrival in Scotland

The anonymously written manuscript *Vita Sancti Servani* ("The Life of St Serf") dates from the 1150s. Curiously it lives side by side with the life of St Kentigern which it contradicts! It was freshly translated by Dr Alan MacQuarrie, who published in the *Innes Review* of the Autumn of 1993: Volume 44 No 2 pp122-152. This paper is readily available online.

As it stands it would be easy to discard it as evident rubbish. But if we are careful to sift through and if we compare the claims with what else we know of the secular history of the time, we may form quite a useful understanding of what actually went on.

Let us begin by summarising the main chapters of St Serf's life leading to his arrival in Fife:

- He was born the son of the King of Canaan and named Malachi (= "my angel/messenger") as well as Serf/Servanus (evidently, therefore, a translation);
- His father died when he was seven years old;
- At the age of 13 he became a monk – leaving his brother to take the crown;
- At the age of 30 he became a priest;
- Soon(?) thereafter he became the Bishop of the Canaanites to whom he ministered for 20 years;
- He then spent 7 years as Patriarch in Jerusalem;
- Travelling, he spent three years in Constantinople before leaving for Rome;
- In Rome he was elected Pope and reigned for 7 years before abdicating to come to Scotland.

According to this story he was, therefore, about 70 years of age (or more!) when he reached the Firth of Forth. However there is, of course, no reason to place any credence whatsoever on any part of this nonsense.

Dating the arrival

According to the Vita, at the beginning of his ministry in Fife he had discussions with Adamnan (in his role as Abbot of Iona) and Bruide map Der-Ilei as King of the Picts. So let us consider the feasibility of this:

Name	Position	Assumed office	Died
Adamnan	Abbot of Holy Isle	679	704
Bridei map Der-Ilei	King of Picts	695/7	705/6

As can be seen the dates for Bridei's reign are in minor dispute, but this is trivial. What we can see is that there is a window of time which allows Serf to have had discussions with both these important figures – broadly 695-704.

As we can see the Vita claims that his post immediately before his journey to Fife was as Pope. There was, of course, no Pope Servanus, but now that we have a fairly precise date to work from, let us examine the roll of Popes from that era:

Pope	Date of Election	Date of Death
John V	685	686
Conon	686	687
Sergius	687	701
John VI	701	705
John VII	705	707

Immediately our attention is drawn to Sergius – born in Sicily about 650, elected as Pope aged 37 and dying aged about 51. So it is quite possible that the anonymous author conflated the arrival of Serf in Scotland with the death of Pope Sergius which he had misunderstood as resignation, giving us an even more precise date for Serf's arrival in Fife as 701/702.

There is, however, a major problem with this pre-Scotland biography for Serf in that almost exactly the same story is told of a St Boniface. For a discussion of this see below – the section on St Curetan.

My assumption is that this "front end" of Serf's life was tacked on to explain (a) that he was a foreigner and (b) that he was already an older man when he arrived – and why, therefore, his mission is Scotland was a short one (I conclude that he was already dead by 710, see below). It may even be that Serf was the same age as the Pope Sergius (and so early 50s on arrival and c60 when he died) – which seems more likely than the 70+ implied by his back story (above).

St Serf's activity in Scotland

MacQuarrie's translation of the *Vita* runs to just over 8 pages; of this, the section discussing his mission to Scotland is not more than four, including substantial footnoting – altogether under 1200 words.

He was met on arrival by Adamnan who assigned to him "the land of Fife, from the Hill of the Britons to the Ochil Hills". Places mentioned as having been visited by him include Kinneil, Culross, Lochleven, Dysart, Tullibody, Tillicoutry, Alva, Airthrey, and Dunning (where he died). The *Vita* is very specific in stating that Serf himself chose the site at Culross for his base and that it was virgin territory – thus rendering impossible the contortionist efforts of James E Fraser (*"From Caledonia to Pictland"* p 254 &c) to suggest that an earlier St Serf – or indeed anyone else, sainted or otherwise – had first occupied that site. [For further discussion of this see discussion of Kentigern in Part 4.]

Why Serf came to Culross

I was very surprised by what I came to understand as Serf's mission. For this we have to recognise the politics – both clerical and lay – of the era.

Background 1 – Tides in Religion

Christianity was already present (albeit quite tenuously) in Strathclyde and amongst the Picts of Galloway in the time of St Patrick (ie pre-500), gaining a foothold in Lothian in the early 500s under British influence (see chapters on Arthur). Dalriada and the kingdom of the Picts came under serious Christian influence in the time of Columba (c563-597). Starting in Inverness it spread South and East.

- Edwin of Northumbria (king c616 – c632) was converted to Christianity in 627 due to Southern influences,
- but it was to Iona that his successor Oswald (king 634-642) turned very soon into his reign to establish the centre at Lindisfarne, installing Aidan as the first bishop. [This should come as no surprise as Oswald had spent his formative years in exile north of the Antonine Wall.]
- It was Oswald's brother Oswiu (king 642-670), also a previous exile, who convened the Synod of Whitby in 644. It was as a result of this synod, particularly the influence of St Wilfrid speaking there that Oswiu turned away from Iona in favour of Canterbury and Rome.
- Bede ("Eccl. Hist." v. 15. 2 Ibid. v. 15, 21) tells us that in 688 on a visit to Aldfrith (king of Northumbria 685-704) Adamnan was convinced of the primacy of Roman rule and practices, but was very much less than generally successful in seeking thereafter to convince Christians under his aegis of this. Robert H Story ("The Church of Scotland, past and present: its history, its relation to the law and the state, its doctrine, ritual, discipline, and patrimony" 1890 (Volume 1) p205) suggests that this was before 692. [Bishop Ceolfrid of Jarrow (tenure 674-716) later reminded King Nechtan of Adamnan's views in a letter.]

Background 2 – Tides in Politics

- While we tend to see conquest as necessarily including the replacement of the ruling families/apparatus, even in British imperial times much of the empire was controlled by leaving the existing structure in place whenever it was willing to pay homage and taxes to their new overlords. And so it was, clearly, with the Picts. The increasing power of the Angles of Northumbria in general – and Bernicia in particular – over the Picts is perhaps best illustrated by the fact that the Pictish king Talorgan (ruled 653-657) was the son of Eanfrith sometime, albeit briefly, Anglian king of Bernicia. Bede claims that it was Oswiu (642-670) who largely brought the Picts under his sway.

- In 671 the Picts took the opportunity of what they saw as the power vacuum created by Oswiu's death to launch an attempt to wrest independence back from the Angles; but this effort was misjudged, for they had not reckoned with the Lothian strongman Beornhaeth. The result was that the Bernicians took more active control of Fife in particular. One aspect of the assertion of control was the establishment in 681 of Trumwine as the Bishop of a new see of the Picts based at Abercorn – an interesting choice of site with a clear escape route South!

- By 685 the Picts had regrouped – Bridei son of Bili had been king since 672 – and inflicted a heavy defeat on the Angles at Dun Nechtain (Dunnichen in Angus). This was followed up by another victory in 698 in which Berhtred, son of Beornhaeth fell (Fraser p254).

- The result of this was that the Picts not only regained all the ground they had lost, but, given that Trumwine felt that he had to flee Abercorn, we may suppose that they at least raided much of what we recognise today as the Lothians. Fraser suggests that this may have been as late as 698 and, if so, this adds detail by further reducing the time window for St Serf.

- Despite the size of this victory, it would appear that Angles remained entrenched in the Lothians with their northern base at Dunbar. As we shall see the Picts appeared not to try to hold any territory South of the Antonine Wall. Lothian became a sort of buffer state governed by Berhtfrith grandson of Beornhaet and son of Berhtred. [In 711 Berhtfrith, acting as regent for the child-king Osred, was to defeat the Picts probably somewhere in the Falkirk/Stirling area but there does not seem to have been any territorial implication (http://en.wikipedia.org/wiki/Osred_I_of_Northumbria).]

[At this point it is well to reinforce the intense frustration of myself and my friends regarding the blind spot within the Scottish Academic community already referred to above. There is an illogical tendency to try to take everything back to Gaelic. Here for Fife, as with the Lothians we see the intrusion of Anglic influence directly onto Pictish communities. Thus in seeking to understand eg placenames the attempt to resort to Gaelic for an explanation or to assume that a Gaelic form ante-dated a Scots/English form is futile (cf my "Scottish Clans: Legend Logic & Evidence" Vol. ii Ch. C1) Even where something or some place is recorded in eg Irish Annals, it is well to suppose that the forms used are a Gaelicisation of a non-Gaelic original.]

So by 698 we have the situation that Adamnan is bent on Romanising Scotland. He hoped that influence would come from every quarter. With regard to south east Pictland he had been relying on Bernician influence based at Abercorn. Now that this was lost and with very frosty relations between the Angles and the Picts, he needed a new tactic and a new champion for his cause on the North shores of the Forth.

Enter St Serf.......

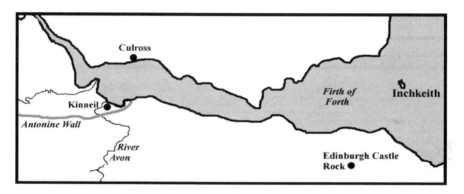

Firth of Forth

How Serf came to and settled in Culross

- The Vita tells us that Adamnan welcomed Serf to Scotland at Inchkeith.

First we should not be surprised that he and his party arrived by sea. Even hundreds of years later the seas were the highways in Britain generally – even more so throughout Scotland. Second we do not know whether the Picts or the Angles had any claim over the island but Adamnan would surely have had a free hand in either case. Like Inchmickery and Inchcolm (and especially the Bass Rock where St Baldred (d. 757) is recorded as living so nearly contemporaneously) it is far from unlikely that these were already in church hands for hermits and/or for burials. There would have been no problem with a landfall in Lothian as the Bernicians were fully on board with Adamnan's intentions, so a whole host of harbours were potentially available. Thus we must assume that Inchkeith was a matter of choice rather than of any real necessity.

- From Inchkeith the party sailed to Kinneil.

The choice of this site was no accident. Kinneil is ON the Antonine Wall..... on the northern side. Had there been any hostility it would have been a matter of a few hundred yards and the party would have been in Bernician territory, under Bernician protection. Given that this was not an armed group, there would have been no real pretext for any pursuit, but they landed without Pictish royal permission so it was better to be safe than sorry.

- From Kinneil Serf saw Culross and decided to settle there

The Vita said that he "cast his staff" across the water and this gives rise to derision – and yes it is nearly 3 miles. But he may well have pointed his staff; we are familiar with "casting one's eye" on something and this is never normally interpreted literally, so I recommend some pedants to get a life! When Serf reached Culross, which, we are told, was a virgin site and so needed clearing, news got to king Bridei and the wisdom of making landfall at Kinneil became clear! Bridei was not pleased and proposed to kill Serf and his team. The Vita says that this was merely because he had no permission; what Bridei's real motivation was we can but guess. In the end Bridei was, however, won round and not only was Serf allowed to carry on with Culross, he was also given the island in Loch Leven. Macquarrie is of the view that the idea of Serf meeting with Adamnan at that island is really no more than a duplication of the Inchkeith meeting anecote. But I see no reason for this. Given that Serf was on a task for Adamnan the idea of plural meetings is far from having been out of order.

- Adamnan allocated Serf his territory

That Serf was there to do a specific job for Adamnan is no better illustrated than by the way he was allocated an area just as sales reps are today. The Vita specifies that Serf's "patch" was "the land of Fife from the Hill of the Britons to the Ochil Hills". We can see from the places mentioned in the Vita it is clear that Serf stuck to his job, notwithstanding that it is far from clear where the "Hill of the Britons" may have been. [It probably represents the most Easterly point of Strathclyde somewhere in the Lennox or Kilsyth Hills.] Indeed the fact that there is no mention of anywhere North of the Lomond Hills of Fife or West or South of Stirling reinforces the idea that Serf's ministry was short and that he was working outwards from his Culross base.

What St Serf did

It is not my purpose to replicate the Vita here. The text is readily available and it is for readers to decide for themselves what to make of the various anecdotes. What I have sought to do is to show the "when" and the "why", thereby to understand Serf's mission and to complete his dissociation from Kentigern.

2. THE CONTEXT

So much for the life and times of St Serf, but so confused has all this been that there are many with a smattering of knowledge in this area who may be tempted to say "Ah.... but what about...." and then bring up some potentially tangential issue which may appear to contradict what I have offered. The biggest of these is the matter of St Kentigern and we have dealt with him above. But there are many other figures/issues and so here follows a miscellany. We can get our retaliation in first, disarm the "What about" ers – and demonstrate that with a proper understanding we can resolve the contradictions.

1. St Curetan "Boniface"

We should begin by noting that the nickname/soubriquet (or adopted name) "Boniface" does not imply any pleasing appearance ("bonny face"), but rather implies the intention to "do good deeds" (from the Latin *bonus* and *facere*).

As noted above the "front end" of the story of St Serf is also attributed to "St Boniface" (see Story Vol. 1 pp 210/1) . In that version of the legend, Serf is just one of Boniface's retinue.

The important thing to note here about these tales of Boniface is that they claim to belong to the era of king Bruide's brother and successor:

| Nechtan map Der-Ilei | King of Picts | 706-724 & 728-729 |

They are normally linked to the date 710 when Nechtan sent word to Jarrow to ask for guidance in religious matters – resulting in a mission as a result of which a church (rather than/reforming the "kil" previously set up by St Kenneth at the behest of Columba) was established at what is now St Andrews. The question then arises as to why Nechtan would have felt the need to seek such advice; the conclusion I draw is that Serf was already dead by this date.

For the sake of completeness we should consider also, therefore, the eras of various Popes called Boniface:

Pope	Date of Election	Death
St Boniface I	418	422
Boniface II	530	532
Boniface III	607	607
St Boniface IV	608	615
Boniface V	619	625
Boniface VI	896	896
Boniface VII	974 & 984	985
Boniface VIII	1294	1303

As we can see there is no Pope Boniface who could possibly "fit the bill".

But Story also alludes to another version of the "Boniface" legend where the protagonist is really called Albanus Kiritanus (St Curetan). This story is not without its problems either, as www.catholic.org gives the date of his death as 660 – even before the synod of Whitby! www.celticsaints.org says that despite dying in 630 he was active in the 700s! It also claims he was born in Italy. The idea that Curetan could have been the leader of a mission from Jarrow to king Nechtan in 710 can be ruled out completely when we appreciate that he was already abbot/bishop of Ross, based in Rosemarkie on the Black Isle, in 697 (whence/when he attended the Synod of Birr).

Thus we may be confident that no-one called Boniface of any other note could have led the 710 mission. If one wanted to be kind to the hagiographers, one might presume that the intrusion of a Boniface into these stories was a misplaced reference to the influence (but NOT the presence – he had died two years previously) of Pope Boniface V in the conversion of Edwin king of Northumbria (in 627).

There is, however, a possible solution: Nechtan may have sent Curetan/Boniface TO Jarrow to get the advice needed first hand – and he could well have returned with a large retinue including at least some of those mentioned in the fabulous stories.

While Adomnan was having his own difficulties securing the agreement of his monks on Iona and was the dynamic figure, generating change in Pictland, it was Curetan/Boniface, who is described as "bishop" who essentially had the principal rank within the church in Pictland. Not only that, but is seems that Curetan outlived Adomnan, if only for a few years. So it is not so unreasonable to suggest that in theory, St Serf came to be one of Boniface's team. Thus we can resolve the dichotomy – Serf did not arrive in Pictland WITH any 'Boniface', but he did serve "under" him.

2. The foundation of Abernethy: Nechtan and Der Lugdach

Regarding the Pictish king Nechtan grandson of Uerb, AO Anderson (*Early Sources*, pp. cxx–cxxi) quotes Skene's *Chronicles of the Picts & Scots*. regarding the foundation of Abernethy (in Fife):

> "So Nectonius the Great, Uuirp's son, the king of all the provinces of the Picts, offered to Saint Brigid, to the day of judgement, Abernethy, with its territories ...

> Now the cause of the offering was this. Nectonius, living in a life of exile, when his brother Drest expelled him to Ireland, begged Saint Brigid to beseech God for him. And she prayed for him, and said: "If thou reach thy country, the Lord will have pity on thee. Thou shalt possess in peace the kingdom of the Picts."

The local legend is, furthermore that Der Lugdach, the Abbess of Kildare who followed St Brigit directly came over in person to establish the site.

The Nechtan to whom this appears to apply is generally credited with the dates 456-480 – when Brigit herself was very much alive (indeed it is not clear that she had even founded the monastery at Kildare by this time), so there is no room here for Der Lugdach. Moreover this is a time, 100 years before Columba and when the conversion of Ireland itself had barely started. Had this Nechtan embraced Christianity in the way implied, Scotland would have been a very different place; the mission of St Columba would have been unnecessary and would have taken a very different course. So we may discount this first King Nechtan.

We should also notice that the reign of Nechtan son of Der-Ilei, to whom we have already made reference, covers the period 706 – 729. Given his other activities it is possible to conceive that it was he who was responsible. There is no doubt, however, that we do have the names of the relevant abbesses of Kildare for this period, so any connection with Der Lugdach can be discounted. Moreover the monastery was a bastion for the Culdees, while Nechtan son of Der-Ilei was very much trying to support Roman practices and thinking. So we may discount this King Nechtan.

And so we are left with the remaining Nechtan. It is not seriously questioned that St Brigit died in the 520s, while this Nechtan's reign covers the period 595-616. It is clearly not feasible that the next abbess would still be in post – and capable of such travel (from Kildare to Abernethy) – 70 or more years later. However if we look at the list of Abbesses of Kildare (see Wikipedia) we find some 25 of them following Brigit covering the period to 1171. Of these the first 5 are:

- Brigit ingen Dubthaig, d. either 521, 524, or 526
- Abbesses of unknown death year alleged to have followed Brigit
  ◦ Der Lugdach, commemorated 1 February
  ◦ Comnat, commemorated 1 January
  ◦ Tuilclath, commemorated 6 January•
- Gnáthnat (or Gnáthat), d. 690
- Sébdann ingen Cuirc, d. 732

If we consider the abbesses from Gnáthnat onwards, we find that they served an average of some 23 years each in post. Applying this average over the whole period from 526 (the latest date for Brigit's death) to 690 (the death of Gnáthnat) we have 164 years – so we should expect there to have been some seven abbesses when only four are named. Clearly there are variations (we see that that Sébdann ingen Cuirc served for 42 years) but we may be confident that there are missing names.

If, then, we assume that the missing abbesses are those immediately following Brigit and if we apply the 23 year average then we find that it is likely that Der Lugdach's died sometime in the period 615x20. Thus

- She could indeed have been broadly contemporaneous with King Nechtan;
- This Nechtan's reign follows the period of St Columba who spent time in this Tayside area of Pictland;
- The Bridei who accepted Columba was Nechtan's predecessor-but-one and had died a decade before Nechtan came to power, so we should have every reason to suppose that this Nechtan did have some positive connection with Christianity;
- She could also have been a contemporary of Pope Boniface IV

While it is true that even today people in crisis ask friends and even prelates to pray for them, if we understand the reference in the chronicle to mean that Nechtan sought the intercession of St Brigit, it would have been more likely that this would have occurred after her death, as with most saints. And this could easily have occurred with the assistance of Der Lugdach.

There was a king of Strathclyde of the same name and the eras of their reigns overlap – the modern fashion is to suppose that these two were one and the same person. This analysis shows this idea to be false – if only on the basis that there would have been no need to go so far away as Ireland for exile. [There are other political objections which need not concern us here.]

Today many people may be tempted to assume that an abbess would be busy running her nunnery – too busy to be making such a long journey eg to Abernethy. However such an objection is easily set aside when one considers the life and activities of other abbots such as Columba, Cuthbert and, perhaps even more so, Adamnan who was so at odds with his own monks after he accepted Roman supremacy that he spent very little time indeed on Iona and so, as we have seen, was able to meet Serf at Inchkeith and commune with him later at Loch Leven.

To summarise: It is reasonable to suppose that it was the king Nechtan who was contemporary with Pope Boniface IV who was responsible for the foundation of Abernethy; there is no strong basis for discounting the influence of Der Lugdach, Abbess of Kildare. On the contrary, what this analysis suggests is that it is the list of Abbesses of Kildare which is deficient, particularly with regard to Brigit's immediate successors, of which there are likely to be 2, 3 or 4 missing. It seems clear that, when he was busy scribing, the Pictish Chronicler had the wrong Nechtan in his mind. We may conclude that when Serf arrived Abernethy was a Culdee centre of Celtic Christianity and that Adamnan's purpose for Serf included diminishing its sway.

This also provides the basis for understanding yet another conflation, for it was, as we have seen, a different Nechtan (map Der-Ilei) who had dealings with a different Boniface (not a pope but St Curetan) which then provided the opportunity for the hagiographer to get his story all mixed up.

3. Triduana

The same clerics seemed unable to make up their minds whether it was St Boniface or St Regulus who led the clerical invasion. However (ironically, as will become evident) we can see our way through this mess by considering St Triduana.

Let us begin by considering her name – which has been so problematic that it has been rendered as Trewell, Tredwell, Tradwell, Trodlin(e) and Trøllhaena! We may parse this name as *þrȳð* = 'strength' (OE) and wunna = blissfulness (OHG). From this we may draw the conclusions (i) that this is likely the name she adopted on taking Holy Orders rather than her birth name and (ii) that the name is Anglo-Saxon in origin (and so we may set to one side the suggestion that she was from Colosse or Constantinople (as in the Aberdeen Breviary)!)

Second we are told that she accompanied St Serf – whether in the retinue of St Boniface (described as 'mythical' by David Farmer in "The Oxford Dictionary of Saints", St Regulus or 'merely' with St Serf. [Alternatively we might interpret the words as implying that she arrived with St Andrew's bones – but this turns out not to be correct for which see below.]

Third we should note a story told about her: "Prince" Nechtan was clearly attracted to her, telling her she had beautiful eyes. Triduana's response was to pluck her eyes out and send them to Nechtan. For my purposes the veracity of this story is irrelevant, what is interesting is the nature of this exchange – clearly one between two young people. Thus we should probably understand "Prince Nechtan" to imply a time before 705 when Nechtan became "king". This then ties Triduana closely to St Serf, reinforcing the idea that this mission came from Bernicia at the behest of Adomnan.

Triduana seems to have made her base at Rescobie, but dedications to her stretch all the way up the east coast to Ballachly in Caithness and Papa Westray in the Orkneys. However at some stage she seems to have felt the need to leave Pictland, as her last base, where she died, was at what is now Restalrig in Edinburgh – safe in Bernician/Anglian hands.

She was clearly far from a child in 700, so let us suppose a birth date for her c670, hence retirement to Restalrig perhaps c730, or earlier if by necessity. Likely occasions would have been 724 and 729 when Nechtan ceased to be king.

Triduana became the go-to Saint for anything to do with the eyes, especially blindness, but it is far from clear when Triduana was linked to eyes specifically in this way. I suspect that it may started with Nechtan's admiration for hers (and especially given how widely she travelled I am sure she did not pluck them out!) and was reinforced in mediaeval times by a supposed miracle healing of Bishop John in Caithness who sought her intercession after maltreatment by King William the Lyon.

Above I used the word "probably" – for although I like the idea that she arrived with St Serf (probably, as we have seen 701/2) it is possible that she did come up from Jarrow with St Curetan/Boniface in 710. In these circumstances we should understand "Prince" in reference to Nechtan quite loosely (but so loose is the rest of the story that we should not necessarily be too determined to place reliance on this terminology).

See also

http://weewhitehoose.co.uk/myth-folklore/triduana/

http://www.caithness.org/atoz/churches/ballachly/

Among dedications to her we may note:

Place	Latitude	Longitude
Triduana Papa Westray	59°20'29.36"N	2°53'13.65"W
Triduana Ballachly	58°23'2.01"N	3°22'53.30"W
Croit Trolla, Dunbeath	58°15'12.82"N	3°26'16.95"W
Cinn Trola Broch	58° 2'54.72"N	3°48'52.78"W
Kintradwell	58° 2'35.12"N	3°49'38.39"W
Kennethmont (Trewel Fair)	57°20'52.69"N	2°45'30.63"W
Cairntradlin	57°12'56.62"N	2°17'52.86"W
Rescobie (ch. & St Trodlin's Fair)	56°39'23.08"N	2°48'30.79"W
Restalrig	55°57'28.59"N	3° 8'57.79"W

4. St Andrews and St Andrew

One does – or should – wonder at the sheer myopic arrogance of the clerics who made up quite preposterous stories they must have known to be lies. It is claimed that "St Regulus" brought the bones of St Andrew to Fife in 345 and that this happened the same year that King Angus defeated the English King Athelstan (which occurred in 832 – some 487 years later)! I will not try to venture into those puny minds who thought that imposing this view on their flocks was acceptable.

The legends seem to agree that such supposed relics of St Andrew as reached Scotland came via a shipwreck at "Mucros" (the pigs' headland). This is supposed to be Fife Ness – the extreme easterly point of Fife, about 9 miles from present day St Andrews, but I do not see any basis for this attribution; far closer to the town (just 2.6 miles away) is Boarhills – the name is a bit of a giveaway! The coast there is rugged but there is a site called "boat haven", so landing is/was far from impossible. We can ignore St Regulus/ St Rule, for by the time the bones got here it was already a "well known fact" (about the truth of which we need not concern ourselves) that it was a St Regulus who had rescued some bones from their original resting place in 345AD. If one were being generous (which I think one should not be) the fact that there were intermediaries who finally brought whatever it was to Fife could be construed as an oversight. It is just about possible to see the journey as continuous from Patras to Kilrymont (where a Christian settlement ("kil") had been founded some time shortly after 565 by Saint Cainnech of Aghaboe (515/16–600) at the behest of St Columba). [Bridei mac Maelchon was king of the Picts 554-584.]

The name "Cennrimonaid" suggests that this was already royal land – which Bridei was, therefore, in a position to allocate for this purpose; the cell (it was not really a "church" as we would understand it today) was, therefore "Kilrimonaid"/"Kilrymont" and the two names were used more or less interchangeably for some time.

It need not concern us why St Wilfrid was a devotee of St Andrew, but he was, and St Acca was a disciple of Wilfrid. Acca became Abbot and Bishop of Hexham, dedicated to St Andrew and endowed with bones which Wilfrid has acquired in the course of his troubles. In 732/3, immediately after the restoration of Ceolwulf to the Kingdom of Northumbria (the names of those who usurped him briefly have not come down to us) Acca felt the need to flee Hexham. It is surmised that Acca had sided with Ceolwulf's opponents. [Ceolwulf abdicated in 737/8, became a monk on Lindisfarne and died in 765.]

There are several mutually exclusive stories as to where Acca went next – complete with the relics of St Andrew – including Galloway, Ireland and Fife, with Fife being the most logical and favoured. So I propose that it was he who was shipwrecked – at Boarhills. The 'obvious' place for him and for the relics to go was Kilrymont. So Acca's time in Scotland was during the reign (729-761) of Angus mac Fergus – and we can see how the careless later scribe confused this Angus with the other Angus mac Fergus (who reigned 820x34), the victor over Athelstan and who, according to yet another legend, made St Andrew his Patron Saint.

Having Acca in charge of Kilrymont suited King Angus as he continued the policy of his predecessors in trying to turn the church away from Iona in favour of Rome. So Acca will have had a real job to undertake in reforming the institution he found there – following his mentor Wilfrid (in England) in establishing the Benedictine Rule (and this in its turn lent confusion – he was referred to as "St Rule"). Just how far the writ of "Bishops" ran in Pictland at that time is hard to assess. As we have seen Curetan is afforded that title, but we have no pattern of them. The first Abbot of St Andrews for whom we have a(n Irish) record is Tuathalan who died in 747, but we may well suppose that Acca, with so much experience in that role already, will have filled that role before him – probably acting also as "bishop". Acca died in the period 740x2; his body taken back to Hexham for burial.

Conclusion

We can now place St Serf in his proper context and it all makes sense. His dates are of the general order 650x715; he cannot have been born until many years after the death of St Kentigern and so had nothing to do with raising him.

In the process we have disentangled many other elements of myth surrounding Serf and the arrival of Christianity in Fife to the point where the fundamental lines of the story are simple and easily understood. Specifically what is set out here are resolutions to various the paradoxes about "St Boniface", "King Angus", "King Nechtan", "St Rule", the shipwreck and the bones of St Andrew.

APPENDIX 4
THE FAROES: THE ISLAND OF THULE IDENTIFIED

[I apologise for any repetition here, but I put this appendix into the public domain as a stand-alone piece.]

Claudius Ptolomeus (otherwise known as Ptolemy) was a geographer who lived and worked in Alexandria, flourishing in the middle part of the second century AD. Although it should be noted that we have no evidence that Ptolemy himself drew maps. He is famous (*inter alia*) for the early maps of Scotland drawn by others based on the coordinates of Latitude and Longitude which he specified for Scotland's capes, bays, river mouths and settlements. He also described the pattern of tribal occupation. As well as information from the Roman occupiers of what is now Scotland he also had access to information deriving from the voyages of discovery (c325BC) of the Marseilles-based Greek explorer Pytheas.

We should begin by considering how Ptolemy developed these figures. Most observers are of the view that Latitude was estimated from the length of the day, but the gnomon was also in widespread use – and where this was the case there should have been little trouble in observing the angles directly to a fair degree of accuracy. Indeed the Greek Eratosthanes, also based in Alexandria, had calculated the circumference of the earth to a truly remarkable degree of accuracy some time around the year 240 BC – some 360 years before Ptolemy's time. Whether a gnomon was available to Pytheas I cannot say, but, carefully measured day length is a good start.

A good indication, however, of how imperfect the latitude information with which Ptolemy had to work was may be gained by his specification for Morecambe Bay – which he defines at 58° 20'N. It is in fact 54° 05'N – an error of 4° and 15', ie 295 miles (475km). Ptolemy also felt bound by the "well known fact" that the island of Thule was at 63° N. This, coupled with his misinformation about eg Morecambe Bay, led him to a complicated process of recalibration to make Scotland fit in to the space available. The net result was to rotate Scotland by about 90° to make it all fit in.

The problem of Longitude was much different. Solving the problem resisted the lure of huge rewards offered by many monarchs into the 1700s. Ptolemy's 0° was based on the so-called Fortunate Isles or Isles of the Blessed –

and there is to this day substantial dispute as to whether these might be supposed to be Madeira, the Canaries, Cape Verde or even the Azores. However it maybe that we can narrow this down. Christian Marx (Survey Review (2014) Vol 46 pp 231–244) has done the most effective job yet in trying to undo Ptolemy's recalibration. He has positively identified an island Ptolemy calls Aebuda as Islay in the Inner Hebrides. Ptolemy places Islay at 15° E of his Prime Meridian, while we define its longitude as 6° West of Greenwich. This should make the Fortunate Isles around 21° west of Greenwich – roughly half way between the Canaries (which stretch as far west as nearly 18°) and the Cape Verde islands (whose most easterly point is about 22° 30') illustrating the basis of the confusion and the level of inaccuracy involved.

Any places further east of Jura have suffered even more badly from Ptolemy's recalculations. Thus the Orkneys and the Isle of Lewis are shown as having the same Longitude – 30° East of his Prime Meridian. The Orkneys are actually centre on 3° W of Greenwich and Lewis 6° 45' W. If Ptolemy's 30° E really corresponded to 3° W then his Prime Meridian should be substantially beyond the Azores. If 6° 45' W were correct then the landfall for the Prime Meridian is on the north coast of Brazil!

We must presume therefore, that the Longitude which Ptolemy offers to us is itself a calculation based on (i) stadia (units of length), (ii) estimates of the distance coverable by "a day's sailing", (iii) where feasible, triangulation and (iv) his system of recalibration – which will have served also to confirm and/or refine the Latitude.

As we have seen, one of Ptolemy's axioms was his information from Pytheas that Thule was at 63°N. As of today it seems that everyone with an opinion supposes "The Island of Thule" to be unreal – mythical. I decided to look into this.

I started by plotting out Scotland for myself, including Thule, using the graticule developed by Barri Jones and David Mattingly ("An Atlas of Roman Britain" 1990 p19) which was good enough for Alistair Strang to use in his own paper (Britannia Vol. 28 (1997) pp1-30).

Ptolemy is remarkably detailed about the dimensions of the island of Thule:

The part of this which extends much toward the west is in	29°00	63°00
that which is farthest eastward is	31°40	63°00
that which is farthest northward is	30°20	63°15
that which is farthest southward is	30°20	62°40
the middle is in	30°20	63°00

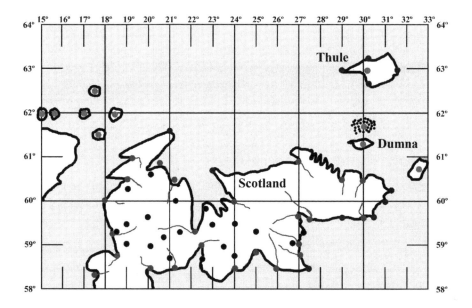

(from http://roman-britain.co.uk/ptolemys-geography.htm, accessed 21/10/16)

I think that these numbers are Ptolemy's calculations. what he really had (from Pytheas) was (a) the identification of 63° N and (b) estimates of the number of stadia North/South and East/West. From these he derived the numbers he presents to us.

We can "undo" Ptolemy's local calculations quite easily. Ptolemy reckons the "width" of Thule (North/South) is 35' of latitude corresponding to just over 40 miles (65km). Using the graticule we can estimate the "length" (East/West) at about 5/3 of this – ie about 67 miles (108 km).

By looking at Ptolemy's other locations we find that Thule is directly North of the Island of Dumna. Christian Marx' transformations shows that there is no doubt that Dumna is Lewis and Harris in the Outer Hebrides. Strang (op cit) was already of this view.

So we need to look for an island due north of Lewis measuring 40+ miles by 65+miles......

The Faroes are of the right size and almost exactly in the right place.

The Faroes actually stretch from 61°20N to 62°20 N (66.5 miles) and (from the Greenwich Meridian) 6°14'W to 7°40'W (46.5 miles – c40 miles if the island of Mykines is excluded). So Pytheas' estimate of Latitude (which is supposed to have been calculated from length of daylight only) is strikingly exact. As for his longitude we have already noted that the Faroes are indeed due North of Lewis – so whatever the basis of the errors with regard to Ptolemy's Prime Meridian there may be have been applied consistently in both cases.

There are two obvious problems with this identification:

(1) Like Scotland, Ptolemy has rotated the Faroes by 90°

I have no doubt that this is a product of the same recalibration process which Ptolemy used for places in Scotland. Thus his 450 year old data – the raw distance numbers (of stadia) – have been transposed.

(2) Ptolemy understood Thule to be a single island, but the Faroes are an archipelago.

Here there are two possible ways to explain this away. The fjords in the Faroes are mostly exceptionally narrow, so Pytheas may not have spent sufficient time exploring to spot this. Even today it is only a close inspection on eg Google Earth which will allow the viewer to notice that the northern group of islands are not one single landmass. The alternative is that at some stage over the 450 years some copyist scribe whose work Ptolemy came to rely on failed to make a word plural.

One objection which some people have made is that if we choose to consider Thule not to be due north of Lewis but rather due north of Orkney, then the "obvious" conclusion should be that Thule should refer to the Shetland Islands. I think that this fails on three grounds

(1) The North of Shetland is less than 61° N making for what would have been a far more substantial error on Pytheas' part.

(2) While, like the Faroes, the Shetlands are just short of 70 miles long, they are a mere 20 miles east to west, half the breadth of the Faroes and a far more substantial discrepancy to explain away.

(3) Unlike the Faroes, there is no way any explorer could fail to notice that the Shetlands are an archipelago.

The Faroese People may thus be delighted to have their history extended by about a millennium – from the c600AD, the current starting point when Irish Monks are supposed to have landed, back to c325BC when we can say with confidence that Pytheas identified them, named them (as Thule) and recorded their location and size with a truly remarkable degree of accuracy.

APPENDIX 5 – NOTES ON THE COVER ILLUSTRATION

The cover illustration is intended to demonstrate several aspects of the story to unfold.

Nennius specified that at the battle at Guinnon Fort, Arthur bore the image of the Virgin Mary on his shoulder. Here we see it – not like a pirate's parrot, but on a cavalry shield of the correct dimensions (1.2m high, 60cm wide).

The reader will note that this shield varies from both the curved testudo and the circular shields of the Roman infantry.

The image of the Blessed Virgin Mary is taken from that of the church at Morano (an island close to Venice) dedicated to the dragon slaying St Donatus of Arezzo who was martyred in the 360s. [See https://wanderwisdom.com/travel-destinations/Venice-Murano.] The image dates to substantially before 1150 and is likely to be a reproduction of a much earlier image on an earlier building on the site. It resembles fairly closely the earliest extant Marian images (see https://churchpop.com/2015/03/13/8-of-the-oldest-images-ofthe-blessed-virgin-mary/), so there is a fair chance that it not too dissimilar to the image Arthur would have used.

Readers may consider it a pure coincidence, but it is interesting to note that at just this time St Pabo Post Prydein, King of the Pennines, Arthur's second cousin and exact contemporary, named one of his sons Dunaut – a variant of the relatively rare name Donatus just mentioned.

At the base of the shield is the Chi-Rho symbol within a laurel wreath - a design adopted by the Roman emperor Constantine for use by his troops on standards and on shields. As noted elsewhere, I suggest that Arthur will have seen himself in the tradition of Constantine. This association remaining long enough in the Scottish psyche that several Scottish kings bore this name. [The Greek letters Chi and Rho are supposed to represent "Christ"; in fact the symbol was in use some centuries BC and so, in reality, are likely to represent the ancient Egyptian god Horus (see Wikipedia ~/Chi_Rho) before being adopted by Constantine.]

In the middle of the shield are the letters Alpha and Omega – widely used in Christian circles at that time.

The sword is a spatha – of the sort typically used by cavalry officers at this time. It is significantly longer than the gladius used by the Roman infantry, but shorter than the longsword of mediaeval times.

David Crone, featured, is also the artist who painted the shield to my general specifications but using his own judgement. He is a member of The Antonine Guard (http://www.theantonineguard.org.uk/) His uniform is accurate for the Antonine period – but not necessarily the Arthurian.

At 14.2 hands "Schiehallion Sundance" is a few inches taller than the normal size of the cavalry horse of the day (13.2 – 14), but David too is taller than most men of that time, so this gives the reader a fair appreciation of the relative size of man and beast. Unfortunately such has been horse-breeding in the 1500 years since then that horses of this size cannot now bear the weight of a full grown man in armour!

CONCLUSION

The true figure who has come down to us as the legendary "King Arthur" has been known to historians all the time, but has been ignored because he did not suit their pre-conceived narratives. He was born near Leeds in 475AD. He was a direct descendant of Old King Cole and a younger son of Masgwid Gloff ("The Lame"), king of Elmet.

The kingdoms of the "Hen Ogled" – the Old North – were exasperated by attacking raids on their territories by Picts and Scots, sometimes reinforced on their journey south. So it was decided that an expeditionary army from the Old North would reinforce the armies of the combined "foederati" tribes – the Damnonii and the Gododdin – who had been friendly in Roman imperial times, provided that the Pendragon – the Commander in Chief – was from the Old North. At the young age of 15, Arthur was selected to be this figurehead, so a dynastic marriage was contracted for his sister Anna to King "Lot" of the Gododdin, whose territory was what is now lowland Eastern Scotland south of the Antonine Wall. Arthur accompanied her also to look after her interests (as was the common practice in those days and long afterwards). Although the selection of Arthur as Pendragon was probably in the first instance no more than a condition of military support from kingdoms of the "Old North", Arthur more than grew into the job, showing exceptional military prowess in the successful campaign which took place in the period 495-517.

During the period 517-537 there is time and scope for several of the legendary deeds to have taken place, but other stories which are incorporated into the legend were no more than satirical entertainments performed at his court and in royal courts thereafter. These matters are left largely unexamined here, but it is hoped that others, now given a very clear basis and time window for their research, will take up the investigation.

After Badon Hill 20 years elapsed until Arthur's death in 537 at the age of about 62. This death occurred because Arthur wanted to reassume the power he had held, while his nephew Mordred, the rightful king of the Gododdin, was unwilling to abdicate the office he had filled properly for most of that intervening time.

With the general story now in its proper historical and geographical context, several of the characters and places in the legend can be understood – so these are identified where possible. In other cases where specific identification is not possible the options can be narrowed down considerably, providing focus for future research by others. Some of the characters are anachronistic – being added by later story tellers for reasons of their own and of their paymasters, a practice which continues to this day.

POSTSCRIPT: WHAT IF...?

If we are to appreciate Arthur's place in history we should give some consideration to the questions "What if he had never lived?" or "What if he had not been the champion he became?"

What actually happened was that there was a sort of dynamic stalemate with incursions one way and the other between the various parties not amounting to anything substantial until, in the face of Viking aggression, the Picts and the Scots allied (c850) subsequently absorbing Strathclyde (from c950) and then (after 1018) Lothian and the Borders. Despite this the Vikings were close to taking over the whole of Scotland until Malcolm III fought them back, his success wholly dependent on massive English support.

So might it all have gone differently? Let us suppose that the military objectives had not been gained... what then?

Scenario A

It is possible that the kings of the Old North would have selected some other princeling and that Arthur's personality did not really count for anything. Thus the war would have gone very largely the same way as it actually went and so nothing would have been different. The most important factor was the bolstering of the forces of the foederati from Britannia, giving them the edge over their adversaries, the Picts and the Scots. But such is the legendary nature of the man that I think that we may give this relatively little credence.

Scenario B

The British were so sick of the raids that they would have ceded more control to the incoming Angles and Saxons. In this scenario it is likely that the Angles who were already in Bernicia as guests of the British kings would have assumed direct rule over the Gododdin and the Damnonii and they would have led the prosecution of the war against the Picts and Scots.

Bearing in mind the later success that the Angles had against the Picts unassisted, we may suppose that they could have taken control from the Tay and the Gask Ridge to Loch Lomond. Like the Romans before them they would not have been willing to stretch themselves to controlling the Highlands, so the Picts would have remained in a way reduced as in Roman times. Meanwhile the Scots would have continued to advance to complete their control of the western shores of Loch Lomond.

Frustrated the Picts would have turned even more on the Scots who may have continued to fight each other mainly in Glen Falloch.

Thus, as it coalesced, "England"'s northern border might well have been from Old Kilpatrick on the Clyde to Loch Lomond, the Gask Ridge and the Tay. It is highly unlikely that The Picts or the Scots would have been able to beat the other decisively and even if, eventually, they united they would not have been able to resist the Vikings. Thus I suggest that the Highlands and Islands and Argyll would have been absorbed fully into the Viking empire.

As history shows the Vikings were unable to sustain an integrated overseas empire, so a single kingdom of the Highlands, Islands and Argyll is likely to have split away, having a relationship to Scandinavia somewhat similar to that of Iceland.

It seems unlikely that this would have given the Vikings any more leverage over Ireland who already had what is tantamount to a free hand from their Hebridean base. It is similarly unlikely that the greater size of Northumbria would have had any impact on its ability to resist the Vikings – on the contrary even in its smaller size it Northumberland was unmanageable as a single political entity and so there would have the danger of subsequent balkanisation. However the new geography would have made it far less likely that the Scots would have attained the overall power that actually did come to them. In particular the greater Anglian influence over central Scotland would have prevented the development of an sense of a Gaelic culture there, with the lowlanders identifying themselves as Anglic.

Scenario C

As we have seen, the Angles had great difficulty in retaining control. While they did extend into Cumberland, Galloway and even Ayrshire, the grip was tenuous. They did invade up the east coast also – the extent of how far they reached being reflected by the location of Nechtansmere where they finally lost ground following the battle there in 685. So what if Arthur had failed AND the Angles proved weak?

The Picts and the Scots were used to allying with each for expeditions to the south, so we should have no doubt that in the aftermath of a failed campaign against them surely they would have been muscular in taking revenge. We should expect that the Damnonii would have fallen to the Scots with the Gododdin being made subject to the Picts. From there it would be a fairly small step for the Scots to have annexed Galloway while the Picts would at least have come to an arrangement with the Selgovae. Bearing in mind that even centuries later the Scots had the habit of invading Northumberland it would be reasonable to suppose that the Picts would have reached Hadrian's Wall in reasonably short order.

At this point the Scots would have been marginalised with little or no point of contact with the wall. Had they been intelligent at this point they would have united with the Picts – this time under them – and the way would have been open for further advance at least as far as Morecambe Bay if not the Mersey on the West and the Humber (perhaps not as far as The Wash) on the east.

As we can see from history, for a very long time Northumberland remained at least semi-autonomous – too hard for kings in the south to control – so we may expect that the Anglo-Saxons may have accepted a Mersey/Humber border so this could have been quite stable for some considerable time.

So how might the Vikings have acted under this scenario? Primarily they wanted good land and wealth – and this was to be found predominantly in the south, so while one should not doubt that they would have raided all over the coasts of "Greater Pictland" the new political geography would have allowed them to concentrate their invasion plans on their real goal, significantly increasing their chances of success. But just as Canute required Scotland to be a client kingdom, so too, earlier Viking kings of "Lesser England" would have had to subjugate "Greater Pictland". The greater wealth of the south, even more united under Viking rule, would have provided the resources for them to push the border north – and given the political structure that would then pertain, the victory would have been over the whole island. But the problem of exercising day-to-day control would still have been there, so it is likely that the existing political structures would have remained in place, but 'managed' as actively as possible by the Viking kings. Not only that but the very substantial population between Hadrian's Wall and the border would have been likely to dominate – and they were not "Cruithni". So the culture would have been significantly different.

Conclusion

It is long since that I came to the view that one of the main governing principles of the universe is irony.

In the introduction to this book I referred to the unhelpful review of "Scottish Clans...". It is true, but is and was irrelevant, that the kilt as we know it today was designed by an Englishman. So too the earliest extant mention of haggis is in an English cookery book which has nothing to say about Scotland. And so it goes on.

And now I conclude that the very existence of Scotland as we know it today is entirely dependent on a man born in Leeds.....

The Scots were always grateful for Arthur's securing their position via a generous peace treaty – and this is reflected by the retention of the name "Ben Arthur", by the name Arthur mac Aedan and the existence of the Clan Arthur. And now too many seek to claim him as their own.

The Picts seem to have been much less enamoured of Arthur – it has been a real struggle to find the echo of his deeds in Pictland. Their adherence to failed strategies (eg the Highland Charge which time and again lead to their own rout) may be indicative of their world view. I suppose that from the Picts' point of view, Arthur really did humiliate them in a way that had not happened since Mons Graupius.

Just as the Epidii disappeared from history through a peaceful take-over – their language and culture largely overtaken by their new masters/protectors – so too was the fate of the Britons at the hands of the Anglo-Saxons and so too was that of the Picts following union with the Scots. So perhaps we may attribute the lack of true (as opposed to legendary) regard for the hero Arthur to the destruction of British culture generally at the hands of Angle, Saxon and Scot.

ACKNOWLEDGEMENTS

David Arbuthnott
Geoff Bagley
Tom Barclay
Cllr Jonathan Bentley
Alasdair Black
Dr James Bell
Neil Buchanan
David Caldwell
Dr Ian Cameron
Sybil Cavanagh
Pauline Connor
Stephen Cowan
Adrian Cox
Eileen Cox
David Crone
Jacqueline Eccles
Alex Forbes of Druminnor
Jonathan Forbes
William Gardiner
Eddie Geoghegan
Dr Stewart Gillan
Liz Glasgow
Cllr Eric Gotts
Chic Grant
Chloe Grant
Paul Grant
Cllr Ann Gaunt
Ron Greer
Francis Hagan
J Martin Haldane
Petronella Haldane
Rev Roddy Hamilton
Gill Harkin
Robin Herne
Jenny Hutcheson
Malcolm Kelly
Pru Kennard
Neil Kennedy
Mary Knight
Michael Knowles
Bill Lennox
Ken Lussey
Hugh MacArthur
Diarmid MacAulay
Walter MacAulay
Maureen MacGregor
Neil Macgregor
Rev. John McGrorry
Dr Mary McHugh
Ian Mackay
Willie MacLaren
Irene McLaughlan
Carol McNeill
Dr Alan MacQuarrie
Sandra McRitchie
Rev Graham McWilliams
Johnathon Menzies
Jo Mackintosh
Christian Marx
Laura Masterton
Simon Miller
George Moore
Claire Mullan
Prof. Caitriona O'Dochartaigh
Martin O'Hare
Maurice Paxton
Ralph Peters
David Potter
Adrian Prior
Emma Rankine
Derek Read
Peter J Robertson
Nicki Scott
the late Romilly Squire
Amanda Samuels
Mitchell Scott
Dan Shadrake
Graeme Sinclair
Harold Smith
Louise Speller
Bill & Shonagh Stewart
Dr Bill Thayer
Joan Thompson
Michael TRB Turnbull
Patricia Weeks
Adam Welfare
John L Williams
Alex Woolf

BIBLIOGRAPHY

The inclusion of any entry in this bibliography should not be taken as approbation in any way. Several of these books are rubbish and I would advise anyone not to waste their time consulting them. Nevertheless I have had to pick my way through them if only to be able to reject their underlying proposition. In most cases I have been able to identify the emotional drive behind the wishing to demonstrate a hypothesis which is in fact false.

Anderson AO "Early Sources of Scottish History" Watkins 1990,

Aneurin, "Y Gododdin" http://www.maryjones.us/ctexts/a01b.html

Anonymous "The Annals of the Four Masters" http://www.rootsweb.ancestry.com/~irlkik/ihm/ire100.htm Anonymous, "Welsh Annals" ("Annales Cambriae")

http://sourcebooks.fordham.edu/source/annalescambriae.asp

Ardrey, Adam "Finding Merlin", Mainstream 2007

Ardrey, Adam "Finding Arthur", Overlook Duckworth 2013

Ashe, Geoffrey "The Discovery of King Arthur", Sutton 2003

Bede, The Venerable "Ecclesiastical History of England" http://www.gutenberg.org/files/38326/38326-h/38326-h.html#toc39

Black, George F "The Surnames of Scotland" Birlinn 1999

Breeze, David J "The Antonine Wall" John Donald 2006

Buchanan, William of Auchmar "The History of the ancient surname of Buchanan" 1743 https://books.google.co.uk/books?id=Ht5EAAAAYAAJ&pg=PP9&redir_esc=y#v=onepage&q&f=false

Caradoc of Llanfarcan "Life of Gildas" http://www.maryjones.us/ctexts/gildas06.html

Chrétien de Troyes, "Erec et Enide" http://www.gutenberg.org/files/831/831-h/831-h.htm

Clare, Tom "King Arthur and the Riders of Rheged" Rheged 1992

Dennistoun, James "Cartularium Comitatus de Levenax", (Kessinger Reprint) 1833

Duggan, Joseph "The Romances of Crétien de Troyes" 2001

Dunbavin, Paul "Picts and Ancient Britons", Third Millennium 1998

Dwelly, Edward "Illustrated Gaelic-English Dictionary" Birlinn 2001

Evans & Thomas "Y Geiriadur Mawr" Gomer 2001

Ford, David Nash http://www.earlybritishkingdoms.com

Fraser, James " "From Caledonia to Pictland" EUP 2009

Fraser, James E "The Roman Conquest of Scotland", Tempus 2005

Fraser, William "The Chiefs of Colqhoun and their country" 1869

Fraser, William "The Lennox" 1874, https://archive.org/details/lennoxvol1memov100fras

Geoffrey of Monmouth "History of the Kings of Britain" (books 7-11) http://www.indiana.edu/~dmdhist/arthur_gm.htm#7.1

Geoffrey of Monmouth, "Vita Merlini" c1150 http://www.sacred-texts.com/neu/eng/vm/index.htm

Grant, Adrian C "Scottish Clans: Legend, Logic & Evidence" Fastprint 2012

Gildas, Saint "The Ruin of Britain" ("*De Excidio et Conquestu Britanniae*") http://www.vortigernstudies.org.uk/arthist/vortigernquotesgil.htm#_ednref42

Hanks & al., "The Oxford Names Companion" OUP 2002

Jocelyn of Furness, "Life of Kentigern" http://sourcebooks.fordham.edu/basis/Jocelyn-LifeofKentigern.asp

Jones & Mattingly, "An Atlas of Roman Britain" Blackwell 1990

King (Ed), "Pocket Modern Welsh Dictionary" OUP 2000

Keegan, Simon "Pennine Dragon" Newhaven 2016

Kincaid, Peter, http://kyncades.org/Alwin_not_Ail%C3%ADn.pdf

Konstram, Angus "Strongholds of the Picts", Osprey 2010

Laycock, Stuart "Britannia, the Failed State", The History Press 2008

Macbain, Alexander, "Outlines of Gaelic Etymology". Mackay 1909

Macquarrie, Alan "Vita Sancti Servani" Innes Review Vol 44 #2 (1993)

Malden & Scott "An Ordinary of Scottish Arms pre-1672" Heraldry Society of Scotland (2016)

Malory Thomas "Le Morte d'Arthur" http://www.sacred-texts.com/neu/mart/index.htm

Marie de France, "Lanval" http://www.arthuriana.org/teaching/Marie_Lanval_Shoaf.html
http://users.clas.ufl.edu/jshoaf/Marie/lanval.pdf

Marx, Christian "Rectification of position data of Scotland in Ptolemy's Geographike Hyphegesis" Survey Review 46: 231–244, DOI (2014)

Moffat, Alistair "Arthur & The Lost Kingdoms" Phoenix 1999

Nennius, "History of the Britons" ("Historia Britannorum")
http://www.yorku.ca/inpar/nennius_giles.pdf
http://sourcebooks.fordham.edu/halsall/basis/nennius-full.asp

Neville, Cynthia "Native Lordship in Medieval Scotland...." Four Courts Press 2005.

Nisbet, Alexander "System of Heraldry" 1722

O'Hart, John "Irish Pedigrees" Vol I Duffy, 1892
https://archive.org/stream/irishpedigreesor_01ohar#page/62/mode/2up

Owen & Morgan, "Dictionary of the Place-Names of Wales" Gomer 2007

Read, Derek http://www.derwas-read.co.uk/old_king_cole_descendants.htm

Rivet & Smith, "The Place-Names of Roman Britain" Batsford 1979

Robinson (ed), "Concise Scots Dictionary" Polygon 1985

Ruys, "Life of Gildas" http://www.maryjones.us/ctexts/gildas07.html

Stirling, Simon Andrew "The King Arthur Conspiracy", The History Press 2012

Strang, Alastair "Explaining Ptolemy's Roman Britain" Britannia Vol 28 (1997)

Story, Robert H "The Church of Scotland, past and present: its history...." (Volume 1) Mackenzie 1890

Swanton (ed & tr), "The Anglo-Saxon Chronicle" Dent 1997

Thomas, Charles "Christian Celts", Tempus 1998

Thomson, Derick "The New English-Gaelic Dictionary" Gairm 2003

Tolkien & Gordon (eds) "Sir Gawain and the Green Knight"
http://quod.lib.umich.edu/c/cme/Gawain/1:1?rgn=div1;view=fulltext
http://d.lib.rochester.edu/camelot/text/weston-sir-gawain-and-the-green-knight

Turnbull, Michael "Saint Andrew, Myth, Legend and Reality" Neil Wilson 2014

Various, "The Old Statistical Account of Scotland 1791-99"
http://stataccscot.edina.ac.uk/static/statacc/dist/home

Various, "The New Statistical Account of Scotland 1834-45"
http://stataccscot.edina.ac.uk/static/statacc/dist/home

Wagner, Paul "Pictish Warrior", Osprey 2002

Way & Squire, "Scottish Clan & Family Encyclopedia" Harper Collins 1994

Wells, Edward Randolph "Ardincaple Castle and its Lairds" (1930)

Williamson, David "Brewer's British Royalty" Cassell 1996

http://forbesclan.com/main.html

https://en.wikipedia.org/wiki/

http://roman-britain.co.uk/ and

http://www.antoninewall.org/

http://www.arthuriana.co.uk/n&q/myrddin.

http://www.druidcircle.org/library

http://fmg.ac/Projects/MedLands/SCOTTISH%20NOBILITY%20LATER.htm#_Toc359672175

http://www.hull.ac.uk/php/cssbct/genealogy/royal/

https://thewildpeak.wordpress.com/2013/04/01/who-was-the-cumbrian-earl-gospatric/